Commonsense methods for children with special needs

It is now common practice for many students who experience difficulties in learning, or who have disabilities, to be placed in ordinary schools and, where practicable, to receive their education in the mainstream. This situation presents a challenge to regular class teachers who must develop confidence and competence in dealing with the personal, social and educational needs of such students, and who often feel inadequate when faced with students with special needs.

This text is based on the premise that there is actually very little which is unique or 'special' about the teaching required by students with mild to moderate difficulties. Most so-called special techniques or special methods are just good basic teaching procedures applied with intensity and precision. The ideas presented throughout the book seek to illustrate this point by giving practical advice which can be incorporated into the mainstream programme in order to cater more effectively for a wide range of student ability. By adding some or all of the strategies described in the book to their normal repertoire of skills, teachers should become more versatile and adaptable in their approach to *all* children.

This new, enlarged edition provides a wealth of useful advice for the busy teacher and for the student teacher in training. Issues of self-management and self-regulation are central to the book's detailed coverage of behaviour problems, learning difficulties, and social skills development. Five chapters are devoted to basic academic skill improvement, and attention is given to ways in which the regular curriculum can be adapted to enable students with learning difficulties to experience some measure of success. Advisers and co-ordinators of special services will also find the advice on school-based and regional support service operation highly relevant to their work.

Peter Westwood is Senior Lecturer in Special Education at Flinders University, Adelaide. His distinguished career in special education spans more than thirty years, and includes experience as a teacher, educational psychologist, college and university lecturer and administrator. He has written more than forty articles for professional journals, three books for teachers and six books for children.

Commonsense methods for children with special needs

Strategies for the regular classroom

Second Edition

Peter Westwood

London and New York

First published 1993
by Routledge
11 New Fetter Lane, London EC4P 4EE

Simultaneously published in the USA and Canada
by Routledge
29 West 35th Street, New York, NY 10001

Reprinted 1993 and 1995

© 1993 Peter Westwood

Typeset in Bembo by Michael Mepham, Frome, Somerset
Printed and bound in Great Britain
by Biddles Ltd, Guildford and King's Lynn

British Library Cataloguing in Publication Data
A catalogue record for this book is available from the British Library

Library of Congress Cataloging in Publication Data
A catalog record for this book is available from the Library of Congress

ISBN 0-415-08772-4 (hbk)
ISBN 0-415-08773-2 (pbk)

Contents

Introduction

This text is based on the premise that there is very little which is unique or 'special' about the type of education needed by mildly to moderately disabled children. It is true that there are a few unusual techniques and approaches which may be appropriate, for example when working with blind or deaf students or those with communication problems; but in general the teaching strategies used with atypical children are not exotic.

We must acknowledge that children with learning problems or disabilities are more like all other children than they are different from them; and while they may have some special needs, their general needs are identical to those of all other children.

Unfortunately, special education is still surrounded by what Meyen, Vergason and Whelan (1972) referred to as 'esoteric mysticism'. This obscures the fact that most so-called special techniques and tricks of the trade are just good basic teaching procedures, applied with common sense and precision. The mystique surrounding special education has regrettably served to make regular classroom teachers feel inadequate when faced with atypical children. They assume that they lack the necessary knowledge and skills to teach such children. This is largely untrue. 'Special educational needs are not to be regarded as a secret garden into which only the initiated may venture' (Thomas 1986: 101) The current trend to integrate students with quite severe disabilities into regular class-rooms makes it essential that teachers accept the challenge.

Throughout this book an effort has been made to deal with children in a non-categorical manner. Much overlap exists in terms of special educational needs across all categories of disability and exceptionality. For this reason it is of more practical value to tackle teaching and management in a general way. Only where it is really relevant is reference made to specific disabilities. The 'Further Reading' section at the end of each chapter provides more detailed coverage of particular disabilities or problems.

This second edition of the book has been expanded and updated to include coverage of recent viewpoints on learning difficulties, on methods of remediation and on programme planning.

ACKNOWLEDGEMENTS

I wish to thank the following individuals and organizations for permission to quote from or reproduce sections of their work in this book.

The Australian Council for Educational Research, for permission to quote from Sophie Bloom's book *Peer and Cross-age Tutoring in the School*.

Merrill Jackson of the Department of Special Education, University of Tasmania, for permission to describe his 'visuo-thematic' approach for remedial reading. It is taken from his book *Reading Disability: Experiment, Innovation and Individual Therapy*, published by Angus & Robertson, Sydney.

William McCormick, State Supervisor for Elementary Education, Dover, Delaware, for permission to quote extensively from his article 'Teachers can learn to teach more effectively' in *Educational Leadership*.

Geoff Rogers, Principal, Heathfield Primary School, for permission to reproduce a section of his reading programme *Truckin' with Kenny*.

My sincerest thanks also to Jane Horgan for preparing the manuscript for this second edition, and to Brian Matthews for his help with the graphics.

Peter Westwood
Coromandel Valley
South Australia

Chapter 1

Learning difficulties

Students classified as having learning difficulty are a heterogeneous group and have a wide variety of characteristics, ranging from academic difficulties to cognitive and social-emotional problems.

(Kraayenoord and Elkins 1990: 110)

The term 'learning difficulties' is a very general one, used widely and without much precision to refer to the general problems in learning experienced by some 15 to 20 per cent of the school population (Taylor and Sternberg 1989). Usually the term is applied to students whose difficulties are not directly related to a specific intellectual, physical or sensory disability, although students with disabilities often do experience problems in learning and in social adjustment. Students who have, in the past, been referred to as 'slow learners', 'low achievers', or simply as 'the hard to teach', certainly fall within the category of those with 'learning difficulties'. So too do the children described as 'learning disabled' (LD); those of at least average intelligence who, for no obvious reason, experience great difficulty in learning the basic academic skills (Richardson 1992). It seems likely that only 1 to 2 per cent of the school population should be regarded as *specifically* learning disabled (Elkins 1991); their unique problems will be addressed later in the chapter.

It is important to realize that students with general and specific learning difficulties comprise by far the largest group of students with special educational needs. These students require some measure of additional support and special consideration if they are to achieve success in regular classrooms.

PLACEMENT

Increasingly over recent years students with learning difficulties have been retained in mainstream classes, rather than segregated or withdrawn into special groups. They have been joined, too, by students with intellectual, physical and sensory disabilities and those with emotional or behavioural problems. This move toward the integration of children with special needs, which began in the 1970s and gained momentum in the late 1980s, has changed dramatically the nature of special educational provision. It has become the responsibility of the regular class teacher to cater for the needs of these students, with occasional assistance from special education personnel, if available. In America, the Regular Education Initiative (REI) is based on the premise that regular teachers will accept this challenge and will become better skilled in meeting the needs of students with widely different abilities and aptitudes (Jenkins, Pious and Jewell 1990). The same assumption has underpinned policy-making in Britain, Australia, New Zealand and most European countries, where integration is now the accepted placement model (Ashman and Elkins 1990; Gross and Gipps 1987; Murray-Seegert 1992).

In order to meet this challenge teachers will have to move toward an approach to teaching which combines effective instruction, personalization and inclusive practices.

Effective instruction

In the first edition of this book, information from McCormick (1979) was presented in support of the view that effective teaching not only raises the attainment level of all students but also reduces very significantly the prevalence of learning failure. More recent evidence fully supports this viewpoint (Simmons, Fuchs and Fuchs 1991). Articles by Yates (1988) and Dyson (1990) indicate clearly that special educators in advisory roles in the 1990s need to be advocates for effective teaching approaches and need to influence regular class teachers to adopt such approaches. Their brief should be 'to improve the quality of schooling for all students' (Butt 1991).

Effective teaching practices are those which provide students with the maximum opportunity to learn. These practices increase student achievement levels through maintaining on-task behaviour. The term 'academic engaged time' is often used to describe such on-task behaviour and refers to the proportion of instructional time in which students are actively involved in their work. This active involvement includes attending to instruction from the teacher, working independently or with a group on assigned academic tasks, and applying previously acquired knowledge and skills. Studies have shown that students who are receiving instruction directly from the teacher spend more time attending to the content of the lesson than students who are expected to find out for themselves. Effective classroom lessons which maintain high levels of academic focus contain the following elements:

- daily review of previous day's work;
- clear presentation of new skills and concepts, with much modelling by the teacher;
- guided student practice, with high success rates and with feedback to individual students;
- independent student practice, applying the new knowledge and skills appropriately;
- systematic cumulative revision of work previously covered.

It is particularly important that *all* students experience a high success rate during the guided practice phase of the lesson. The teacher must be expert in monitoring performance at the level of each student in the class, as corrective feedback is then geared to individual needs and learning rate.

Effective lessons, particularly those covering basic academic skills, tend to have a clear structure. Evidence suggests that students with disabilities integrated in regular classes do best in structured programmes (Gow and Ward 1991). In particular, students with behaviour problems, or with some degree of emotional disturbance, require an environment which is well-organized and predictable, and a programme which is presented clearly and with abundant opportunities for success.

McCormick's guidelines for more effective teaching[†]

McCormick (1979) identified a number of characteristics in teachers who helped children to achieve at better-than-expected levels. His summary provides a valuable framework against which to design effective pro-grammes to meet the needs of children with and without disabilities. His advice is as valid now as it was in 1979.

In schools where students achieve better results than expected, teachers demonstrated a greater understanding of the structure and substance of the content being taught. In particular they:

- were more specific about lesson objectives;

† Based on McCormick 1979; 60 and reproduced with permission.

- were better able to judge accurately the time needed to accomplish these objectives;
- made more frequent use of structuring comments as instruction proceeded;
- successfully broke the lessons into manageable and logical sequences;
- more ably anticipated problems in reaching the objectives and made accommodations for them.

Teachers also demonstrated a greater understanding of the special characteristics of their students. In particular they:

- more often modified instruction on the basis of student responses;
- used a vocabulary, oral and written, more appropriate for the age or ability level;
- adjusted the level of questions for different ability levels in the class;
- presented materials at an appropriate level of difficulty.

Furthermore, the teachers demonstrated a greater understanding of the principles of learning. They:

- made frequent use of opportunities to create and maintain an appropriate mind-set for pupils;
- frequently encouraged students to set appropriate and realistic goals for themselves;
- spent time and effort in creating an atmosphere of concern about the importance of learning the lesson content;
- more often provided opportunities for learner success;
- more often provided immediate feedback to learners; more often checked the level of mastery being achieved (and proceeded only if an acceptable level of learning was evident);
- gave more appropriate consideration to the length and spacing of practice;
- in general provided more meaningful and coherent presentations.

Personalization and inclusive practices

When teachers are urged to cater for students' individual needs, including those of students with significant disabilities and learning problems, it should not be taken to mean that each and every child must be given an individual work programme for most of the school day. Such an arrangement would be both unworkable and unnecessary. Group work and whole-class activities can be used frequently, provided that different outcomes are expected for different students. For example, within a whole-class lesson one child may write three pages of his or her own thoughts unaided; another may manage only three sentences with much help from the teacher; yet another may manage only a picture. All these responses are acceptable. A classroom activity is 'inclusive' if it allows every child to make an attempt, and to achieve some degree of success alongside others. The integration of students with special needs into regular classes must involve inclusive curricula rather than, or in addition to, individual programming. Where individual educational plans (IEPs) are required, they should indicate quite clearly not only what the student needs to do which is different from the rest of the class, but also the areas of the curriculum where he or she can be counted in with the others. Ideally such inclusion will be for most of the school day.

Even within whole-class or group sessions, teachers can and do 'personalize' their approach. For example, when questioning a group the teacher directs a straightforward and simple question to Child A in the expectation that he or she will manage to respond to it. A more searching question is directed at Child B. Similarly, when a teacher provides additional work at the same level for one child in order to help that child master the topic, while at the same time setting something different and more complex for another child, that teacher is personalizing the approach. Other examples of personalization, which reflect a thorough knowledge of the students in the class, include waiting longer for certain students to respond to a question; praising specific students; drawing upon the interests and abilities of individuals when discussing a topic; delegating responsibilities within the group; setting short-term goals; providing more (or less) direct assistance; revising topics more frequently for some students; and selecting different resource materials.

Effective instruction, combined with personalization and the use of inclusive activities, will reduce the frequency with which a teacher needs to devise separate programmes for students with disabilities or learning difficulties. In addition to knowing their students extremely well, teachers also need to be aware of the factors which may cause or exacerbate learning difficulties. In particular, they need to recognize the factors over which they have most control.

FACTORS ASSOCIATED WITH LEARNING DIFFICULTY

In their chapter entitled 'Dimensions of learning problems', Wallace and Kauffman (1986) support the view that seldom is a *single* cause found for a particular student's learning problem; and they also stress that sometimes it is impossible to identify *any* predisposing or precipitating factors. Certainly diagnosis of learning difficulties remains a very inexact science.

Over to you: Possible causes of learning difficulty

Before moving to the next section, try to list as many possible reasons for learning difficulty as you can think of. For example, 'difficulty with English as a second language', 'hearing impairment', 'school absence', etc.

Now move to the categories below and analyse your list. Place a tick against the appropriate category for each item on your list. For example, 'difficulty with English as a second language' would score a tick against 'family background'; 'hearing impairment' would score a tick against 'within the student'. Some items may need a tick in more than one category.

- Within the student
- Within the family background or culture
- Within the peer group
- Within the curriculum
- Within the teaching approach
- Within the student–teacher relationship
- Within the school/class-room environment
- Other

The results of your analysis above will probably show far more ticks in the 'within the student' category than in any other. A common reaction when faced with a student who is failing is to look for problems or 'deficits' within the learner, rather than elsewhere. 'What's *wrong* with him (or her)?' we ask. Yet such a question is unlikely to yield a useful answer, since at best it will give only a partial explanation for the problem. Even parents tend to assume that there is something 'wrong' with their children if school progress is unsatisfactory (Elkins 1991), and it is common to find such children referred to educational psychologists and general practitioners for evaluation or diagnosis. However, it is usually much more productive to examine factors external to the child, such as quality and type of instruction given, teacher expectations, relevance of the work set, class-room environment, interpersonal dynamics within the class social group, and rapport with the teacher. These factors are much more amenable to modification than are factors within the child or within the family background or culture.

An 'ecological perspective' on this situation recognizes that a learning problem is almost always due to a complex combination of interacting factors, all of which merit attention when seeking to provide additional help for the student concerned. If teachers do not consider these factors, and if they do not seek to teach effectively and personalize their approach, they may easily precipitate a child's entry into the failure cycle.

The failure cycle

The basic message of the failure cycle is, 'If at first you don't succeed, you don't succeed!'

Observation of young children suggests that, even at an early age, children begin to regard themselves as 'failures' in given learning situations. If, for whatever reason, a child finds that he or she cannot do something which other children are doing easily, there is a loss of confidence. This loss of confidence leads to deliberate avoidance of the type of activity associated with the failure; and sometimes even avoidance of any new or challenging situation. Avoidance leads to lack of practice. Lack of practice ensures that the individual does not gain in proficiency or confidence, while other children forge ahead. Constant failure results in poor self-esteem and lowered motivation.

The effects of early failure are thus cumulative (Walberg 1988), and probably account for many instances of learning difficulty in particular school subjects. While there are almost certainly different thresholds of tolerance for failure among any group of students, it must be acknowledged that failure is not a pleasing experience, and given sufficient exposure to it, almost any student will develop avoidance strategies. It must be noted, too, that the failure cycle is not confined to early school experiences, but can be established at any time in life. For example, the present writer associates failure, pain, avoidance and dislike with attempting to learn to water-ski!

The implications of the failure cycle for the teacher are twofold. First, it is evident that to reduce the possibility of early failure in a new learning situation, teachers must prepare and present new tasks very clearly indeed, with as much direct guidance and support as necessary to ensure success. This issue will be discussed fully in Chapter 3. Second, the only way of breaking the failure cycle is to devise some way of providing successful practice in which the learner recognizes that he or she is improving. Strategies for achieving this goal, and for helping the learner to become more independent in his or her learning, are presented in the following chapters.

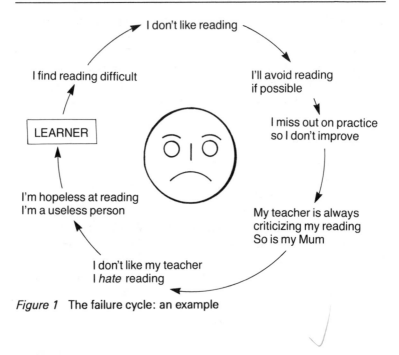

Figure 1 The failure cycle: an example

Students who are most likely to have learning problems and to experience frequent failure are those often described by their teachers as slow learners.

The slow learner

There is no official definition of a 'slow learner', yet most teachers have no difficulty at all in identifying such children in their own classes. Clearly there is a general understanding of the most obvious characteristics of this population.

Like many labels used to describe students with learning problems, the term has acquired its own odium in recent years. Dyer (1991) suggests that it should be abolished, as it is a derogatory term and tends to colour the attitudes of teachers. It also implies that such students should be 'taught slowly', quite the reverse of their actual need. It is unfortunate that for many years teachers have clung unquestioningly to the trite principle that 'children should be allowed to learn at their own rate'. What of the children who learn too slowly and *could* learn more rapidly? Brandt (1985) has cautioned teachers that allowing students to progress at their own rate actually creates an ever-widening gap between the faster and the slower learners. Certainly, the evidence is that slow learners fall increasingly behind and experience fewer and fewer successes if they are not given special consideration (Walberg 1988). 'Special consideration' should mean more rapidly-paced, effective instruction which teaches them more, not less, in the time available.

Two viewpoints have emerged concerning slower learners. One viewpoint can be termed 'The Deficit Model'.

Slow learners: The Deficit Model

A number of writers have attempted to summarize the characteristics of 'slow learners'. The following list represents a compilation from those sources.

It is argued that slow learners have difficulties in learning because they have:

- below average intelligence;
- poor concentration span;
- poor powers of retention for knowledge and skills;
- underdeveloped listening skills;
- difficulties in understanding complex language structures;
- a meagre vocabulary;
- lack of ability to generalize and transfer new learning;
- little desire to go beyond the information given in any lesson at school;
- inability to use reading as a means of acquiring information, extending knowledge, and for enjoyment;
- major problems in written language;
- poor self-esteem;
- lack of self-management skills;
- behavioural and emotional reactions to failure.

It is easy to see why the list tends to be described as a 'Deficit Model': all the comments are negative and pessimistic. There is a danger that teachers may shrug their shoulders and feel that such students are impossible to teach. However, it can be argued that if a teacher is aware of these areas of difficulty experienced by the student, he or she can take account of them when preparing classroom work. Each of the above so-called 'deficits' has an immediate implication for *what* we teach and *how* we teach it to slower students.

Many years ago Gulliford made a comment which is as true in the 1990s as it was then: 'Though slow learners and the socially disadvantaged often appear to have less to offer, this is a measure of their need rather than an indication of their limits' (Gulliford 1969: 48).

The second viewpoint on slow learners attributes their problems to inefficiency in learning style. A common definition of learning style is that it is the sum total of the mental processes, emotions, motivations and coping strategies which a learner brings to a learning situation. Some students are observed to have very poor task-approach skills. They do not have effective ways of attempting new tasks, but rather employ hit-and-miss strategies which have high failure rates. They do not plan ahead or monitor their own performance. Frequently they become locked into a failure cycle, even in the first year at school; and their problem is exacerbated by the rapid development of behaviour patterns detrimental to good learning. Early failure undermines confidence and the child develops avoidance strategies which further reduce the opportunity to learn. Stott, whose work in the 1970s gave the first insights into these problems, suggested that many students regarded as mildly intellectually disabled, or specifically learning disabled, are not lacking in potential ability. He considered that their poor approach to learning prevents them from attending to or working at anything for very long. They need to 'learn *how* to learn' (Stott 1978; Stott, Green and Francis 1983). The evidence is that students *can* be helped in this direction (Gloeckler and Simpson 1988).

The 'learning style' viewpoint presented by Stott certainly strengthens the argument that students with learning difficulties benefit most from explicit teaching of new concepts and skills. They need to be placed in well-managed classrooms, with clear, active teaching and where students spend productive time-on-task, experiencing successful practice and knowing that they are reaching mastery.

LEARNING DISABILITIES

Learning disability (LD) is the term applied to students whose difficulties cannot be traced easily to any lack of intelligence, to sensory impairment, to cultural or linguistic disadvantage or to inadequate teaching. This small group, perhaps no more than 1 to 2 per cent of the school population, exhibits chronic problems in learning, particularly within the academic skill areas of reading, writing, spelling and mathematics.

Although the field of 'learning disabilities' (LD) is often said to date back only to the 1960s, with the name Samuel Kirk mainly associated with pioneering work in identification and classification of students with chronic learning problems, the initial recognition of unusual learning difficulties actually began well before the turn of the century (Richardson 1992). Since those early days, the field of learning disabilities has represented something of a growth industry, with more research, more publications, and more public interest generated than in almost any other field of education. Nevertheless, learning disability remains a controversial issue. Many educators deny that there *is* a form of learning difficulty distinct from the general learning problems which are known to impede the progress of some students (Franklyn 1987). Other experts argue strongly that a form of learning disability does exist which is qualitatively and etiologically different from the more general forms of academic failure. Even after many decades of research, no final consensus has been reached concerning a precise and unambiguous definition of learning disability (Kavale, Forness and Lorsbach 1991).

The best-known form of specific learning disability is, of course, dyslexia. This form of reading problem is thought to be present in just under 1 per cent of the school population (although some reports place the prevalence rate much higher). It is often defined as a disorder manifested by difficulty in learning to read despite conventional instruction, adequate intelligence and sociocultural opportunity. Other forms of learning disability have been identified as dysgraphia (problems with writing), dysorthographia (problems with spelling), and dyscalculia (problems with arithmetical calculation). However, such quasi-medical terms are not at all helpful in educational decision-making related to placement and teaching of the students concerned.

Some authorities in the learning disability field tend to attribute the learning problem to neurological or constitutional deficiencies within the student. For example, Adelman and Taylor (1987) devote several pages to a discussion of possible neurological dysfunction as a causal factor. They suggest that the LD student may have sustained very minor, subclinical brain damage before or during birth; or may have a nervous system which is maturing at a slower rate than is normal (maturational delay theory) or which exhibits biochemical irregularities. The CNS dysfunction theory is supported by Hynd, Marshall and Gonzalez (1991). However, even if some of these factors do apply in a particular student's case, two comments must be made. First, the diagnosis does not provide useful information for educational intervention: it doesn't tell us what we should do. Second, it is most unlikely that such a factor can operate alone to cause the learning difficulty.

Although much emphasis has been placed upon the organic or biological causes of learning disability, and interest has also been shown in possible genetic factors in some cases, recent studies have suggested other possible causes. In particular, attention has been directed towards learning style. In many cases of learning disability the children exhibit very inefficient learning styles – for example, not approaching a task such as word recognition or phonic decoding or arithmetical computation with any adequate system. The important thing to note is that current evidence suggests that these children can be taught more efficient strategies and can then function at a significantly higher level (see Chapter 3).

One of the major problems which has been evident in the learning disabilities field for some years is that of accurate identification. Any list of symptoms used to describe the learning disability syndrome creates problems. It has been asked, 'How can child A be described as a learning-disabled child [or more specifically, perhaps, a dyslexic child] when he or she shows only three of the so-called symptoms?' The inability to identify a list of characteristics which were 'always present' in cases of specific learning disability was one of the main factors which weakened the argument for the existence of a particular form of learning difficulty which is different from a general learning problem. To some extent this confusion was reconciled when it was proposed in the late 1960s that subtypes of dyslexia exist. More recent studies have confirmed the existence of such subtypes (McKinney 1988; Flynn et al. 1992). It was found that the symptoms or characteristics presented by dyslexic children tended to cluster into syndromes or patterns of difficulty – for example, subtypes with major auditory and linguistic problems, or with visuo-spatial difficulties, or with emotional blocks to learning.

Characteristics of students with LD

Over the years, children with learning disabilities have been described as having, in addition to the problems with reading, writing, spelling and arithmetic, some of the following difficulties:

- a history of late speech development (and continuing immaturities in articulation and syntax);
- visual perception problems (frequent reversal of letters and numerals – distorted or blurred word shapes);
- auditory perceptual problems (including difficulties in identifying sounds within words and blending sounds into words);
- poor integration of sensory information (for example, can't easily learn to associate and remember printed symbols and their spoken equivalent);

- weak lateralization (for example, underdeveloped hand–eye preferences; directional sense confusion);
- some signs of neurological dysfunction;
- hyperactivity;
- weak sequencing skills (as reflected in jumbled letter sequences in spelling or in word-attack skills in reading);
- poor co-ordination;
- low level of motivation;
- secondary emotional problems due to learning failure and poor school progress.

Studies have tended to show that far more LD students have auditory and language problems (60 per cent) than have problems with visual perception and motor skills (10 per cent); some have mixed difficulties, or no obvious difficulties in either area.

General advice on methods and approaches for LD children will be found in later chapters dealing with literacy and numeracy. Here it is only necessary to state the main principles which emerge from the literature on teaching learning disabled children.

- Reading, writing, spelling and maths skills should be thoroughly taught, leaving nothing to chance.
- At the same time, the skills must be utilized in a meaningful way so that reading and writing and arithmetic are used for a real purpose, not merely as drill exercises.
- More attention must be given to phonic skill development than is currently the case in contemporary approaches to the teaching of reading. However, in a few cases, a predominantly phonic approach may be contra-indicated if the child has significant auditory problems. As a generalization, training in phonological awareness is now regarded as an essential component of remedial teaching (see Chapters 6 and 7).
- Metacognitive and cognitive training strategies, such as those described in Chapter 3, must be used alongside skill-building and practise.
- Ideally, special tuition will be provided, perhaps by withdrawing the child from the regular class for brief, intensive sessions. Where this is not possible, individual help should be given daily within the classroom setting. Parents often make use of tutors who work with children after school hours. It is unrealistic to expect a child with a learning disability to make optimum progress if not given individual tutorial help.

- There is little evidence to support the view that identifying sub-types of learning disability will easily lead to the selection of a particular method of instruction for a specific type. This diagnostic-prescriptive approach has yet to prove itself (Snider 1992).
- The use of any training programme which seeks to improve an underlying skill or process, such as visual perception, has been discredited in recent years (Hallahan and Kauffman 1991). Such training appears not to result in improved achievement levels in reading, writing or spelling.

SUMMARY

This chapter has presented an overview of the problems encountered by students with general and specific learning difficulties. It is suggested that, rather than concentrating solely upon so-called deficits within the learner, it is more productive to identify other factors over which a teacher can exert much greater influence when planning an educational programme. Attention was given to exploring what is meant by 'effective instruction for all students', and to notions of a personalized approach within an inclusive curriculum to reduce failure rate.

A conclusion can be reached that within the whole-class context slower learners and those with specific learning disabilities need to be taught more effective ways of managing themselves and regulating their own learning. These issues are developed fully in the next two chapters.

Discussion points

- Finding topics and activities within the daily programme which are 'inclusive' of all children across a wide ability range presents a real challenge. Discuss some examples of inclusive practices from your own experience.
- How might a teacher break in to the 'failure cycle' and help a student to improve?
- What needs do slow learners and learning-disabled students share in common?
- Refer back to 'The Deficit Model'. Discuss the teaching implications for each item in the list said to be typical of a slower learning student.

Further reading

Anderson, V. and Stanley, G. (1992) 'Ability profiles of learning disabled children', *Australian Psychologist* 27, 1: 48–51.

Ashman, A. and Elkins, J. (eds) (1990) *Educating Children with Special Needs*, Sydney: Prentice Hall.

Association of Independent Schools of N.S.W. (1992) *Effective Teaching: Techniques for Students with Special Needs in Regular Classrooms*, (video package), Sydney: A.I.S.

Bowd, A. (1990) *Exceptional Children in Class*, Melbourne: Hargreen.

Gaylord-Ross, R. (1989) *Integration Strategies for Students with Handicaps*, Baltimore: Brookes.

Gloeckler, T. and Simpson, C. (1988) *Exceptional Students in Regular Classrooms*, Mountain View: Mayfield.

Mastropieri, M.A. and Scruggs, T.E. (1987) *Effective Instruction for Special Education*, Boston: College-Hill.

Rieth, H. and Evertson, C. (1988) 'Variables related to the effective instruction of difficult-to-teach children', *Focus on Exceptional Children* 20, 5: 1–8.

Scruggs, T.E. and Wong, B.Y. (1990) *Intervention Research in Learning Disabilities*, New York: Springer-Verlag.

Stainback, S. and Stainback, W. (1992) *Curriculum Considerations in Inclusive Classrooms*, Baltimore: Brookes.

Young, R.M. and Savage, H.H. (1990) *How to Help Students Overcome Learning Problems and Learning Disabilities*, Danville: Interstate Publishers.

Chapter 2

Helping children develop self-management skills

Children need to be taught self-management skills for planning and carrying out learning experiences with increased independence just as they need to be taught to read.

(Wang 1981: 201)

The term 'self-management' refers in this chapter to the child's ability to function independently in any given learning environment. In the classroom it relates to such behaviours as knowing how to organize one's materials, knowing what to do when work is completed, knowing how and when to seek help from the teacher or a peer, how to check one's own work for careless errors, how to maintain attention to task without constant supervision or reassurance, how to observe the well-established routines in the class, such as ordering lunch, having sports equipment or books ready for a specific lesson, knowing when a change of lesson or room is to occur, and so on. The actual self-management skills required by a child will tend to differ slightly from classroom to classroom, according to a particular teacher's management style, routines and expectations. For example, in some classrooms a premium is placed upon passive listening, note-taking and sustained on-task behaviour, while in other classrooms initiative, group-working skills and co-operation with other children are essential prerequisites for success. The self-management skills required in an informal setting tend to be different from those needed in a more formal or highly structured setting. Knowing how to respond to the demands and constraints of different lessons or settings is an important aspect of self-management.

Evidence exists to show that the type of classroom learning environment created by the teacher, and the instructional approach used, can both markedly influence the development of self-management and independence in children. Teaching approach and learning environment determine how effectively available learning time is used by the children to increase their independence (Wang and Walberg 1985; Wang and Zollers 1990). Some teachers seem to operate with students with special needs in ways which foster their *dependence* rather than their independence. For example, they may offer too much help and guidance for these children in an attempt to prevent possible difficulties and failures. They may virtually spoon-feed the child, using an individual worksheet programme which offers few challenges and calls for no initiative on the child's part. Too much of this type of approach is not what mainstreaming of special-needs students should be about. Not only does it not foster independence, it may well operate in such a way as to segregate the child from the mainstream curriculum and from the peer group for too much of the day.

SELF-MANAGEMENT CRUCIAL FOR INTEGRATION

Why are self-management skills important, and why have they been given priority early in this book? The reason is simple: the possession of adequate self-management skills by a child with a disability or a learning problem seems to be one of the most important factors contributing to the successful integration of that child in a regular class. A study comparing children with a mild intellectual disability, who were successfully integrated in regular classes in the upper primary school, with similar children who were not successfully integrated, revealed the following. The successfully integrated children:

• exhibited significantly more initiative and self-management in their classroom behaviour;
• spent significantly more time usefully engaged upon tasks set by the teacher;
• spent significantly less time off-task in inappropriate or disruptive behaviour;
• demonstrated significantly better awareness of classroom rules and routines.

(Westwood 1984)

It could be argued that a child with special needs should only be placed in a regular class when he or she has acquired adequate levels of independence in work habits, self-control, social skills and readiness for basic academic learning. Some of these requisites were identified by Salend (1984) in a review of successful mainstream programmes and have been confirmed as essential prerequisites for positive integration by Centre and Bochner (1990).

Self-management is closely allied to a much broader phenomenon, that of adaptive behaviour.

The concept of adaptive behaviour

Adaptive behaviour has been defined by Butler (1990: 707) as 'The individual person's skill in adjusting to the environment at adequate levels of independence and responsibility through maturation, learning and social adjustment.'

Adaptive behaviour manifests itself in at least three ways:

- as the acquisition of age-appropriate self-help skills to permit independent functioning;
- as the development of patterns or codes of behaviour which are appropriate for different social contexts;
- as the ability to benefit and learn from direct personal experiences.

The extent to which an individual's behaviour is appropriately adaptive in any given situation is gauged by the degree to which the behaviour is compatible with the standards of personal and social responsibility and self-sufficiency expected in a person of that age and within that culture (Baroff 1991).

Some students, for example those with intellectual disability, or with social, emotional or psychological disorders, frequently exhibit poor adaptive behaviour (Thurman and Widerstrom 1990). Indeed, impairment in adaptive behaviour, combined with sub-average general intelligence, is still used as a criterion in identifying individuals with an intellectual disability (Grossman 1983).

One of the major goals of intervention with such students is to increase their independence by improving their skills in self-management. Even students with milder forms of disability or learning difficulty often display ineffective self-management and need positive help to become more independent learners (Weinstein et al. 1989; Cole and Chan 1990).

SELF-MANAGEMENT CAN BE TAUGHT

Evidence is accumulating in support of the view that deliberate training in self-management can be effective in promoting independence, even in students with intellectual disability (Hughes, Korinek and Gorman 1991) and with learning difficulties (Taylor and Sternberg 1989; Gloeckler and Simpson 1988; Lovitt 1991). What can be done to teach self-management? Firstly, teachers must believe that such teaching is important, and that it is possible to teach self-management skills to children who lack them. Secondly, teachers need to consider precisely which skills or behaviours are required by their students in order to function independently in their particular classrooms.

Let us examine a very simple example of teaching self-management in a regular classroom. Obviously the routine involved, the amount of modelling and specific direction, and the complexity of the language used, will be adapted to the age and ability of the class.

Teaching students what to do when a piece of work is completed

Establish attention. Call upon specific students for responses, particularly those known to be lacking in self-management and initiative.

'Let's make sure that we all know what we do when we finish a piece of work in this class. Perhaps you finish your maths assignment, or you complete your first draft of a story and you don't need to see me to check it at once. This is what you do. First, you read through the work carefully yourself.'

Write on blackboard: 'READ YOUR OWN WORK CAREFULLY'.

'Why do we do that Allan?'
'Good! To check that we have the heading and date and your name. I'll write that on the blackboard.'

Write: 'CHECK HEADING, DATE AND NAME.' Perhaps have the class read this aloud.

'Good. Any other reasons, Karen?'
'Yes, to check for careless mistakes.'

Write: 'CORRECT ANY ERRORS.'

'Now that you have checked those things you place your work in this tray on my desk. So, what do I write about that on the blackboard?'

Write: 'PLACE IN Mr W's TRAY.'

'Good.'
'Then you go back to your desk and you can do one of these things.'

Write: 'MOVE ON TO THE NEXT EXERCISE, OR COMPLETE ANY UNFINISHED WORK FROM PREVIOUS LESSON, OR

FIND A BOOK TO READ SILENTLY, OR TAKE A PUZZLE
SHEET, OR MOVE TO THE COMPUTER AREA.

*Review: 'Let's read those rules through together; then we'll start our writing
lesson. When you've finished I want you to do exactly what it says on the
blackboard without me needing to remind you. Sally, come out and point to each
one of our rules as we read them together once more.'*

When a child fails to do the correct thing after completing work you are
now in a position to refer him or her to the routine previously established.
Teaching a student the appropriate way to manage himself or herself in the
classroom links closely with the establishment of general classroom rules.
This matter is discussed further in Chapter 4.

Over to you

Consider your own class setting (pre-school, primary, middle or
senior school) and the subjects you cover within the curriculum.
Write down a comprehensive list of the knowledge and skills needed
by a child to function independently in your setting. The examples
provided in the first paragraph of this chapter may serve as a starting
point.

Write down the steps and procedures you might use in teaching
any two of the skills needed for self-management in your list above.

In some situations a teacher might employ a 'star chart' or other visual
recording system to reward at regular intervals all those students who
demonstrate the specific self-management skills expected of them. Rewarding would be most frequent immediately after the teaching of the rule
(as above, for example), but would not be phased out totally even after
several weeks for those who are generally lacking in initiative.

It is important to establish the idea of maintaining the appropriate
performance *without prompting*. Remember, when you are constantly
reminding the class of what to do you are maintaining the students'
dependence. You may need to remind the children with special needs
more frequently than the others to begin with, and reward more frequently
their correct responses; but your long-term aim is to help these children
to function independently. When they *do* function independently you have
helped them to become more like other children in the class, and that is a
goal of integration.

LOCUS OF CONTROL

The whole issue of self-management and initiative in children links closely with the personality construct known in psychology as the locus of control. To explain locus of control one needs to understand that individuals attribute what happens to them in a particular situation either to internal factors (e.g. their own efforts or actions) or to external factors (e.g. luck, chance, things outside their control). Children with an internal locus of control recognize that they can influence events by their own actions, that to some extent they control their own destiny. Or to bring it down to classroom level, that when they concentrate and try hard, they get better results.

The internalization of locus of control (i.e. the development of responsibility and self-reliance) usually increases rapidly with age if a child experiences normal satisfaction and reinforcement from his or her efforts and responses. However, it has been found that many children with learning problems, and with negative school experiences, may remain markedly external in their locus of control, feeling that their efforts have little impact on their progress, and that what happens to them in learning tasks is unrelated to their own actions (Walden and Ramey 1983). In its extreme form the externality is usually described as 'learned helplessness', where the individual anticipates failure immediately any new situation occurs, and cannot conceive of being able to change this outcome (Canino 1981; Schunk 1989).

The child who remains largely external is likely to be the child who fails to assume normal self-management in class and who is prepared to be managed or controlled by 'powerful others' such as the teacher, parent, teacher's aide or more confident peers. There exists a vicious circle wherein the child feels inadequate, is not prepared to take a risk, seems to require support and encouragement, gets it, and develops even more dependence upon others. The teacher's task is one of breaking into this circle and quite deliberately causing the child to recognize the extent to which he or she has control over events and can influence outcomes. It is natural for a teacher to wish to help and support a child with special needs; but it should not be to the extent that all challenge and possibility of failure are totally eliminated. Failure must be possible and children must be helped to see the causal relationship between their own efforts and the outcomes, and to accept responsibility for both. Children will become more internal in their locus of control when they recognize that effort and persistence can overcome failure (Lovitt 1991).

STRATEGIES FOR INCREASING INTERNALITY

Much of the research on matching teaching style or learning environment to a child's perceived or measured locus of control suggests that children who are markedly external respond best at first in a highly structured, predictable, teacher-directed setting, particularly for the learning of basic academic skills. It also suggests that strongly internal students are able to cope well with open or child-centred programmes (Bendell, Tollefson and Fine 1980). Regardless of this, teachers must recognize that for some children with a markedly external locus of control there is a need to help them develop greater internality. This development is likely to be a gradual process, therefore such strategies as suddenly placing external children in a very open, child-centred teaching environment may only increase the number of occasions when they fail and develop an even greater feeling of helplessness and lack of ability. There is a need to work slowly towards the children assuming slightly more responsibility for their work and effort over a period of time. Consideration should be given to the fact that a structured teaching approach, which itself does little to increase internality, may be necessary for a while before a child can become independent enough in school work and study to survive in an open situation. For example, a very teacher-directed programme may be needed initially in order to raise the child's level in basic academic skills. Evidence suggests that such an approach is certainly required by students with behaviour problems if they are to be integrated successfully into regular classes (Conway 1990).

Wang and Stiles (1976) first experimented with a system whereby seven- to eight-year-old children were gradually encouraged to plan more and more of their own work (including how long to spend on each task) within the constraints of available classroom resources and the timetable. Their conclusion was that the self-scheduling system was effective in developing the children's abilities to take increased responsibility for their own learning. It also increased their perceptions of personal responsibility for achievement and success. In other words, the gradual increase in the use of self-directed learning may increase the self-management skills and internality of locus of control. This is certainly one of the underlying principles embodied in the Adaptive Learning Environments Model (ALEM) developed by Wang and her colleagues as a system for integrating students with special needs in regular classrooms (Wang and Zollers 1990). It is also evident in the emphasis now placed upon allowing students to work collaboratively in such subject areas as mathematics (Holmes 1990).

What are some of the strategies a teacher might use to increase internality? The following list may provide a few clues.

Increasing internality of locus of control

- Individual 'contracts' between teacher and child can be introduced in a fairly simple form. These may specify the tasks assigned for a two-hour period or for a morning, but allow the child to decide in what order to tackle the work, how long to spend on each section, and when to seek assistance.
- The use of self-instructing material (e.g. programmed kits or computer programmes) may also help a child to gain an awareness of the extent to which his or her own efforts result in progress and achievement.
- Situations may be contrived where children are given a range of graded tasks, some of which will be a little beyond them. When they begin to fail on these tasks they can be shown that with a little more effort on their part, and if they seek help when necessary, they can complete the work successfully. The children are taught how to try rather than to give up.
- Teachers who provide only direct correction for school work (i.e. simply marking responses right or wrong, without giving feedback and extra practice) are merely establishing a feeling of lack of ability in the child. Feedback to children should be corrective when possible and they should be given the opportunity to prove that they can solve similar items to those that were initially incorrect. Teachers should plan to provide corrective feedback in such daily activities as mental arithmetic or spelling if they want the lower achievers to improve in these areas. Too much testing without follow-up teaching may increase externality.
- If at some time it is necessary to punish a child for some misdemeanour, the punishment should be given immediately following the incident and the child must fully understand the reasons for it. Punishment which is divorced in time and place from the event is likely to exacerbate feelings of helplessness. The child should also be given the earliest opportunity to act appropriately in a similar situation and should be rewarded and specifically praised for doing so.
- While every opportunity should be taken to praise or reward a slower or poorly motivated learner for genuine progress, teachers must avoid rewarding success if no real effort was required.

- Employ the notion of 'wait time' when orally questioning the less-able students within a class lesson. Too frequently a teacher moves quickly from the less-able student, probably to avoid embarrassment when he or she does not immediately answer. This can create a feeling of frustration and uselessness in the students; and after a time they don't make any effort to reply. Studies have shown that if teachers wait only a few seconds longer, many of these students will make a response which can be accepted and praised (Rowe 1986).

Praise

The whole issue of teachers' praise merits fuller comment. Teachers' use of praise has been well researched, but its overall effects are still somewhat uncertain. It appears to have a differential effect according to the characteristics of the children being praised. Brophy (1979) reviewed studies in this area and concluded that praise does seem important for low-ability, anxious, dependent students, provided that it is genuine and deserved and praiseworthy aspects of the performance are specified. A child should know precisely why he or she is being praised if appropriate connections are to be made in the child's mind between effort and outcome. Trivial or redundant praise is very quickly detected by children and serves no useful purpose. Descriptive praise, however, can be extremely helpful:

'That's good work, Leanne. I really like the way you have taken care to keep your letters all the same size.'
'Good, David! Those lines are really straight today because you pressed hard on the ruler.'
'I'm very glad you asked me that question Sara. It shows you are really listening very carefully to the story.'

Thompson, White and Morgan (1982) carried out observations in third-grade classrooms and noted that high-achieving students received significantly more praise than less able or difficult students. For example they received up to 50 per cent more praise than children with behaviour problems. These researchers also made the telling observation that *all* children received far more neutral comment, criticism and warnings than they did praise. They state that teachers were far more disapproving than approving and tended therefore to create a negative classroom climate which was not conducive to learning or self-esteem.

Attributional retraining

It is important to recognize the negative impact which an external locus of control can have upon a student's motivation to persist in learning. It is easier for the child to give up and develop avoidance strategies rather than persist if the expectation of failure is high. In the instructional approach known as 'attributional retraining' (Cole and Chan 1990) students are taught to appraise carefully the results of their own efforts when a task is completed. They are taught to verbalize aloud their conclusions: 'I did that well because I took my time and read the questions twice'; 'I listened carefully and I asked myself questions'; or 'I didn't get that problem correct because I didn't check the example in the book. Now I can do it. It's easy!'

The main purpose in getting the students to verbalize such attribution statements is to change their perceptions of the cause of their successes or failures in school work. It helps to focus their attention on the real relationship between their efforts and the observed outcomes.

Attributional retraining seems to have maximum value when it is combined with the direct teaching of effective task approach strategies to use in a particular task. This strategy training is discussed fully in the next chapter.

Assessing locus of control

Questionnaires exist for the assessment of locus of control in children of various ages, but it is usually possible to recognize from classroom observation those children with a markedly external locus. Teachers should be on the look-out for such children and should attempt to intervene to improve the situation.

Lawrence and Winschel (1975) have concluded that children with intellectual disability being considered for integration into regular settings should demonstrate an internality for both success and failure which is not less than the average level in the regular class. While such judgement may need to be made rather subjectively, locus of control is certainly one learner characteristic which does need to be taken into account. It may need specific attention once the student with a disability is integrated (Rogers and Saklofske 1985).

SUMMARY

This chapter stressed the importance of teaching all children the most effective ways to manage themselves in the regular classroom, to show initiative and to become self-reliant. These attributes are of particular importance in the case of children with disabilities, since self-management appears to be a crucial prerequisite to successful integration and functioning in the mainstream.

Helping children develop self-management skills also involves assisting them to develop a more internal locus of control and to recognize the extent to which their own actions influence their successes and failures. Techniques for fostering this development were discussed.

Everything which has been said in this chapter applies across all categories of disability and across all ability levels. For example, the visually impaired student with above-average intelligence needs specific self-management skills quite as much as the sighted child with some degree of hearing loss. Appraisal of each individual's level of self-management should be a starting point for assisting children with special needs to cope more adequately in regular settings.

In the next chapter the notion of self-management is extended to include the even more important issue of self-regulation in the actual process of learning.

Discussion point

Jason is twelve years old. He has been assessed as moderately intellectually disabled and he spends most of his time at a special school. However, on two mornings each week he attends a regular class in the local school, with some assistance provided in the form of a teacher aide. The intention is, that over a period of time, Jason will be integrated into the regular school on a more permanent basis.

Jason has difficulty in coping with the demands of the regular school and clearly needs help in adjusting to the routines and expectations there. He is a friendly boy and has no emotional or behavioural problems. His family is very supportive.

Consider some of the actions you might take in order to maximize his chances of success when integrated into the regular school.

Further reading

Cohen, S. and de Bettencourt, L. (1983) 'Teaching children to be independent learners', *Focus on Exceptional Children* 16, 3: 1–12.

Cole, P. and Chan, L. (1990) *Methods and Strategies for Special Education*, New York: Prentice Hall.

Crandall, V., Katkovsky, W., and Crandall, V.J. (1965) 'Achievement responsbility questionnaire', *Child Development* 36: 91–109.

Gupta, R.M. and Coxhead, P. (1990) *Intervention with Children*, London: Routledge.

Hughes, C.A., Korinek, L. and Gorman, J. (1991) 'Self-management for students with mental retardation in public school settings', *Education and Training in Mental Retardation* 26, 3: 271–91.

Licht, B.G., Kistner, J.A., Ozkaragoz, T., Shapiro, S. and Clausen, L. (1985) 'Causal attributes of learning disabled children', *Journal of Educational Psychology* 77, 2: 208–16.

Little, A.W. (1985) 'The child's understanding of the causes of academic success and failure', *British Journal of Educational Psychology* 55: 11–23.

Nowicki, S. and Strickland, B.R. (1973) 'A locus of control scale for children', *Journal of Consulting and Clinical Psychology* 40, 1: 148–54.

Chapter 3

The development of self-regulation in learning

> Self-regulated learning means that individuals manage their cognitive abilities and motivational effort so that learning is effective, economical and satisfying
>
> (Paris and Oka 1986: 103)

In Chapter 2 attention was given to the development of basic self-management skills in children. Self-management was defined as the child's ability to function independently in any given learning environment. Discussion in that chapter focused mainly upon the importance of teaching students how to organize themselves, physically and mentally, for classroom learning. In particular, work habits, attention, on-task behaviour, self-control and initiative were stressed as vitally important prerequisites if a student is to benefit fully from an educational programme. Self-management in organizational practices helps a student to become a more independent learner (Bowd 1990).

In this chapter the term 'self-management' is expanded to include not only the elements above, but also the learner's ability to regulate his or her own thinking processes while involved in a learning task. Such self-regulation requires that students play an active role and monitor closely the effects of various actions they take and decisions they make while learning. This involves the capacity to think about one's own thinking (metacognition) and to apply appropriate cognitive strategies necessary for tackling the particular learning task.

One of the common observations concerning many students with learning problems is that they have become 'passive' learners (or even non-learners). They show little confidence in their own ability to control learning events in the classroom, or to bring about improvement through their own efforts or initiative. Teaching a student how to learn and how to regulate and monitor his or her own performance in the classroom –

how to become a more self-regulated learner – must be a major focus in any intervention programme. It is pertinent for teachers to ask, 'Can we teach students how to learn? When a student lacks effective learning strategies can we provide instruction which will develop such strategies?' These questions are answered, at least in part, by the mainly positive results which have emerged from research into self-regulated learning (Zimmerman and Schunk 1989), metacognitive training (Chan 1991) and cognitive behaviour modification (Cole and Chan 1990; Paris and Winograd 1990). These approaches will be discussed in this chapter, and their practical applications for students with learning difficulties will be explored.

METACOGNITIVE INSTRUCTION

'Metacognition' can best be described as 'understanding and controlling one's own thinking'. It refers to an individual's capacity to monitor and regulate his or her mental processes while approaching a new learning task or solving a problem (Ashman and Conway 1989). Metacognition has two main components: an awareness of the skills needed to perform a specific task effectively (i.e. a knowledge of the appropriate attack-strategies to use); and the ability to use self-regulation to ensure successful completion of the task (i.e. planning one's moves, evaluating the effectiveness of one's actions, checking progress), and coping with any difficulties as they arise (Cornoldi 1990).

It is considered that metacognition helps a learner to recognize that he or she is either doing well, or is having difficulty learning or understanding something. A learner who is monitoring his or her own ongoing performance will detect the need to pause, to double-check, perhaps begin again before moving on, to weigh up possible alternatives or to seek outside help. In this respect, metacognitive strategies are an essential part of what are traditionally referred to as independent study skills. But metacognition also enters into many areas of classroom performance, and the conscious use of appropriate self-monitoring strategies makes for more effective learning. 'Metacognitive strategies are plans we use to direct our own learning and include setting objectives, listing resources needed, planning a sequence of actions, and using an appropriate yardstick to judge success' (Bowd 1990: 41).

The view is now widely held that many learning problems that students exhibit are related to metacognitive deficits, that is, the learners lack the ability to use effective strategies when faced with a learning task, and cannot monitor or regulate their responses appropriately. Some students undoubtedly develop their own efficient strategies without assistance; others do not. Paris and Oka (1986) have observed that often cognitive strategies are not taught explicitly in classrooms and may remain obscure or totally misunderstood by many students. Quite clearly, some teachers don't make their instruction explicit enough for these students. They add to their students' learning problems by failing to demonstrate effective ways of approaching a new task. A teacher needs to provide clear modelling of the most appropriate strategies to use to minimize the chances of failure and to maximize the chances of early success. A teacher who says, 'This is how I do it, and this is what I ask myself as I do it. Watch and listen', is providing the learner with a sound starting-point. The teacher who says, 'See if you can find out how to...', is often providing an invitation to failure and frustration. Perhaps a useful example to consider here is that of teaching early handwriting skills to young children. This is one area where teachers do provide modelling, verbal cues, and corrective feedback, and do invite the students to monitor their own performance. Few teachers would invite beginning writers to discover efficient letter-formation for themselves. Similar direct instruction should also be provided in such skills as mathematical problem-solving, reading comprehension, spelling, and story writing.

It is important to indicate that there is a difference between cognitive instruction and metacognitive instruction. Cognitive instruction involves teaching the student the specific steps to follow and the skills to use when tackling a particular task – for example, the exchanging rule in subtraction, the 'look-cover-write-check' method of learning to spell an irregular word, or the appropriate way to read a six-figure reference to locate a point on a map. This type of instruction embodies what is often called 'attack-strategy training'. Metacognitive instruction goes beyond this, focusing on techniques which require the learner to monitor the appropriateness of his or her responses and to weigh up whether or not a particular strategy needs to be applied in full, in part, or not at all in a given situation. For example, to recognize that there is no need to use the exchanging rule in a particular subtraction problem because there is obviously a short-cut solution; or recognizing that the application of the 'look-cover-write-check' method to learn a simple phonetically-regular word is unnecessary. Most teachers tend to focus almost entirely upon cognitive training, which is a necessary but insufficient procedure in itself to ensure independence in learning. It is essential that teachers realize the need to devote time and effort to encourage students to think about their own thinking in a variety of learning situations. In particular, students need to be shown how to use what Conway and Gow (1990) refer to as 'self-interrogation' and 'self-checking'. They need to be taught appropriate questions to ask themselves as they carry out a specific task and monitor their own progress.

According to several authorities a variety of intellectual tasks can be more easily accomplished if students use metacognitive skills and are provided with instruction in how to do so (Ashman and Conway 1989; Paris and Winograd 1990; Chan 1991). The curriculum areas of reading and mathematics are often cited as examples of academic skills which can be improved by metacognitive training. Students should be taught how to approach these areas 'strategically' and then given abundant opportunity to practise the application of these key strategies. For example, in Chapter 10 some mainly cognitive strategies for improving problem-solving in mathematics will be discussed. Similar cognitive and metacognitive strategies can be taught to students to improve their reading comprehension. The PQRS strategy described below provides an example.

The PQRS reading comprehension strategy

P = Preview   Scan the chapter or paragraph, attending to headings, subheadings, diagrams and illustrations. Gain a very general impression of what the text is likely to cover. Ask yourself, 'What do I know about this already?'

Q = Question   Generate some questions for yourself: 'What do I expect to find out?' 'Will it tell me how to make the object?' 'Will it tell me how to use it?' 'Will I need to read this very carefully or can I skip this part?'

R = Read   Read the passage or chapter for information: 'Are my questions answered?' 'What else did I learn?' 'Am I understanding this?' 'Do I need to read this again?' 'What does that word mean?'

S = Summarize   Briefly state in your own words what the text is saying. 'What was the main idea?' 'Does my statement sound correct?' 'Do I need to add anything else?' 'What reaction am I getting from the person who is listening to me?'

The teacher models good application of the PQRS approach, demonstrating how to focus on important points in the passage, how to check on one's own understanding, how to back-track or scan to gain contextual cues. This modelling assists students to internalize particular strategies and self-questioning techniques. They are then helped to apply the same approach, with corrective feedback from the teacher. Strategies of this type are best taught through dialogue between teacher and students working together to extract meaning from the text. Peers can facilitate each other's learning in small groups. This 'dialogue approach' has been termed 'reciprocal teaching' by Cole and Chan (1990). Dialogues allow students and teachers to share their thoughts about the process of learning, and to learn from the successful strategies used by others. Dialogues also serve a diagnostic purpose by allowing teachers to appraise students' levels of understanding and their unaided use of certain strategies.

Over to you

Read again the PQRS strategy described above.

- Which of the questions are metacognitive, rather than simply cognitive?
- Generate a few more metacognitive questions for that example.

Generalization of the application of a particular strategy to a new situation can be a problem. This fact needs to be recognized and transfer of training needs to be planned for, rather than assumed. Chan (1991) has recommended that teachers ensure that specific strategies taught are actually *needed* in the daily curriculum to facilitate immediate application. It is also necessary to provide a variety of new contexts (e.g. different texts, different problems) over a period of time and to discuss fully with students the various situations in which a particular strategy can be used effectively.

Research studies seem to provide the following tentative conclusions:

- Metacognition is developmental in nature. As children grow older they become involved more actively in their own learning. Children following normal developmental patterns develop strategies to facilitate their learning and become able to monitor the effects of their own efforts (Sileo 1985).
- Metacognitive training can assist students with learning problems to develop appropriate strategies in given contexts (Cole and Chan 1990).
- The effects of metacognitive training are often task-specific, especially with low-ability students. Provision must be made for training to be applied across a variety of tasks, to aid generalization (Ashman and Conway 1990).

- Cognitive and metacognitive training has been effective in improving aspects of performance in mathematics such as computation and problem-solving, in improving reading comprehension and recall of information from texts, in the writing of summaries, in preparing essays and in spelling (Cole and Chan 1990).

Over to you

Identify the strategies needed when a student is required to prepare and write a concise factual report following a simple science experiment.

Taking Conway and Gow's (1990) point that metacognition involves self-checking and self-interrogation while completing a task, write down some questions which students might ask themselves while writing this report.

COGNITIVE BEHAVIOUR MODIFICATION (CBM)

Cognitive behaviour modification, or verbal self-instruction, is a closely related approach to metacognitive training. It involves the application of a set of procedures designed to teach the students to gain better personal control over a learning situation by use of self-statements or directions which guide their thinking and actions. The students are taught an 'action plan' in which they talk themselves through a task in order to control their performance and monitor their results. 'Inner language' is seen as very important for both cognitive and metacognitive development, and the learner is taught to use language to control his or her own responses.

Cognitive behaviour modification: basic principles

The training procedure for a typical cognitive behaviour modification programme usually follows this sequence:

Modelling The teacher performs the task or carries out the new procedure while 'thinking aloud'. This modelling involves the teacher asking questions, giving directions, making overt decisions and evaluating the results.

Overt external guidance The student copies the teacher's model and completes the task with the teacher still providing verbal directions and exercising control.

Overt self-guidance The learner repeats the performance while using verbal self-instruction as modelled by the teacher.

Faded self-guidance The learner repeats the performance while whispering the instructions.

Covert self-instruction The learner performs the task while guiding his or her responses and decisions using inner speech.

Typical covert questions and directions a student might use would include: What do I have to do? Where do I start? I will have to think carefully about this. I must look at only one problem at a time. Don't rush. That's good. I know that answer is correct. I'll need to come back and check this part. Does this make sense? I think I made a mistake here, but I can come back and work it again. I can correct it.

These self-questions and directions cover problem definition, focusing attention, planning, checking, self-reinforcement, self-appraisal, error detection and self-correction. They are applicable across a fairly wide range of academic tasks. Sometimes the instructions, cue words or symbols to represent each step in the procedure may be printed on a prompt card displayed on the student's desk while the lesson is in progress.

Training in self-instruction techniques of this type are considered to be particularly useful for students with mild intellectual disability as part of their improvement in self-management (Conway and Gow 1990). The application of cognitive behaviour modification to cases of chronic behaviour disorder is discussed in the next chapter.

Over to you

- Construct a set of self-instructions which a student might use when copying a diagram from a textbook.
- Devise a sequence of instructions which a student could use when reading a chapter from a novel which he or she must later summarize.
- How might cognitive behaviour modification be used to slow down the performance tempo of a student who is impulsive?

SUMMARY

Students with learning difficulties are often perceived as passive, powerless, incompetent and without motivation to succeed. In this chapter a case has been argued for changing this situation by placing students more actively in control of their own learning processes. Research has shown that students can be taught to become self-regulated learners, capable of taking the initiative and controlling their own responses more effectively.

The teacher's role involves the explicit modelling of effective ways of approaching a learning task or solving a problem. Students must be helped to internalize appropriate task-approach strategies and must be given abundant opportunity to practise and master these across a wide range of new concepts. The aim is to ensure that students learn how to learn. The value of metacognitive instruction and cognitive behaviour modification in achieving this goal has been discussed in this chapter.

Self-regulated learning can build the confidence of a student and thereby increase motivation and self-esteem as well as producing higher achievement within the curriculum. As Harris and Pressley (1991: 401) have said 'Used appropriately, cognitive strategy instruction is an exciting and viable contribution to the special educator's repertoire'.

Discussion point

Given that the methods used in the early years of schooling have tended to become less structured and more child-centred in the mainstream of education, how might the specific strategy training advocated in this chapter be included in general classroom practice?

Further reading

Ashman, A. and Conway, R. (1989) *Cognitive Strategies for Special Education*, London: Routledge.

Borkowski, J.G. (1992) 'Metacognitive theory: a framework for teaching literacy, writing and math skills', *Journal of Learning Disabilities* 25, 4: 253–7.

Chan, L. (1991) 'Metacognition and remedial education', *Australian Journal of Remedial Education* 23, 1: 4–10.

Cole, P. and Chan, L. (1990) *Methods and Strategies for Special Education*, Sydney: Prentice Hall.

Graham, S., Harris, K. and Reid, R. (1992) 'Developing self-regulated learners', *Focus on Exceptional Children* 24, 6: 1–16.

Rowe, H. (1989) 'Teaching learning strategies', *SET Research Information for Teachers* 1, 14: Australian Council for Educational Research.

Chapter 4

The management of behaviour

Classroom behaviour problems interfere with instruction and with social interactions.

(Lewis and Doorlag 1987: 114)

Many teachers report that one of their main concerns in the regular classroom is the child who disrupts lessons, seeks too much attention from the teacher or peers and who fails to co-operate when attempts are made to provide extra help or to construct an individualized programme. In other words, the teachers feel that although they may know what the child needs in terms of basic instruction, it is impossible to deliver the service because the child is totally unreceptive.

While it is true that some students exhibit behavioural problems in school which are a reflection of stresses or difficulties outside school (e.g. in the family), it is also evident that in some school situations disruptive behaviour and apparent social maladjustment result directly from factors within the learning environment. The student who is bored by work which is trivial and lacks challenge may well become troublesome. The child who is teased or ignored by the peer group may either withdraw or become attention-seeking or aggressive. The atmosphere in some schools, and the approach of some teachers, tend to alienate certain students; and therefore maladjustment and the development of poor self-image can be caused by factors within the system, rather than within the child. Unfortunately, as Conway (1990) suggests, teachers are more likely to see the problem as lying within the student and his or her background than within the school curriculum or the methods used.

When cases of disruptive or deviant behaviour are reported, particularly in secondary schools, it is important to consult with other teachers to discover whether the student is also a problem when in their classes. All the teachers who have contact with the maladjusted student will usually need to get together to agree upon a common approach to be used in dealing with the problem behaviour. One of the factors which can add to a maladjusted student's problems in secondary school is the frequent change of teachers for different subjects. Within the course of a single day a student may encounter quite different treatment, ranging from the authoritarian to the permissive. This lack of consistency needs to be minimized. It is one of the reasons why some schools have established 'sub schools' with a smaller but consistent pool of teachers to cater for specific groups of students through in-class support at a more personal level (Lavers, Pickup and Thomson 1986). With younger children the problem of inconsistent management is not as great, since most of the curriculum is planned and implemented by a single teacher who gets to know the children well. In senior schools, however, many more difficulties can arise.

Occasionally, of course, it is necessary to seek expert advice when a child's deviant behaviour does not respond to consistent forms of management set out below; but in many cases behaviour can be modified successfully within the school setting. A starting point is the establishment of good classroom rules.

CLASSROOM RULES

Classroom rules are essential for the smooth running of any lesson and should be formulated by the children and the teacher together very early in the year. The application of rules should be consistent, and should recognize both the rights and responsibilities of the students and the teacher. Rules should be few in number, clearly expressed, displayed where they can be seen by all, and formulated in positive terms (what the students *will do*, rather than *must not do*). Students must understand why the rules are necessary and must know exactly what will happen if a rule is broken (Calf 1990).

Classroom-based research on the management style of teachers has yielded a clear indication that the most effective teachers establish rules and procedures as a top priority at the beginning of the year. They discuss the rules with the students, and apply them systematically and fairly. Such teachers were also more vigilant in the class-room, used more eye contact, were more proactive than reactive to prevent behaviour problems, set appropriate tasks for students to attempt successfully, avoided 'dead spots' in lessons, kept track of student progress, checked work regularly and provided feedback to the whole class and to individuals (McManus 1989; Lovitt 1991).

William Rogers (1989a, b) suggests that all teachers should develop their own discipline plan to enable them to know in advance what to do when classroom behaviour is disruptive. The plan gives a teacher confidence when the pressure is on. Corrective actions which a teacher can decide to use might include:

- tactical ignoring of the student and the behaviour (low-level disruptions);
- simple directions ('Ann – get back to your work please');
- positive reinforcement ('Good, Ann');
- question and feedback ('What are you doing, Mark? I'll come and help you');
- rule reminders ('David, you know our rule about noise. Please work quietly');
- simple choices ('Excuse me Joanne. You can either work quietly here, or I'll have to ask you to work at the corral. OK?');
- isolation from peers (take the student aside and discuss the problem; then place him or her in a quiet area with work to do);
- removal from class (time out in a different room, under supervision, may sometimes be needed).

Teachers may also use strategies such as deflection and defusion to take the heat out of a potential conflict or confrontation. Teacher: 'Sally, I can see you're upset. Cool off now and we'll talk about it later; but I want you to start work please.' The judicious use of humour, without sarcasm, can also help to defuse a situation, without putting the student down (Rogers 1989b: 54).

Classroom rules, rights and responsibilities

Valuable advice is given by William Rogers (1989) in his programme called 'Decisive discipline' and in his book *Making a Discipline Plan*. He suggests that the goals of discipline in school should be to assist students to do the following:

- accept responsibility for their own behaviour;
- exercise self-control;
- respect the rights of others;
- adopt the principles of fairness and honesty;
- face the logical consequences of their own behaviour.

Clear, consistent rules must be democratically established by all members of the class, based on the rights of others and on personal responsibility. Respect for the rights of others includes the right of other students to learn and the right of the teacher to teach.

Rogers illustrates well the principle that, while the actual rights and the rules which protect the class are important, the process by which these are developed is just as important. Classroom discussion, early in the first week of a new term, should focus upon rights, rules and responsibilities. There must also be open discussion of the consequences for breaking a rule. Rules should include matters like communication (e.g. hand up and wait), and treatment of others' ideas (e.g. listening and praising), movement in the room, noise levels, safety, personal property, school equipment. Rules should be stated in positive terms – what the students will do, not in negative 'must not' terms. Students should feel a sense of ownership for rules through contributing to their formulation.

In Rogers' approach, three steps are taken when any problem arises:

- give a warning in the form of a rule reminder;
- give time out for five minutes;
- student gives an apology to the class.

When it is not possible to find an appropriate consequence for a particular disruptive behaviour, the students should be encouraged to write about the behaviour. They must say what they did, what they should have done and what they are going to do to put matters right.

CHANGING BEHAVIOUR: AN OVERVIEW

In order to change undesirable behaviour in a specific student it is usually necessary to consider all factors which may be supporting the behaviour both directly and indirectly. For example, a girl who openly defies a teacher's request to work quietly on an assignment and not disturb those around her may actually be seeking peer group approval for provoking and standing up to the teacher. She may also be successfully avoiding a situation where she is forced to admit that she cannot do the work which has been set. She may later gain more attention, albeit critical, from her parents if a letter of complaint is sent home from school. These factors combine to reinforce the status quo. In addition, the girl may be preoccupied with the outcome of some confrontation she had with another teacher in the previous lesson or with another student at lunch-time. Finally, if the work appears to her to have no real significance, she will have little motivation to attempt it. In order to bring about change here the teacher must work to ameliorate the various influences of as many of the factors as possible. This type of global attack on the problem, an attempt to manipulate variables within the total context in which the child operates, has been termed the 'ecological approach' by Hallahan and Kauffman (1991).

A somewhat different approach, but one which is commonly used in conjunction with the ecological approach, for maximum impact, is the 'behavioural approach', more often referred to as 'behaviour modification'.

In this approach three assumptions are made:

- all behaviour is learned;
- behaviour can be changed by altering its consequences;
- factors in the environment (in this case the class-room) can be engineered to determine which behaviours will be rewarded and which will be ignored or punished.

Typically a problem behaviour is targeted for change. The factors which are maintaining it are identified. A programme is devised to reshape this behaviour into something more acceptable or more productive through a consistent system of reward, reinforcement or punishment. Attention must also be given to improving the student's own self-monitoring and decision-making in order to increase self-control relative to the problem behaviour (Conway 1990).

Rather emotional criticism is sometimes levelled at behaviour modification programmes. It is suggested that the manipulation of the individual's behaviour and reactions is somehow impersonal and thus out of keeping with humanistic views on the value of interpersonal relationships. However, the precise planning and management of a behaviour modification programme requires very careful observation of how the child, the teacher and other children are interacting with each other and influencing each other's behaviour. Far from being 'impersonal' the techniques used to bring about and maintain change are highly interpersonal.

Some teachers are also deterred from attempting behaviour change programmes because they have been told that very accurate record-keeping and charting of frequency and duration of particular behaviours will be required. While data sheets and accurate monitoring of responses are of definite value in clinical settings, or where an aide or paraprofessional assistant is available, it is usually unrealistic to expect the busy classroom teacher to maintain such detailed records.

Some examples of behaviour modification techniques will be presented in the following sections of the chapter, together with suggestions for manipulation of the classroom environment to achieve specific results. First it is timely to quote Hallahan and Kauffman, to place such strategies in context:

Good behaviour management for disturbed children has a lot in common with good behaviour management for all children. The best preventive action any teacher can take is to make sure that the classroom is a happy place where children take pride in their work and learn to treat others with respect.

(Hallahan and Kauffman 1986: 184)

IDENTIFYING THE PROBLEM

As previously stated, teachers are often troubled by the child who is constantly seeking attention, interrupting the flow of a lesson and distracting other children. Naturally, many teachers feel threatened by the child who is a constant challenge to their discipline. That feeling of threat can cause the situation to get out of hand as the teacher becomes trapped in confrontations with the child and an ongoing war is waged, rather than possible solutions being sought.

All too often one observes the teacher reacting overtly to undesirable behaviour and at once reinforcing it. Many behaviour problems in the classroom, particularly disruptive and attention-seeking behaviours, are rewarded by the adult's constant reaction to them. For example, the teacher who spends a lot of time shouting at children or threatening them is in fact giving them a lot of individual attention at a time when they are behaving in a deviant manner. This is a misapplication of 'social reinforcement' and the teacher unintentionally encourages what he or she is trying to prevent. Some control techniques used by teachers (e.g. public rebuke or punishment) can have the effect of strengthening a child's tough self-image and status in the peer group.

If you have a child who is presenting problems to you in terms of control and behaviour it would be useful if you took the necessary time to analyse the possible reasons for this within your classroom setting. These questions may be helpful when attempting to draw up a complete picture of disruptive behaviour.

- In which lesson is the behaviour less frequent (e.g. the more highly structured sessions, or the freer activities)?
- At what time of day does the behaviour tend to occur (a.m. or p.m.)?
- What is the noise level like in the room before the problem arises?
- How is the class organized at the time (groups; individual assignments, etc.)?
- What am I (the teacher) doing at the time?
- How is the child in question occupied at the time?
- What is my immediate response to the behaviour?
- What is the child's initial reaction to my response?

- How do other children respond to the situation?
- When I have successfully dealt with the problem in the past, what strategies have I used?

Notice that the analysis deals with issues which are immediately observable in the classroom. Behaviour analysis does not need to examine the child's past history or search for deep-seated psychological problems as causal explanations for the child's behaviour (Conway 1990).

Sometimes changes as simple as restructuring the working groups, reducing noise level in general and closer monitoring of work in progress will significantly reduce the occurrence of a particular behaviour.

STRATEGIES FOR REDUCING DISRUPTIVE BEHAVIOUR

Deliberate ignoring

Ignoring the child is an approach which can be used far more frequently than most teachers are prepared to accept. If a child begins some form of disruptive behaviour (e.g. calling out to gain attention) the teacher ignores completely that child's response by turning away and giving attention to another student who is responding appropriately. If the peer group can also be taught to ignore a disruptive student and not reinforce the behaviour by acknowledging it and reacting to it, the planned ignoring technique will be even more successful. This technique is frequently sufficient on its own to modify the behaviour of, for example, an intellectually disabled child in a regular class who is merely acting up in ways typical of a younger child.

Clearly it is not sufficient merely to ignore disruptive or inappropriate behaviour. It is essential that planned ignoring be combined with a deliberate effort to praise and reinforce appropriate behaviours at other times in the lesson. While it is common to view the frequency of undesirable behaviour in a child as something to reduce, it is more positive to regard the 'non-disruptive' or appropriate behaviours as something to reward and thus increase. It is a useful guideline to be more positive and encouraging than critical and negative in your interactions with students.

A teacher cannot ignore extremely disruptive behaviour when there is a danger that someone will be hurt or damage will be done. Nor can a teacher go on ignoring disruptive behaviour if it is putting other children at educational risk through lost learning time. The teacher must intervene to prevent physical danger, but should do so quickly, quietly and privately. Private reprimands, coupled if necessary with time out, are less likely to bring the inappropriate behaviour to the attention and approval of other children.

Reinforcement and rewards

In order to modify behaviour, particularly in young or immature children, it may be necessary to introduce a reward system. If social reinforcers such as praise, smiles and approval are not effective, it will be necessary to recognize and cater for individual differences. If possible find several reinforcers which may be used to provide variety over a period of time. It may be that the child likes a stamp, a sticker or coloured star, a chance to play a particular game, build a model, construct a puzzle, listen to a taped story on a cassette, or even clean the blackboard! Some teachers use tokens. Tokens are simply a means of providing an immediate and tangible reward. Tokens are usually effective because of their immediacy, and students can see them accumulating on the desk as visible evidence of achievement. Tokens can be traded later for back-up reinforcers such as time on a preferred activity, early minutes, or a positive report to take home to parents. While not themselves sensitive to individual preferences for particular types of reinforcement, tokens can be exchanged for what is personally reinforcing.

A token chart or star chart may be drawn up for the classroom wall, and both individual and group efforts can be rewarded quickly and visibly during the day. Some teachers find the use of a points system helpful in general classroom management; e.g. rewarding the first group ready for work, a group showing high levels of self-management, the children with the highest levels of work output, individuals working quietly, individuals who exhibit helpful behaviour to others.

Initially we need to reinforce every small step in the right direction, but the reinforcement can be reduced over a period of time. Most textbooks on behaviour modification provide some general rules for using reinforcement. It is worth repeating them here:

- First, reinforcement must be given immediately after the desired behaviour is shown and must be given at very frequent intervals.
- Second, once the desired behaviours are established, reinforcement should be given only at carefully spaced intervals after several correct responses have been made.
- Third, the teacher gradually shifts to unpredictable reinforcement, so that the newly acquired behaviour can be sustained for longer and longer periods of time without continuing feedback.

Time out

'Time out' refers to the removal of a student completely from the group situation to some other part of the room, or even to a separate but safe setting for short periods of isolation. While time out may appear to be directly punishing it is really an extreme form of ignoring. The procedure ensures that the child is not being socially reinforced for misbehaviour.

It is important that every instance of the child's disruptive behaviour should be followed by social isolation if the time-out technique is being used. The appropriate behaviour will not be established if at times the inappropriate behaviour is tolerated, at times responded to by punishment and at other times the child is removed from the group. It is essential to be consistent.

Avoid placing a student outside the classroom if in that situation he or she gets other interesting rewards; e.g. being able to peer through the window and attract the attention of other students in the room, making contact with other students in the corridor, watching more interesting events in other parts of the school.

Explosive situations may develop with some disturbed children, and a cooling-off period will be necessary. A set place should be nominated for this (e.g. a corner of the school library, where worksheets may be stored for use by the student). The student will not return to that particular lesson until he or she is in a fit state to be reasoned with and some form of contract can be entered into between teacher and student. The student, should, however, be under supervision for all of the time spent out of the classroom.

Punishment

Punishment, if administered appropriately, is yet another way of eliminating undesirable behaviours. At times punishment is necessary and its consequences do modify behaviour. Punishment, when needed, should be given immediately the deviant behaviour is exhibited. Delayed punishment is virtually useless. Punishment is most effective if it is combined with positive reinforcement. This combination brings about more rapid and effective changes than the use of either procedure alone. The child who pushes or punches other children will learn appropriate behaviour if he or she receives positive reinforcement (praise or tokens) for friendly and co-operative behaviour as well as punishment (loss of privileges, verbal reprimand, time out) for the inappropriate behaviour.

The principal objection to punishment or 'aversive control' is that, while it may temporarily suppress certain behaviours, it may also evoke a variety of undesirable outcomes (fear, a feeling of alienation, resentment, an association between punishment and schooling, a breakdown in the relationship between teacher and student). Punishment may also suppress a child's general responsiveness in a classroom situation besides eliminating the negative behaviour.

As has been stated previously, punishment should not be used as the sole method for modifying behaviour and controlling certain students. Punishment has as many unfortunate side-effects as it has benefits.

Behavioural contracts

A behavioural contract is a written agreement signed by all parties involved in a behaviour change programme (Fletcher and Presland 1990). The student agrees to behave in certain ways and to carry out certain obligations. The staff and parents agree to do certain things in return. For example, a student may agree to arrive on time for lessons and not disrupt the class. In return the teacher will sign the student's contract sheet indicating that he or she has met the requirement in that particular lesson, and adding positive comments where possible. The contract sheet accompanies the student to each lesson throughout the day. At the end of each day and the end of each week, progress is monitored and any necessary changes are made to the agreement. If possible, parental involvement is negotiated by the school, and the parents agree to provide some specific privileges if the contract is observed for two consecutive weeks, or loss of privileges if it is broken. When behaviour contracts are to be set up it is essential that all teachers and school support staff are fully informed of the details.

The contract system is strongly advocated by Lovitt (1991) who suggests that the daily report card can specify precisely which features of behaviour are to be appraised each lesson by the teacher. A simple yes/no response column makes the recording task quick and easy for a teacher to complete at change of lesson. For example:

Arrived on time	Y	N
Had completed homework	Y	N
Followed instructions	Y	N
Stayed on task	Y	N
Did not disturb others	Y	N
Completed all work	Y	N

Lovitt (1991) also suggests sending a copy of the report home, and liaising regularly with parents by telephone or letter.

Over to you

Identify some problem behaviour which is giving you cause for concern in your present class. Write down as objectively as possible the main features of this behaviour. What are the most obvious characteristics? Why is the behaviour troublesome?

Try to identify the specific situations which seem to trigger off the behaviour. What do you do when the behaviour occurs? What do the other children do when the behaviour occurs?

Keep this information in mind as you read the remaining sections of this chapter and attempt to select intervention strategies which might be helpful for bringing about the desired changes.

Read the following description provided by a teacher when referring a child for assessment by an educational psychologist.

David never seems to be able to keep quiet in my lessons. He always keeps shouting out answers without thinking and he does almost anything to get the attention of other children; shows off almost non-stop. He's on the go all the time. He is a pest before school, too. Before I can get out of my car he is waiting to tell me about something that's happened and to carry my bag to the staffroom. He clings on to me when I'm on yard duty and hangs back after school to talk. I sometimes give him jobs to do just to get him out of my hair, but half the time he doesn't finish them. The thing that really annoys me is that he keeps asking me for help during quite simple activities. He doesn't need help and he stops me from attending to those who do. Then, when I do sit down with another group he deliberately does something to interrupt or to make me cross. He really never gets stuck into his work. He produces very little and I have to virtually stand over him to get him to concentrate. Of course, I can't do that all the time. He's really hopeless when we start on something new. He doesn't listen to the instructions so just jumps in and guesses wildly at what has to be done – hit or miss, he doesn't care. Some of the other kids don't like him much because he messes up their team games in the yard. He can't stand losing either! He cheats if he gets the chance. When he's in a group at lunch time I've seen him do really stupid things. The others lead him on and he just does anything to impress them. He's even damaged another teacher's car just because the others dared him to do it.

What would *you* do to assist a boy like David?

REDUCING AGGRESSIVE BEHAVIOUR

Teachers are bothered most by aggressive behaviour in children (Church and Langley 1990). Increase in teacher stress is now considered to be closely linked with an increase in misbehaviour and aggression in school (Conway 1990; Wragg 1989). Some of the strategies suggested above for reducing generally disruptive behaviour are applicable also to the reduction of aggression. The following supplementary points may be helpful where aggression is the major concern. If episodes of aggressive behaviour continue, it is essential that the teacher obtain specialist guidance, counselling or similar support services. Work with the family as well as the child may be indicated.

Prevention

Knowing that you have a potentially aggressive child in your class should make your aware of the need to control or limit situations where aggression might be provoked. Too much unstructured time, too many dead-spots in lessons, too much unsupervised movement within the room, must be avoided. It may be necessary to give particular thought to the layout of the classroom to allow ease of supervision and access to desks and resources. The establishment of predictable routines and basic rules in the room will help. The teacher, knowing the class well, should be able to anticipate and divert misbehaviour and aggression by a well-timed question, a change of activity, or the delegation of a small duty to the problem child.

Proximity

When a child appears to be on the point of losing control, move physically closer to him or her, even invading the child's personal space, as a means of reducing or preventing the aggressive action. Quickly direct the child's attention to something new and move him or her to a different part of the room. Give the student something easy but productive to do and stay with him or her until the work is commenced. Make positive comments about the student's attention to the new task.

Provide physical outlets and other alternatives

In educational settings it is important for some children to have extra opportunities for physical exercise and movement in order to 'burn off' excess energy in acceptable ways (e.g. competitive races, circuit training).

Sometimes it is useful to have some video tapes of basic aerobics or fitness programmes available to be used in the classroom or activity room when the need arises for a quick change of activity. For certain children this cathartic 'get it out of your system' strategy seems very successful although there is no scientific basis at the moment. The present writer found it very useful with both primary and secondary students with major behaviour problems, as a strategy for preventing difficulties.

Teach children to express their anger verbally

Students who are poor communicators, perhaps through language difficulties, often don't know how to handle their own anger and aggression, and their reactions are therefore inappropriate. Part of any programme to improve behaviour and reduce the frequency of outbursts should be aimed at helping the student to verbalize the problem. Talking through a threatening situation helps the child to establish control and thus reduces impulsive misbehaviour. Accept the child's angry feelings but offer other suggestions for expressing them. For example say, '*Tell* her you don't like her taking your book.' '*Ask* David politely to return your paintbrush.' Then ensure that the child *does* use this approach at once. Cognitive behaviour modification programmes may also be helpful.

Assertiveness training

Assertiveness training is designed to lead children to understand that they have the right to be themselves and to express their feelings openly. Assertive responses generally are not aggressive responses, but they are open and honest. Simply stated, assertive behaviour is being able to express yourself without hurting others.

Dissolve explosive situations through humour

A joke can help to ease a child out of a temper tantrum or outburst without losing face and can avoid placing teacher and child in confrontation. The joke or humour must not be at the child's expense and must not hint at ridicule or sarcasm.

Improving self-control in cases of conduct disorder

A cognitive behaviour modification programme developed by Wragg (1989) has proved very successful with some students who exhibit chronic conduct disorders. The programme uses individual coaching and rehearsal with cue cards to establish self-instruction strategies in the student. These self-instructions are used to help the student monitor his or her own reactions to daily problems, and to control and manage such situations more effectively.

The first stage in intervention is to help students analyse their inappropriate behaviour and to understand that what they are doing (e.g. lashing out at others; arguing with staff) is not helping them in any way. Next the student is helped to establish both the desire to change and the goals to be aimed for over the next week, (to stop doing this and to start doing that). An 'emotional temperature chart' provides a graphic point of reference from which the student can begin to monitor his or her own level of arousal, anger or discomfort.

Over a number of sessions the student is helped to change negative thoughts and beliefs to more appropriate positive equivalents. A key ingredient in the programme is teaching the student to use covert self-control statements which serve to inhibit inappropriate thoughts and responses, allowing time for the substitution of more acceptable responses – for example, to be assertive but not aggressive. The programme can be extended to improve such essential classroom behaviours as increased time on-task.

Wragg notes that school counsellors and psychologists can also use the programme with conduct-disordered children in clinical settings.

HELPING WITHDRAWN OR TIMID CHILDREN

Merrett and Wheldall (1984) have indicated that teachers are much more likely to notice and respond to aggressive and disturbing behaviour than they are to quiet and withdrawn behaviour in the average classroom. The quiet, withdrawn children who cause no problem to the teacher may even be overlooked. They are likely to go unnoticed because their behaviour never disrupts the classroom routine. They annoy no one and they do not constantly come to the teacher's attention.

Teachers are becoming more aware of the significance of extreme shyness and withdrawal as signs of maladjustment. However, quiet children are not necessarily emotionally disturbed and may have no problems at all. For example, children reared in families where the parents are quiet and reflective are themselves likely to learn similar patterns of behaviour. Reticent and quiet children may be quite happy; and it is a questionable practice to force such children to be assertive.

If a child does have a genuine problem of withdrawal from social interaction with other children, the teacher does need to intervene. This may apply particularly to children with physical or intellectual disabilities where social acceptance may be a major problem. Some of the strategies for teaching social skills described in the next chapter will be very important in such cases. Let it suffice here to suggest that the lonely or rejected child may need to be helped to establish a friendship within the class by judicious selection of partners for specific activities (e.g. project work, painting, completion of a puzzle, etc.) and by planning frequent opportunities for the child to experience some very positive outcomes from working with another child. Sometimes the teacher can encourage the child to bring some unusual toy or game from home which can be shared with another child. Once established, even a very tentative friendship must be nurtured by the teacher.

Highly formal classrooms, where much silent deskwork is expected, will do little to foster social development in children lacking these skills. Equally, highly individualized programmes for special needs children may attend to their cognitive needs at the expense of their social skills development.

When the social isolation is extreme it may be the result of an almost total lack of social skills, from a history of rejection, from childhood depression, or from some combination of these factors. Verbal communication can be minimal with such children; even eye-contact may be virtually absent. In many such extreme cases the social isolation may be maintained by negative reinforcement, that is, the behaviour is continued because it avoids unpleasant contact (e.g. ridicule) from other children.

In the literature on socially isolated children it is usually suggested that careful observation be made within the classroom and in the playground in order to find the point at which some cautious intervention might be attempted (e.g. getting the child to engage in some parallel play alongside other children as a preliminary step to later joining the play of others, taking a turn, etc.). The teacher will need to guide, support, prompt and reinforce the child through these various stages. In almost all cases the co-operation of the peer group will need to be enlisted if the child is to become an accepted member of that group. Studies have shown that social skills training, together with peer involvement, can have lasting effects on improving social adjustment of primary age children (Slavin 1991).

Studies which have focused on the integration of children with disabilities into regular classes have indicated that social acceptance of these children into the peer group does not occur spontaneously (Stainbeck, Stainbeck and Wilkinson 1992). Most children with disabilities need to be taught how to relate to others, (how to greet them, how to talk with them, how to share things), quite as much as the students without disabilities need to be taught tolerance and understanding of those who are different from themselves.

HYPERACTIVITY

This form of behaviour is considered to be present in approximately 2 per cent of the school population. The term is often misused and applied to children who are merely bored and restless, or who are placed in a class where the teacher lacks good management skills. However, there are genuine cases of hyperactivity where the child experiences great difficulty in controlling his or her motor responses and exhibits high levels of inappropriate activity throughout the day (Levy 1990). Hyperactivity is also present sometimes as an additional problem in certain other forms of disability (e.g. cerebral palsy, congenital or acquired brain injury, specific learning disability, attention deficit disorder).

No single cause for genuine hyperactivity has been identified, although the following have all been put forward as possible explanations: central nervous system dysfunction (perhaps due to slow maturation of the motor cortex of the brain), subtle forms of brain damage too slight to be confirmed by neurological testing, allergy to specific substances (e.g. food additives), adverse reactions to environmental stimuli (e.g. fluorescent lighting), inappropriate management of the child at home, maternal alcohol consumption during pregnancy ('foetal alcohol syndrome'). 'Most investigators now agree that the hyperactive syndrome encompasses a heterogeneous group of behaviour disorders having different symptom clusters and etiologies' (Cohen and Minde 1983).

Hyperactive children usually exhibit below-average achievement levels in most school subjects. They may also be poorly co-ordinated. Some have problems with peer relationships. The literature indicates that most hyperactivity diminishes with age, even without treatment. However the impaired concentration span and restlessness associated with the condition may well have seriously impeded the child's progress during the important early years of schooling.

Four main approaches are used to treat hyperactivity.

Pharmacological treatment

This is perhaps the most common form of treatment, especially in America. Approximately 80 per cent of hyperactive children do seem to respond positively to drug treatment, but the others do not. The main drugs used in America are Ritalin, Dexedrine and Cylert. The reduced hyperactivity which accompanies medication does not always result in increased scholastic achievement, perhaps because the child is not provided with remedial tuition to help make up the leeway. Hallahan and Kauffman (1991) reviewed a number of studies of the progress made by students with hyperactivity. They concluded that medication alone is rarely, if ever, an adequate answer. Some form of extra tuition is needed, together with one or more of the approaches described below. However, in some cases medication can significantly improve attention span. Dramatic changes in behaviour and a reduction in family stress have been reported by some parents (Keith and Engineer 1991).

Some undesirable side effects have been reported from prolonged use of drugs (slow growth rate, short stature, disturbed sleep patterns).

Nutritional treatment

This involves the avoidance of specific foods containing, for example, artificial colourings or preservatives. The Feingold Diet is the best known of these treatments, although its use remains somewhat controversial. Diet control certainly doesn't prove effective with all hyperactive children, but some parents have claimed that it has been extremely helpful in specific cases.

Catharsis ('Get it out of your system')

This is merely the application of the strategy described earlier in the chapter whereby children 'burn off' excess energy through vigorous physical activity provided at frequent intervals.

Behaviour modification

The hyperactive child's on-task behaviour, attention to work, completion of assignments, reduction of disruptive outbursts, all need to be reinforced and rewarded. The over-active behaviour should be ignored where possible, or at least played down in importance. Where this is not possible, time out, removal of the child from positive reinforcement, has been shown to be effective in reducing hyperactivity, and is regarded as considerably safer than medication or strict diet regimes (Boyle 1990).

Wragg (1989) advocates self-management training to improve on-task behaviour. In this 'cognitive behaviour modification' approach the child is taught to control his or her own responses and behaviour by strategies such as verbal rehearsal or verbal regulation: 'I must work for five minutes on this, then take a break for one minute'. Sometimes video recordings of a child's actions are played back to him or her to focus on and discuss what must be modified (Lovitt 1991). Cognitive behaviour modification is mainly applicable to children of at least average intelligence since they are more able to understand the method and utilize it consistently.

Owing to the possibility that hyperactivity is caused by different factors in different individuals, it is not surprising to find that quite different forms of treatment are advocated, and that what works for one child may not work for another. The conclusion must be that any approach to the treatment of hyperactivity must attend to *all* factors which may be maintaining the behaviour (Gurry 1990).

SUMMARY

This chapter has presented some specific techniques for controlling and modifying children's behaviour.

In general, a combined ecological-behavioural approach has been advocated, whereby a child's problems are not treated in isolation but instead are tackled within the total context of the curriculum, the peer group, the classroom environment, and the family.

Particular attention has been devoted to disruptive and aggressive behaviour since this causes the most concern for teachers at all age levels. The problems of hyperactivity have been discussed mainly for the benefit of teachers of young children or of those with specific learning disabilities.

Consideration has also been given to the difficulties encountered by shy, timid or withdrawn children. This latter topic leads to a more detailed coverage of social skills training in the next chapter.

Discussion points

- Do you agree with the use of tokens to reward and modify behaviour?
- 'Teacher stress' has become a major problem in recent years. Discuss the factors which may be responsible for stress in teachers, and suggest ways in which the problem may be reduced.
- Every school should have a written and enacted policy which addresses behaviour management. What would a new member of staff hope to find in the written policy?

- 'You will never help a maladjusted student to develop appropriate behaviour by removing him or her from the class.' Is this statement true? Discuss.

Further reading

Alberto, P. and Troutman, A.C. (1990) *Applied Behaviour Analysis for Teachers* (3rd edn), Columbus: Merrill.

Balson, M. (1988) *Understanding Classroom Behaviour* (2nd edn), Hawthorn: Australian Council for Educational Research.

Bull, S.L. and Solity, J.E. (1987) *Classroom Management*, London: Croom Helm.

Canfield, J. (1990) 'Improving students' self-esteem', *Educational Leadership* 48, 1: 48–50.

Gordon, T. (1989) *Teaching Children Self-Discipline*, New York: Random House.

Hundert, J. and Houghton, A. (1992) 'Promoting social interaction of children with disabilities in integrated settings', *Exceptional Children* 53, 4: 311–20.

Jackson, M. (1991) *Discipline: an Approach for Teachers and Parents*, Melbourne: Longman-Cheshire.

Lerner, J.W. and Lerner, S.R. (1991) 'Attention deficit disorder: Issues and questions', *Focus on Exceptional Children* 24, 3: 1–20.

McManus, M. (1989) *Troublesome Behaviour: a Teacher's Survival Guide*, London: Routledge.

Morgan, S.R. and Reinhart, J.A. (1991) *Interventions for Students with Emotional Disorders*, Austin: Pro-Ed.

Workman, E.A. (1982) *Teaching Behavioural Self-control to Students*, Austin: Pro-Ed.

Wragg, J. (1989) *Talk Sense to Yourself*, Hawthorn, Australian Council for Educational Research.

Chapter 5

Improving social skills and peer group acceptance

Placing handicapped students in the regular classroom is the beginning of an opportunity. But like all opportunities it carries with it the risk of making things worse as well as making things better.

(Johnson and Johnson 1980: 10)

The quotation above applies most particularly to the issue of social acceptance of children with special needs when placed in a regular class. The results of most integration studies do not support the belief that integration into the mainstream will spontaneously improve the social status of children with disabilities; in some cases the child's positive social interactions are greatly reduced by such a placement (Gresham 1984; Slavin 1991). There are three basic problems:

- disabled children, contrary to popular belief, do not automatically observe and imitate the social models which are around them (Stobart 1986);
- teachers do not tend to intervene positively to promote social interaction on the disabled child's behalf;
- children without disabilities do not readily demonstrate high levels of acceptance of those with disabilities (Stainbeck, Stainbeck and Wilkinson: 1992).

Research studies indicate that it is common for children with significant speech problems, physical disabilities, intellectual impairment, emotional disturbance and poor scholastic achievement to be rejected by their more fortunate peers (Horne 1982). Admittedly the problems of social acceptance tend to be fewer for the mildly disabled than for those with more severe and obvious forms of disability (Espiner, Wilton and Glynn: 1985), but even the mildly disabled may have personality problems, communication difficulties or other characteristics which make it likely that they will be ignored if not openly rejected by the peer group.

Since one of the principal goals of integration is that of enhanced social development for children with disabilities and learning difficulties, it is vitally important that the regular class teacher recognizes the need to plan for improvement in this area (Lovitt 1991). Since the late 1970s a great deal has been written concerning social skills training for shy and unforthcoming children and for those with disabilities. Some of these techniques will be discussed in this chapter. At the same time increased attention has also been given in many schools to including 'social education' or 'human relationships' as an identifiable strand within the curriculum. For example, Wildlake (1983) quotes the following topics contained within the Scottish Social Education Project, a fairly typical programme of this type.

Social education

1. Coming to terms with yourself
     the development of a sense of personal identity
     self-confidence
     personal accountability.
2. Coming to terms with other people
     the development of tolerance
     the development of adaptability
     the ability to co-operate with others
     an understanding of the nature of authority and the need for
         social order.
3. Concern for other people
     the development of sensitivity towards others
     sympathy with others
     the development of a sense of social responsibility.

In schools where specific attention is given to matters such as these, particularly if issues of disability are openly discussed under section 2 and 3 above, there is a much greater likelihood that differences among individuals will be more readily accepted, and that rejection and hostility will be minimized.

Even with these positive advances some teachers still inadvertently deal with children, emotionally and physically, in ways which contribute to the social exclusion of some class members (Byrnes 1984). Some examples will illustrate this point.

- Teacher A always selects two team-leaders for outdoor games, with the instruction to 'choose your own teams'. Guess who is always chosen last or excluded because she is poorly co-ordinated and rather slow? This situation could be avoided by the use of a different organizational strategy.

- Teacher B always has Wayne sitting near her table so that she can more easily control his behaviour and also provide help when needed. While serving to 'maintain' Wayne in the classroom and attending to two of his educational needs, the approach inevitably isolates the boy from normal interaction with other children during deskwork time. This may not be a problem if he is programmed into group work and pair-activities at other times in the day; but the chances are he may not be.

- Teacher C believes that Lynette must have individual work assignments set because she can't cope with the general level of classwork (and this teacher never uses ability or friendship grouping for any purposes). The teacher spends time and effort in programming appropriate material for Lynette and even provides a carrel for her to work in, away from the other children. While this is totally defensible as a method of catering for this child's scholastic needs, it must be recognized that it virtually eliminates any social interaction. Is this 'integration'?

- Teacher D rarely ventures into the playground unless on duty. If Teacher D spent a little time observing David he would find that this boy is always ignored by other children at lunch time and at morning break. He spends his time by the door waiting to come back into the classroom (Westwood 1982).

Obviously some teachers need to be more aware of such situations and also to recognize failures in peer relationships. They must then be prepared to implement suitable strategies to bring about improvements. These strategies will now be discussed. It must be clear that, although reference is made frequently to children with disabilities, the approaches are equally applicable to any child who needs help in personal/social development.

IDENTIFICATION OF CHILDREN WITH PEER RELATIONSHIP PROBLEMS

Naturalistic observation

The most obvious strategy for identifying children with particular problems is informal observation of social interactions within and outside the classroom. A teacher who takes the trouble to note the ways in which children play and work together will quickly identify children who are neglected by their peers, or who are openly rejected and become an object of ridicule and teasing. It is very important also to try to observe the surface reasons which appear to give rise to this situation. For example, is the child in question openly obnoxious to others through aggression, hurtful comments, a tendency to spoil games or interfere with work? Or at the other extreme, does the child seem to lack motivation, confidence and skills to initiate contact with others, remaining very much on the outside of any action?

Naturalistic observation is probably the most valuable method of identification for the teacher to use since it focuses on the child within the dynamics of peer group interactions and can thus indicate a number of factors which might be modified.

Sociometric survey

Naturalistic observation tends to identify the most obvious cases of popularity or rejection, although it may not pick up all of the subtleties of social interaction in the class. For this reason some teachers find it useful to carry out a whole-class survey in order to get all the children to indicate, in confidence, their main friendship choices. The teacher may interview each child privately or, if the children can write, may give out slips of paper with the numerals 1 to 3 printed on them. The teacher then requests that each child write down first the name of the person he or she would most like to play with or work with as a partner in a classroom activity or at lunch-time. The teacher may then say, 'If that person was away from school who would you choose next?' and that name is listed second. A few teachers might also say, 'If there is anyone in the class you really don't like to work with or play with you can write that person's name against number 3. You don't *have* to write any name there if you get on well with everyone, just leave it blank.' (This last procedure is sometimes criticized by teachers, who fear that children may afterwards discuss what they wrote. If handled carefully, however, this problem should not arise.) When the papers are collected the teacher calculates the score for each child on the basis of 2 points for a first choice and 1 point for a second choice. The results for each individual in the class can then be tabulated. Some teachers go so far as to map the choices in the form of a sociogram, showing the 'stars' (most popular), the 'isolates' (not chosen by others), mutual pairs and cliques, etc.

The information gained from a sociometric survey may help a teacher to determine the composition of certain working groups in the class (Gronlund 1985; Bowd 1990). It can sometimes be helpful in identifying which children are named as first preference or second preference by the isolates, even though the choice was not reciprocated; there may be a chance to pair these two children for some activities. However, it is often found that isolates merely name the stars in the class, and the choice is not realistic. Children who are not chosen or who are listed as 'not liked' should obviously become the target for some of the intervention strategies described in this chapter.

Rating Scales

Gresham (1982) advocates the use of a peer rating scale rather than a sociometric survey, since he feels that this provides a better measure of 'likeability'. Also it ensures that some children are not forgotten or overlooked, as may happen with a sociometric survey of the type described above.

The children are provided with a list of the names of all the children in the class and required in confidence to place a score from 1 (not liked very much) to 5 (liked a lot) against each name. Summation of the completed scores will reveal the children who are not liked by most class members, as well as showing the level of acceptance of all other children. The result may sometimes correlate highly with naturalistic observation, but occasionally quite subtle positive or negative attitudes appear which are not immediately obvious to outside observation (Asher and Dodge 1986).

Parent nomination

Sometimes a child's social relationship problems at school may be brought to the teacher's attention first by the parent, who says, 'I'm worried about Paul. He doesn't bring any friends home and doesn't play with other children after school', or 'Marion has been coming home from school saying that the other girls are making fun of her in the playground and on the bus.' This type of information should be followed up by the teacher and treated in a sensitive manner.

Over to you

Use either the sociometric survey or the rating scale procedure described above with your own class. Before charting the results try to predict those children who will obtain low scores.

(continued...)

- How accurate was your prediction?
- Did your survey reveal any unexpected information?
- How might the results of this exercise help you in your day-to-day work with your class?

CREATING A SUPPORTIVE ENVIRONMENT

To facilitate social interaction for children with special needs in regular classrooms, three conditions are necessary.

- The general attitude of the teacher and the peer group needs to be made as positive and accepting as possible.
- The environment should be arranged so that the child with a disability has the maximum opportunity to spend time socially involved in a group or pair activity, during recess and during academic work in the classroom.
- The child needs to be taught the specific skills that may enhance social contact with peers.

Influencing attitudes

Lack of previous experience with disabled children and a lack of knowledge about handicapping conditions can lead children (and even teachers) to feel uncomfortable in the presence of a person with a disability. This, in turn, causes them to avoid contact where possible. Where the disabled individual has a marked speech and communication problem, looks grossly abnormal, and is poorly co-ordinated, the difficulties are greatest. Gow and Ward (1991) have noted that students with moderate intellectual disability and language problems are the most difficult to integrate successfully. In extreme cases, ignorance concerning disability can result in quite damaging prejudice, hostility and rejection (Hickson 1990).

Fortunately evidence is accumulating to show that attitudes can be significantly changed in teachers and in the peer group. Teachers and peers tend to become more accepting of children with disabilities when they better understand the nature of the disability (Lewis and Doorlag 1991). Experience has shown that a combination of information about, and direct contact with, disabled children provides the most powerful positive influence for attitude change (Gloeckler and Simpson 1988).

Improving attitudes

The following approaches have all been beneficial, particularly when used in combination, in improving attitudes towards disabled children. Throughout these awareness-raising techniques, the stress should be upon 'How can we help?' and 'How would we treat someone like that in our class?'

- Viewing films or videos depicting disabled children coping well and doing everyday things.
- Factual lessons and discussion about particular disabilities.
- Having disabled persons as visitors to the classroom or as guest speakers.
- Simulation activities, e.g. simulating deafness, or visual impairment, or being confined to a wheelchair. (Note that unfortunately two conditions which cannot be simulated are intellectual disability and emotional disturbance. These are also the two which produce the greatest problems in terms of social isolation and rejection in the peer group.)
- Reading and discussing stories about disabled persons and their achievements.
- Regular visits as helpers to special schools or centres.

Creating opportunities

If social learning is to take place, it is essential that the socially inept child has the opportunity to be truly involved in all group activities, both inside and outside the classroom. If disabled children are to be socially integrated then group work situations and co-operative learning should be used frequently in pre-school, primary and secondary settings (Slavin 1991). Unfortunately, while grouping and activity methods are common in the early years of schooling they are less common in the middle school or upper primary school. They are used even less in the later years, when children are faced with a mainly academic curriculum and a fairly rigid timetable.

Much of the work which has supported the value of co-operative learning and grouping within the classroom has been carried out by two brothers, Roger and David Johnson (1990, 1991). They make two assumptions: that teachers create classroom environments where competition is not a dominant element; and that teachers use grouping strategies to encourage co-operation among students for at least part of each day. Regrettably, both assumptions prove to be false when applied to certain teachers. Some use too much competition among their children on a regular basis. Some teachers make no use at all of grouping. They keep all the children in formal settings working on the same material for the same time, regardless of individual differences, actively discouraging any talking or collaboration. The implications here are that if a teacher rarely, if ever, uses grouping as an organizational option, it is unlikely that much will be achieved towards social integration in that classroom.

Organization for group work

When utilizing group work as an organizational strategy, it is important to consider the following points:

- Merely establishing groups and setting them to work is not enough. Group members have to be taught how to work together. They must be shown the behaviours which encourage or enable co-operation, e.g. listening to the views of others, sharing, praising one another, offering to help each other. If the task involves the learning of specific content, teach the children how to rehearse and test one another on the material.
- Teachers must carefully monitor what is going on during group activities and must intervene when necessary to provide suggestions, encourage the sharing of a task, praise examples of co-operation and teamwork and model co-operative behaviour themselves. Many groups can be helped to function efficiently if the teacher (or the aide or a parent helper) works as a group member without dominating the situation.
- The ways in which individual tasks are allotted has to be very carefully planned (division of labour) and the way in which each child can assist another is also made explicit, e.g. 'John, you can help Craig with his writing then he can help you with the lettering for your title board.' Contingent praise for interacting with others should be descriptive. 'Good, John. I can see your friend really appreciates you holding the saw for him.' 'Well done Sue. That's nice of you to help Sharon with that recording.'
- The size of the group is also important. Johnson and Johnson suggest a group of two or three members if the children are young or are unskilled in group work. Control the composition of the group carefully to avoid obvious incompatibility. Information from a sociometric survey may help to determine appropriate partners for less popular children.

- The choice of topic and tasks for group work is very important. Tasks have to be selected which require collaboration and teamwork. Themes which have proved very successful include: production of a wall display based on a recent visit to a fauna park, planning and rehearsing sketches or skits to be performed, making a video recording, preparing a carnival, sporting activities such as swimming and bowling, co-operative learning of a mathematics assignment (Madden and Slavin 1983). This latter project (mathematics) involved groups of four or five students, including slower learners, working together to master the set material to a particular standard. The group result was evaluated on the basis of how much each individual member had improved on his or her own initial score. The goal structure set for the task clearly involved co-operation. Under this structure, group members have a vested interest in ensuring that other members learn, as the group's success depends on the achievement of all. Helping each other, sharing and tutoring within the group must all be placed at a premium.

  It is important to realize that while the short-term results from single projects of this type are beneficial, the effects may not be durable. To ensure maintenance over time, any new skills gained must be reinforced constantly and new opportunities created for further interaction.

- Talking should be encouraged during group activities. It is interesting to note that subgrouping in the class has the effect of increasing transactional talk (talk specifically directed to another person and requiring a reply) by almost three times the level present under whole-class conditions.

- Room arrangement is important. Group members should be in close proximity but still have space to work on materials without getting in each other's way.

- Group work must be used frequently enough for the children to learn the skills and routines. Infrequent group work results in children taking too long to settle down.

What other strategies can be used to enhance the disabled child's chances of positive social integration?

- 'Peer tutoring', 'buddy systems' and other helping relationships have all been found effective to a greater or lesser degree; some can result in the development of genuine and lasting friendships.

- A greater use of games and play activities of a non–academic type can place the disabled child in situations where he or she can more easily fit in and work with others.
- Make a particular topic (e.g. 'Making friends' or 'Working together') the basis for class discussion. 'If you want someone to play with you at lunch-time what would you say to that person?' 'If you saw someone in the school playground who had just started at the school today, how would you greet them? How would you make them feel welcome?' Sometimes teachers prepare follow-up material in the form of worksheets with simple cartoon-type drawings and speech balloons into which the children write the appropriate greetings or comments for the various characters. Much of this can be incorporated into a total social education programme.
- It is important to get the peer-group members to reinforce and maintain social interactions with disabled children. Often they are unaware of the ways in which they can help. They, too, may need to be shown how to initiate contact, how to invite the child with special needs to join in an activity, how to help the child with particular school assignments, etc.

SOCIAL SKILLS TRAINING

One of the main reasons why certain children are unpopular is that they lack appropriate social skills which might make them more acceptable. They are in a catch–22 situation, since friendless students have no opportunity to practise social skills, and those with poor social skills are unable to form friendships (Lewis and Doorlag 1991).

Social isolation in childhood may have serious long-term consequences in terms of mental health in adult life, so it is vital that isolated and rejected individuals are helped to overcome some of these problems as early as possible. Fortunately there is growing evidence that social behaviours which contribute to positive personal interaction with others can be taught and can have lasting effects (Hickson 1990; Lovitt 1991).

What are 'social skills'?

Broadly speaking, social skills are those components of behaviour that are important for persons to initiate, and then maintain, positive interactions with others. The following specific behaviours have been identified as important for social competence.

Basic social skills

- Eye contact: being able to maintain eye contact with another person to whom you are listening or speaking for at least brief periods of time.
- Facial expression: smiling, showing interest.
- Social distance: knowing where to stand relative to others; knowing when physical contact is inappropriate.
- Quality of voice: volume, pitch, rate of speech, clarity, content.
- Greeting others: initiating contact or responding to a greeting, inviting another child to join you in some activity.
- Making conversation: age-appropriate conversational skills, expressing your feelings, asking questions, listening, showing interest, responding to questions asked.
- Playing with others and working with others: complying with rules, sharing, compromising, helping, taking turns, complimenting others, saying thank you, saying you're sorry.
- Gaining attention and/or asking for help: using appropriate ways.
- Coping with conflict: controlling aggression, dealing with anger in self and others, accepting criticism, sportsmanship.
- Grooming and hygiene.

The above list represents a fairly complex amalgam of non-verbal and verbal skills which all appear crucial for successful social interaction.

As well as having the appropriate social skills, an individual also needs *not* to have other behavioural characteristics which prevent easy acceptance by others, e.g. high levels of irritating behaviour (interrupting, poking, shouting etc.); impulsive and unpredictable reactions; temper tantrums; abusive language; cheating at games. In some cases these undesirable behaviours may need to be eliminated by behaviour modification or cognitive behaviour modification procedures. Lovitt (1991) advocates the use of metacognitive instruction and verbal self-instruction to modify negative behaviours and improve social skills.

Some writers find it useful to view social skills not as merely 'verbal' or 'non-verbal', but rather as being mainly either 'cognitive' or 'overt'. Cognitive functions include knowing what to do or not to do by interpreting social cues in a situation (e.g. knowing when an adult is ready to be approached and has time to listen); empathizing with or understanding the feelings of others; anticipating the results of your actions. Overt functions include the actual behaviours exhibited: e.g. smiling, gesturing, speaking at an appropriate volume, making eye contact, not standing too close to another person when speaking, etc. Children with intellectual disability and those with genuine emotional disturbance tend to have difficulty in acquiring the cognitive functions even after overt functions have been taught. This is to be expected since the acquisition of these functions (e.g. the concept of what constitutes 'a friend') follows a developmental sequence in all children. Children with special needs will be very much later in reaching a full understanding of such matters (Smith 1982). In some cases the problem is exacerbated by parents who have overprotected the child and have thus reduced social involvement with others.

Attempts have been made to design programmes which will systematically teach any of these skills which are deficient. Examples include, the Catch Project (Sheppard 1990); the Peers Programme (Finch and Hops 1983); the Walker Social Skills Curriculum (Walker 1988). The programme Developing Understanding of Self and Others (Duso), published by American Guidance Service, is also recommended by Gloeckler and Simpson (1988). The results from these programmes seem to be very promising, but even without such programmes teachers can assist children to develop social skills within their daily curriculum (Lovitt 1991).

How are social skills taught?

In an individual case the first step is obviously to decide where to begin, what the priorities are for this child. Csapo (1983) suggests that teachers should observe and analyse not only what the child does and does not do already, but also determine the specific social skills needed and valued in that particular age-group or class. It is pointless to teach skills which in that particular context are not immediately functional.

The most meaningful setting in which to enhance a child's social skills are, of course, the classroom and playground. As suggested in the previous chapter, a teacher needs to intervene at times to assist a child to gain entry to a group activity or to work with a carefully chosen partner. The teacher must also praise and reinforce both the target child and the peer group for all instances of co-operative, helpful and friendly behaviour. However, *in situ* intervention is not always feasible, particularly in extreme cases of withdrawal or rejection. At times it may be necessary for a child to be coached thoroughly in a particular skill away from the class situation before that skill can be used in the peer group setting. Franco *et al.* (1983) provide an excellent example of this from a case study of a very shy adolescent. These practitioners focused on conversational skills as being the most important to establish in this youth. In a withdrawal room they worked on four areas: asking questions of others, making reinforcing comments and acknowledging what others say, showing affective warmth, maintaining eye contact. Sessions were held twice weekly for twenty minutes over a fifteen-week period. After explanations and demonstrations from a tutor, the youth then practised these behaviours with the tutor and applied them in a series of ten-minute conversations with different male and female partners (to aid generalization). The partners were previously instructed to be warm and friendly but to refrain from asking questions of the subject unless he asked one first. They were also told to keep their responses brief so that the onus would be on the subject to maintain the conversation. The subject was instructed to adopt the strategy of finding out as much as possible about the other person's interests and to keep the conversation going. Observations were made at intervals after the coaching sessions had finished, and significant and durable improvements were reported in his classroom interactions.

The Peers Programme (Finch and Hops 1983) also uses coaching in a withdrawal situation first. The child spends fifteen minutes with an adult and one peer, in order to establish such basic skills as how to make friends with others, how to respond to the approaches of others, how to keep interactions going, how to praise others, how to be co-operative. The child is then monitored and rewarded for any evidence of these skills being used during recess time and also during academic work with a partner. Instruction can take several forms including modelling, role-play, sociodrama and direct instruction (Gloeckler and Simpson 1988).

The general training pattern used in most social skills programmes follows a sequence of steps.

Coaching in social skills: six steps

1 **Definition** Describe the skill to be taught. Discuss why this particular skill is important and how its use helps interaction to occur. The skill may be illustrated in use in a film-clip, a picture or cartoon, a simulation using puppets, or pointed out to the child by reference to activities going on in the peer group. The teacher may say, 'Watch how she helps him build the wall with the blocks.' 'Look at the two girls sharing the puzzle. Tell me what they are saying to each other.'

2 **Model the skill** Break the skill down into simple components and demonstrate these clearly yourself, or get a selected child to do this.

3 **Imitation and rehearsal** The child tries out the same skill in a structured situation. For this to occur successfully the child must be motivated to perform the skill and must attend carefully and retain what has been demonstrated.

4 **Feedback** This should be informative. 'You've not quite got it yet. You need to look at her while you speak to her. Try it again.' 'That's better! You looked and smiled. Well done.' Feedback via a video recording may be appropriate in some situations.

5 **Provide opportunity for the skill to be used** Depending upon the skill just taught, small group work or pair work activities may be set up to allow the skill to be applied and generalized to the classroom or other natural setting.

6 **Intermittent reinforcement** Watch for instances of the child applying the skill without prompting at other times in the day and later in the week. Provide descriptive praise and reward. Aim for maintenance of the skill once acquired. To a large extent these behaviours, once established, are likely to be maintained by natural consequences, i.e. by a more satisfying interaction with peers.

Over to you

Select a social skill from the list provided in this chapter (e.g. 'Working with others', or 'Gaining attention'). Plan a series of activities following the six steps above in order to teach and maintain that skill in a child.

Some of your colleagues in school suggest that social skills should be an 'across the curriculum' responsibility and not treated as a separate topic. How do you respond to this suggestion? Is there a place for a social skills curriculum in its own right? How would it be implemented?

SUMMARY

Many children with disabilities or learning difficulties encounter problems of peer group acceptance when placed in regular classes. In addition, some non-handicapped children also experience these difficulties. The ways in which attitudes can be improved, the environment modified to facilitate social interaction and the teaching of specific social skills have been described in this chapter. Evidence suggests that teachers often overlook and therefore neglect this aspect of a child's learning and development in school. Much can be done to assist children with social and personal problems and teachers must recognize their responsibility in this area. To be effective, a mainstreaming programme must include provision for enhancing the social acceptance of special-needs students (Lewis and Doorlag 1991).

Poor scholastic achievement seems to be a factor leading to poor social acceptance, even after social skills have been taught. Unless achievement within the curriculum can also be increased, acceptance may remain a problem for some children. Attention in the following chapters is therefore focused on accelerating the acquisition of basic academic skills.

Discussion points

- Anna is in Year 3 at school and is an extremely shy and timid child. She does not cause any problems in the classroom and her general bookwork is of a good standard. Her teacher has become increasingly concerned that he cannot get Anna to be more forthcoming and assertive both inside and outside the classroom setting. He feels that, if anything, Anna is becoming even more withdrawn. What should he do?

- Many emotionally disturbed children lack the social skills to enable them to relate easily to other children in regular or special classes. A significant number of such children are not only anti-social but also openly aggressive and hostile. Imagine that you have such a child in your class. Describe the steps you might take to modify this child's aggressive behaviour and make him or her more socially acceptable in the group.

Further reading

Atkinson, A. and Green, V. (1990) 'Cooperative learning: teacher's role', *Childhood Education* 67, 1: 8–11.

Bryan. T. and Lee, J. (1990) 'Social skills training with learning disabled children and adolescents', in Scruggs, T.E. and Wong, B.Y. (eds) *Intervention Research in Learning Disabilities*, New York: Springer-Verlag.

Cartledge, G. and Milburn, J.F. (1980) *Teaching Social Skills to Children*, New York: Pergamon.

Curran, J.P. and Monti, P.M. (1982) *Social skills Training*, New York: Guilford.

Hill, S. and Hill, T. (1990) *The Collaborative Classroom*, South Yarra: Curtin Publishing.

Johnson, D.W., Johnson, R.T. and Holubec, E. (1990) *Circles of Learning: Cooperation in the Classroom* (3rd edn), Edina, Minn: Interaction Books.

LeCroy, C.W. (1983) *Social Skills Training for Children and Youth*, New York: Haworth.

Slavin, R.E. (1990) *Cooperative Learning: Theory, Research and Practice*, Englewood Cliffs: Prentice Hall.

Stainbeck, S. and Stainbeck, W. (1990) *Support Networks for Inclusive Schooling*, Baltimore: Brookes.

Stephenson, S. (1990) 'Promoting interaction among children with special educational needs', *British Journal of Special Education* 17, 2: 61–5.

Sutton, G. (1992) 'Cooperative learning works in mathematics', *Mathematics Teacher* 85, 1: 63–6.

Chapter 6

Literacy: where to begin

Ideally, a school's reading program should be able to provide reading
experiences that result in proficient reading skill for all children,
including those who find reading difficult. In practice, schools fall short
of this ideal.

(Omanson 1985: 35)

Learning to read is not a simple task, even for some children of average
intelligence (Gillet and Bernard 1989). It may be a very difficult task indeed
for children with significant disabilities such as impaired hearing, cerebral
palsy, visual impairment, intellectual disability or emotional disturbance.
For example, hearing impairment often limits the child's general vocabulary development and restricts awareness of the phonemic structure of
words. Cerebral palsy, even if not accompanied by intellectual impairment,
may cause visual perceptual problems and a tendency to rapid fatigue in
tasks which require carefully controlled eye movements. Visual impairment may necessitate the use of magnification aids and enlarged print; or
in the case of blindness may require the substitution of braille materials for
conventional print. Intellectual disability results in a much slower learning
rate; and the child will be ready to read at a much later age than is normal.
In some cases the child may never reach this stage during the school years
if the disability is moderate to severe. Emotional disturbance may cause a
child to be so preoccupied that concentration is impossible and motivation
is totally lacking. Yet almost all these children can be helped to master at
least the basic skills of word recognition, if not the higher-order reading
skills. Quite dramatic improvements can result from special coaching of
even the most difficult children.

It has been said that there is no one method, medium, approach or
philosophy that holds the key to the process of learning to read. From this
it follows that the greater the range and variety of methods known to

teachers, the more likely it is that they will feel competent to provide appropriate help for slower learners and children with specific learning difficulties:

> research and our own experience suggests that the approach which is successful with all children with reading difficulties is one which combines features of a number of different approaches and is adapted to a child's individual needs.

> (Gillet and Bernard 1989)

CURRENT LANGUAGE ARTS PHILOSOPHY

The psycholinguistic approach

The current mainstream approach to reading instruction reflects a very strong swing against the teaching of specific component skills such as letter recognition and the sounding and building of words (i.e. a decoding approach). This reaction has come mainly from the field of psycholinguistics (e.g. Smith 1985; Goodman 1967). The psycholinguistic approach is based on the premise that from the very earliest stages of reading the learner makes meaning from print by using his or her experience of language to predict words and phrases; indeed, it has been termed 'a psycholinguistic guessing game' by Goodman (Gollasch 1982). The emphasis is upon the reader constructing meaning from the sentence or paragraph using all available cues to assist with the process. Three main cueing systems are available:

- the semantic (the meaning of what is being read);
- the syntactic (the logical grammatical structure of the sentences or phrases);
- the grapho-phonic (the correspondence between the symbols in print and the speech-sound values they represent).

The meaning-emphasis viewpoint of the psycholinguistic school implies that if a reader is thinking intelligently about what he or she is reading, almost all the 'guessing' is based in semantic and syntactic cues (the 'top-down' approach), and rarely is it necessary to resort to decoding a word from its letters or syllables (the 'bottom-up' approach). For this reason attention to phonics is given a somewhat lower priority than in more traditional approaches to teaching reading (Goodman 1989).

Whole Language

At classroom level, the psycholinguistic perspective now underpins what has become known as the 'Whole Language' philosophy for the teaching of reading and writing. According to Donaldson (1992), Whole Language has five key features which help to distinguish it from other approaches.

Whole Language: Principal features (Donaldson 1992)

The application of Whole Language philosophy to the development of literacy involves at least the following procedures:

- reading good literature to students every day, and having real literature available for students to read for themselves;
- providing time each day for sustained silent reading;
- providing daily opportunities to read and write for real purposes;
- teaching reading skills in context, rather than in isolation;
- integrating the curriculum to allow literacy skills to be utilized across subject areas.

Students learn to read and write while they read and write to learn and solve problems.

(Goodman 1989: 70)

In the Whole Language approach all the language arts, including reading and writing, are treated as one and developed together in meaningful situations. The approach is the antithesis of the hierarchical, skill-based model.

(Wray 1989: 5)

Goodman (1989) denies that Whole Language is a method or an approach. He describes it as a philosophy of curriculum, of learning, of teaching and of language. Reading and writing are defined as integrated processes for making sense out of and through written language. Learners are seen to be capable of actively constructing the meaning for themselves, experimenting with language, making decisions and predicting, taking risks and self-correcting when necessary.

Enthusiasts of Whole Language argue that phonic skills and spelling skills *are* taught with the approach, but not as ends in themselves (Newman and Church 1990). The skills are tackled with individual students at the moment when their use serves an immediate purpose, for example, when a student is needing to spell a particular word correctly or to identify a word which cannot be predicted from context. Phonic decoding skills and spelling skills are not taught through specific drills or exercises used in isolation.

Whole Language often incorporates the use of literature-based programmes, using authentic texts rather than basal readers. Reading materials from other subject areas, such as mathematics, science and environmental studies, are frequently used within the programme. It is believed to be important to offer the student multiple texts and different genres if reading and writing are to be used in truly relevant ways.

Exponents of Whole Language claim that it is a valuable approach, not only for students who learn to read and write easily, but also for students with special needs and for adults with literacy problems (Newman and Church 1990; Crux 1991). However, the Whole Language approach is not without its critics (Taylor 1991; Whitehead 1991). The views of the psycholinguists may hold true for children who learn to read easily – they may well acquire reading skills almost as a natural developmental process. However, teachers who have worked with chronic reading problems know that in the majority of cases, as well as reading for meaning, it is essential to instruct these children in word recognition, letter knowledge and decoding skills if they are to make progress (Westwood 1986). As Heymsfeld has commented when arguing for inclusion of basic skills instruction within the Whole Language approach, 'We cannot depend on haphazard, amorphous lessons to teach something as critical as knowledge of the alphabetic code' (1989: 68).

Decoding skills

Problems arise within an exclusively psycholinguistic approach when a child is not at all skilled in contextual guessing. Perhaps the child's experience with language, particularly the more elaborate language of books, has been very restricted and the child's own vocabulary is limited. No teacher would deny that the purpose of reading is to make meaning, or that the more reading one does the more likely one is to become a better reader and to enjoy the activity. However, can one make complete meaning and read fluently without at some stage having acquired the necessary word-attack skills to employ when context clues are inadequate? Stott (1981) was particularly critical of the extent to which the psycholinguists have actively persuaded teachers to minimize their attention to phonic work. 'Phonics' has become an emotive term. In some educational circles the teaching of phonic skills is regarded as reactionary and therefore to be despised – an attitude which flies in the face of much recent research which highlights the importance of such instruction. Snider states, 'there

is a vast body of research that supports the use of phonics in the early stages
of teaching reading' (1992: 15). (See also Groff 1990; Tunmer 1990;
Chapman and Tunmer 1991; Eldredge, Quinn and Butterfield 1990; Chall
1989).

All methods which concentrate from the beginning on reading for
meaning leave to chance the learning of the code itself, yet children cannot
become independent readers unless they master the code (Naidoo 1981).
Learners differ in the extent to which they pick up phonic principles
incidentally. Many children will deduce the code and its rules for themselves, but some will not. The judgement of just how much emphasis to
give the teaching of phonics needs to be made on an individual basis. As
far as gaining an understanding of the graphic-phonic system, there seem
to be three types of children: those who gain insight on their own, with
little or no direct instruction; those who need some initial instruction and
then make progress on their own; and those who will never master it on
their own, knowing only as much of the system as they have been taught
(Baarda 1982).

The present writer's experience as a remedial teacher and as a teacher
of primary and secondary special classes suggests that the vast majority of
children with reading problems exhibit poorly developed phonic knowledge and inefficient word-attack skills. They benefit from a carefully
structured supplementary phonic approach in order to develop the skills
which they currently lack. In defence of such teaching Eeds-Kniep has
said, 'We do know that this [instruction in phonic skills] is something good
reading teachers do because they find these techniques helpful and effective
when nothing else has been' (1979:916).

It must be stressed here that an *exclusively* phonic approach is not being
advocated for any child, with or without special needs. It is being argued
that within a total reading programme due attention should be given to
the teaching of decoding skills for those children who need this instruction.
The psycholinguistic and literature-based programmes emphasize the
importance of such matters as:

- surrounding the child with stimulating reading material;
- creating a climate where reading is an enjoyable, necessary and
  valued occupation;
- the teacher modelling good reading performance and attitude;
- giving abundant encouragement to any child who makes the effort
  to read independently.

These factors create a necessary *but insufficient* condition to ensure that
all children will become proficient readers. It is when learning is left to

chance that the child with learning problems is at risk. To reduce the possibility that some students will not become good readers the additional factors listed below must be considered when implementing the main-stream reading curriculum.

The priority needs of students with reading difficulties

The child who is experiencing difficulties in learning to read needs to have the following:

- An empathic and enthusiastic teacher.
- Abundant opportunity to read for pleasure and for information.
- An understanding of what the task of reading actually involves and what purposes are served by reading.
- Successful practice, using material which has become familiar to the student.
- An improved self-esteem through counselling, praise, encouragement, success and the recognition of personal progress.
- A carefully graded programme, which may mean the creation of much supplementary material to use alongside the mainstream programme to provide additional practice. If child-produced or teacher-made books are being used either alongside or instead of other literature, they must be used in a structured rather than an informal manner in order to teach effectively.
- More time will need to be spent on early reading activities (e.g. flashcards, word-to-picture matching, simple copy-writing, sentence building, etc.).
- More time must be spent in over-learning and reviewing material at each stage.
- If basal readers are still used, careful preparation of sight vocabulary is needed before each new book is introduced to ensure success.
- Auditory training (e.g. discrimination of sounds, blending sounds into words, segmenting long words into syllables, etc.) may be needed before decoding skills are taught.
- Systematic teaching of phonic knowledge and word-building, unless contra-indicated by speech or auditory problems. Skills taught should stem from, and be applicable to the actual reading material being used by the student.
- Correct letter formation (printing) and handwriting to be taught alongside the reading activities.

- Finger-tracing and other multi-sensory approaches (e.g. textured letters) may be needed by a few children to aid assimilation and retention.

Many of the features listed above are already incorporated in the approach known as Reading Recovery (Clay 1985), described in Chapter 7 in this text. Whatever the approach being used in mainstream classes, these basic needs of the student with learning difficulties must be met. The development of literacy skills must be given very high priority for all children.

In order to cater most precisely for the specific needs of students with learning difficulties, it is necessary to appraise their current skills and knowledge.

DIAGNOSTIC ASSESSMENT

The starting point for any intervention should be based on the results of some form of assessment of the child's current abilities. Such an assessment need not involve the use of highly sophisticated tests, and should not be a lengthy procedure. If a large amount of information is necessary in order to plan a programme, the assessment of the child should be spread over several short sessions. One is basically seeking answers to the following four key questions.

1 What can the child already do without help? What skills has the child developed?
2 What can the child do if given a little prompting and guidance?
3 What gaps exist in the child's previous learning?
4 What skills, concepts or processes are obviously beyond the child's present capabilities and would therefore constitute unreasonable goals in the short-term?

Figure 2 summarizes the key steps involved in implementing a diagnostic approach to an individual learner. It begins with assessment and leads to programme planning and implementation. The procedure is applicable to all the main areas of the curriculum and it will be referred to again in the chapters dealing with writing, spelling and arithmetic.

The various stages in Figure 2 may be interpreted thus:

Stage 1 This may involve the use of check-lists, tests, inventories, as well as naturalistic observation of the learner. In the domain of reading the most useful procedure is to listen to the child reading from an appropriate text

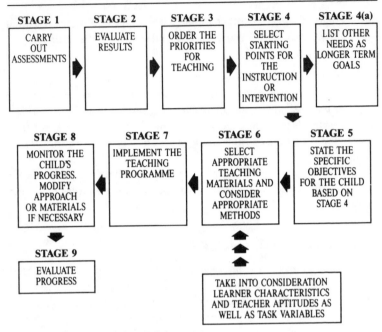

Figure 2 The diagnostic model

and to note the strategies used and the errors made. Is the child confident and fluent? Does the child self-correct? Is the child dependent upon adult assistance? A running record of errors, self-corrections, requests for help, etc, can be noted on a photocopied version of the child's text.

Stage 2   This involves looking at what you have obtained from the assessment of the child performing in a particular skill area (e.g. reading) and applying the four diagnostic key questions referred to above.

Stage 3   This involves the identification of the most serious gaps in the child's previous learning which may need to be remedied.

Stages 4 and 5   These involve the selection of a starting point or teaching aim from the data analysed in Stage 3, and the writing of a specific student performance objective to make that aim operational: e.g. teaching aim: 'to increase the child's basic sight vocabulary'; performance objective: 'given the twelve most commonly occurring words from the key words list presented on flashcards the child will read these aloud without hesitation or prompting.'

Stage 6 This involves the selection of appropriate material (books, kits, apparatus, etc.) to assist in working towards the stated objective, and consideration of the most appropriate method of working with this child, based on a knowledge of his or her characteristics (e.g. learning strategies, interests, concentration span, etc.) and your own personal competencies in dealing with small group or individual tuition.

Stage 7 This involves implementing the teaching programme with the child for a period of sufficient duration and frequency to have some impact on progress. Ideally the programme may be operated within the whole-class setting, rather than in isolation. However, at times it will be necessary to provide such tuition in a withdrawal situation.

Stage 8 This involves an overlap with Stage 7, in that you are required to determine whether your programme is working effectively by the use of an ongoing (formative) evaluation of the child's performance.

Stage 9 This involves some definite procedure for assessing how much real change has occurred in the child as a result of the programme (summative evaluation). This is usually carried out at the end of the teaching block and is linked directly with the stated objectives at Stage 5.

Note that when working with and testing a child, it is important to observe the child's learning strategies and task-approach skills, as well as the actual responses being given. For example, has the child selected a particular answer after careful thought, or was it an impulsive guess? Is the child hesitant and under-achieving because he or she is wary of the adult and unwilling to take a risk?

Diagnosis must eventually involve a consideration of the total situation in which the learner operates. As well as learner characteristics it is important to evaluate also the learning task itself (e.g. level of difficulty, its relevance to the child's interests, etc.), the teaching method being used, and the physical environment in which the child is being taught and the quality of the relationship between the child and the teacher and the child and the peer group. In other words, educational failure (and therefore the means by which to change the situation) is rarely due only to factors within the child. Failure usually stems from a complex interaction among all the above variables.

Diagnostic approaches are referred to as either formal or informal. The term 'formal diagnosis' usually implies that published tests (e.g. reading attainment tests or reading diagnostic tests) are used in order to obtain specific information about a learner's current status in certain selected areas such as comprehension, word recognition and phonic knowledge. Sometimes particular component skills are assessed such as auditory discrimination, visual discrimination, short-term auditory memory or sound blending. Formal assessment may be carried out for a whole class simultaneously, for example by the use of pencil-and-paper group testing. At other times formal assessment must involve the careful and detailed testing of one child alone using standardized or criterion-referenced tests. Formal assessment of this type is useful in indicating where current achievement stops and new learning needs to begin. It is usually supplemented by information from informal testing.

Informal diagnosis involves such procedures as direct observation of learners in action and an examination of what they actually do or what they produce during a lesson. Informal assessment in reading includes, for example, listening to the child read aloud and detecting the presence or absence of particular strategies for word attack, use of context, prediction, comprehension, general fluency and expression. The use of teacher-made informal reading inventories may be of value here. The inventories comprise graded samples (paragraphs) from books available in the classroom. A child's level of success on the inventory will provide a good indication of the readability level of books he or she can cope with independently and for instructional purposes. Performance on the inventory will also indicate the child's general approach to the task of reading (e.g. hasty and careless, hesitant and unwilling to risk a guess, etc.). Accuracy in reading the graded passages should be 95 per cent if the material is to be read independently by the child, and 90 per cent for material to be used for instructional purposes. Material with an error rate of 15 per cent or more is considered to be at frustration level (too difficult).

Over to you

Prepare an informal reading inventory using photocopied passages from appropriate books in your classroom. The material should be carefully graded, beginning at the level of very simple vocabulary and short sentences in passages approximately 50 words in length. Extend this to more complex and demanding material in 150–200

(continued...)

word samples. Prepare six passages and use the inventory with a selected child. Evaluate the results in detail, indicating what the child can and cannot do in terms of word recognition, use of context, self-correction, etc.

The book *Watching Children Read and Write* (Kemp: 1987) provides excellent advice and practical guidance for making and analysing Running Records.

Level 1: Assessing the non-reader

If an individual, regardless of age, appears to be a non-reader it is worth obtaining the following information:

- Can the learner concentrate upon a learning task and attend to the teacher, or is he or she too preoccupied, distractible or hyperactive?
- Has the learner had adequate language experience and sufficient vocabulary development to begin reading?
- Has the learner developed adequate listening skills to attend to the subtleties of speech sounds within words? This is important if the early approach to reading is going to stress phonic aspects and sound blending. (See also 'Auditory skills'.)
- Does the learner understand what reading involves? (Ask, 'What do we *do* when we read to someone? If you had to teach a friend to read what would you tell them to do?')
- Does the learner seem able to grasp that words have unit values in print, that the spaces between words have some significance?
- Does the learner have the concepts of 'letter' and 'word'? Does the learner have an awareness of the left-to-right progression in a printed sentence?
- Is the learner capable of carrying out visual discrimination of pictures, or letters and words? Can he or she correctly perform matching exercises?
- Does the learner recognize *any* words by sight? (E. g. own name; environmental signs such as 'CLOSED' or 'KEEP OUT'.)
- Can the learner complete picture-to-word matching activities correctly after a brief period of instruction?

- Can the learner carry out a simple learning task involving sight recognition of two words taught from flashcards without picture clues (e.g. 'MY' and 'BOOK')?
- Does the child know the names or sounds of any letters when these are presented in printed form?

Marie Clay's (1985) book, *The Early Detection of Reading Difficulties*, is very useful for appraising a child's concepts about print and his or her understanding of the reading task. Her assessment procedures cover several of the factors listed above.

Level 2: Assessment above beginner level

For the child who is not a complete non-reader and who has at least some functional skills, the following areas are worthy of assessment.

Basic sight vocabulary   What can the child already do in terms of instant recognition of the most commonly occurring words in print? The Dolch Vocabulary List, the Key Words to Literacy List, or the lists in the book *Reading Rescue* (Gillet and Bernard 1989) all provide appropriate material for this area of assessment.

Miscues and use of context   When the child is reading aloud from age-appropriate material, what types of error are made? Do the words conform to the meaning of the sentence or are they totally out of keeping with the message? Does the child tend to self-correct when errors are made, in order to restore meaning? (See Kemp 1987.)

Word-attack skills   When reading aloud, does the child attempt to sound-out and build an unfamiliar word even without being instructed to do so? If not, can the child do this when he or she is encouraged to try? Has the child developed a fully functional set of phonic principles? In particular, does the child know all the common single letter sounds, digraphs, blends, prefixes and suffixes? Can the child divide a regular but lengthy word into its component syllables?

Auditory skills   Can the child discriminate between similar but not identical speech sounds when these are presented orally in word-pairs (e.g. mouse–mouth, cat–cap, money–monkey)? Teachers can devise their own word lists for this purpose, or use can be made of Wepman's Auditory

Discrimination Test or that contained in McLeod's Domain Phonic Survey.

Can the child analyse or segment familiar words into their component sounds? This is a listening and oral test, not a reading test. If the child hears the word 'remember', can he or she break this into the units re–mem–ber? If testing this, you must first give some practise so that the child understands what is required.

Can the child blend or synthesize sounds in order to pronounce a given word (e.g. cr–i–sp). Again, this is a listening test and not a reading test; the child does not see the word in print. The following diagnostic test designed by David Moseley[†] is very useful for assessment of this skill.

Instructions
Say: 'I am going to say some words very slowly so that you can hear each letter sound. I want you to tell me what the word is. If I say "O–N" you say "ON".'
Discontinue after five consecutive failures.
Sound the phonemes at a rate of about one each second.

The words

i–t	l–o–t	f–r–o–g	s–p–e–n–d
n–o	m–a–n	w–i–n–k	c–r–i–s–p
w–e	r–e–d	c–o–l–d	p–l–a–n–t
d–o	c–u–p	b–u–m–p	f–r–o–s–t
a–m	b–i–g	r–e–s–t	t–r–u–n–k

Scoring: 1 + total number correct ÷ 5 (e.g. $1 + \frac{15}{5} = 4$).

Interpretation:

Child's age	Normal score	Extreme difficulty
6–7	3 to 4	2 or less
7–8	4 to 5	2 or less
8–9	4 to 5	2 or less
9–10	4 to 5	3 or less
10–11	5	3 or less

Auditory discrimination, auditory analysis (segmentation), and phoneme blending are now regarded as parts of a more general metalin-

---

[†] D.V. Moseley, Centre for Learning Disabilities, N.S.M.H.C., London. Reproduced with permission.

guistic ability termed 'phonological awareness' (Goswami and Bryant 1990; Sawyer and Fox 1991). It is claimed that phonological awareness is essential in helping beginning readers to break the orthographic code; and that training in such skills as segmentation, blending, rhyming, alliteration and isolation of sounds within words, results in improvement in early reading and spelling. Tunmer (1990) has reviewed a large number of studies supporting the value of phonological awareness training of this type (see Chapter 7).

Comprehension Reading can hardly be called true reading unless children are understanding the meaning behind the print; therefore evaluation of this aspect of performance is crucial. Informal questions can be asked after a child has read a passage silently or aloud. The questions should not be solely at a factual-recall level (literal comprehension), e.g. 'How old is the girl in the story?' 'What is the boy's name?', but should probe for understanding at higher levels of inference and critical interpretation (e.g. 'Why did the man act in that way? Was he angry or shocked?', 'When the lady suggested they look for the goods in another shop was she being helpful or rude?', 'What do *you* think of the suggestion the leader of the team makes?').

Exercises using cloze procedure are sometimes useful in both testing and developing comprehension and contextual cueing. A passage of some 100 to 150 words is selected and every fifth or sixth word (approximately) is deleted leaving a gap. Can the child read the passage and provide a word in each case which conforms to the meaning of the passage and the grammatical structure of the sentence?

A particularly valuable instrument for the evaluation of reading rate, accuracy and comprehension is the *Neale Analysis of Reading Ability* (1988, 1989). The test also allows for appraisal of the student's auditory skills in discrimination, blending and simple spelling. An analysis sheet is provided to facilitate the recording and classification of errors.

Level 3: Assessing the child who has reached a reading plateau

Some children appear to reach a temporary plateau in their reading development at or about a reading age of eight years to nine years. Many of the assessment techniques covered in the previous section may help to uncover the possible areas of difficulty in these children. The following procedures are also helpful at this level.

Error analysis   It is with children who have reached a reading plateau that error analysis can be extremely valuable in pinpointing specific gaps in a child's current reading skills. Possibly the child has not yet mastered certain letter clusters as phonic sight habits, and will either make random guesses or will refuse or mispronounce unfamiliar words containing these letter clusters.

To employ the error analysis procedure it is usual to listen to the child reading aloud on several different occasions using material which is reasonably challenging but not at frustration level. The performance is recorded on tape for later analysis.

Kemp (1987) suggests that errors can be recorded on a running record sheet, and classified as: self-correction (S.C.); appeal for help (A); teacher intervention (T. T. A. if the child is told to 'try that again', or T for 'told' if the word is supplied by the teacher); substitutions (S–the substituted word is written above the text word); omissions (line drawn above the word omitted); repetition (underline word each time the child repeats it). Attempts at decoding a word should also be recorded in terms of phonemes and syllables. Kemp's procedure also allows for quantitative evaluations to be made leading to the calculation of error rate, self-correction rate and dependency rate. These measures can be used to compare a student's performance before and after an intervention programme.

Readability of the text   Consider the difficulty level of the material the child is attempting to read. Has he or she selected books which are at frustration level? Reading skills will not advance if the child is constantly faced with text which is too difficult.

There are several procedures which have been used over the years to calculate approximate readability level of texts. One system involves the following steps, using a sample of thirty sentences:

- Count thirty sentences.
- Count the number of words with three or more syllables in those sentences.
- Calculate the nearest square root of that number.
- Add a constant of 3 to your answer.
- The result obtained represents the school year level at which the material would usually be read successfully.

For example, if there are 54 words with three or more syllables, the nearest square root is 7. Add 3, = 10. The material is typical of Year 10 and could be read successfully by the average student of that age level.

However, readability level is determined by more than the number of multisyllabic words. The ease with which a text is read is also related to the reader's familiarity with the topic, the complexity of the syntax used and the sentence length. Even the size of the print and format of the pages can influence readability, especially for students with learning difficulties. The most useful index of readability is a student's actual performance on the text.

A valuable chapter dealing with methods for judging the difficulty of reading material is presented by Burmeister (1978) in the book *Reading Strategies for Middle and Secondary School Teachers.*

When selecting texts for students to read, teachers should consider the following points:

- Is the topic within the experience of the students? Is it meaningful and relevant?
- Is the language used in the text natural and easy to predict? Are there many unfamiliar words? Are the sentences complex? Are the sentences stilted (as they often are in early reading books)?
- Are there many useful contextual and pictorial clues?
- Is the book itself attractive and appealing?
- Will this type of text expand the student's experience of different forms of writing for different purposes?

Affective factors   With a child who has ceased to make progress, it is vitally important to consider affective as well as cognitive factors. For example, has the child developed a very negative, 'couldn't-care-less' attitude towards reading, avoiding the task whenever possible? Does the child derive any enjoyment from reading? Is the material in the book in keeping with the child's real interests? Is the working relationship between the child and the teacher (or tutor) a positive one? Is there any incentive to improve? Where difficulties are detected in these areas, it is just as important to attempt to change matters, if possible, as it is to concentrate on the skills aspect of reading development.

The handbook prepared by Johns (1986) contains some useful questionnaires, inventories and scales for the appraisal of affective and attitudinal factors. Ekwall's (1985) text provides useful advice on counselling techniques.

Over to you

Assemble appropriate materials for use in assessing a student's current ability in:

- phonological awareness;
- sight recognition of commonly occurring words;
- phonic knowledge;
- word-attack skills;
- comprehension.

Use the materials with a student and seek answers to the four key questions presented earlier in the chapter.

SUMMARY

All the procedures described in Chapter 6 for the assessment of a child with reading difficulties are applicable to children with very varied forms of physical, sensory or intellectual disability. A particular disability does not require a specific and unique form of diagnostic evaluation; one is simply attempting to find out with some degree of precision what the child can and cannot do at the present time in this skill area. It may well be that the child with the more severe form of disability, or with multiple handicaps, will be assessed in readiness-type skills typical of a much younger child, but the actual procedure involved in assessment does not differ.

According to how the child performs on the initial diagnostic assessment, a teacher would either focus on the early or pre-reading skills (e.g. sentence building, word-to-picture matching, letter knowledge, etc.), on intermediate skills such as word-attack, contextual cueing, etc., or on higher-order reading skills such as prediction and literal, interpretive or critical levels of comprehension. Activities will then be programmed to assist the child to develop beyond the present stage. The next chapter provides a description of a number of methods which may be employed to assist children with reading difficulties, regardless of the cause of such difficulties. Most of these methods can be used within the regular classroom and do not require children to be withdrawn for remedial assistance.

Discussion point

Imagine that you are appointed to a school where no systematic check is made of children's reading progress at any age level.

You are asked by the head teacher to devise some appropriate system for assessing the overall reading attainment in the school and for identifying those children in need of special assistance.

After considerable time and effort you plan what seems to be a viable set of procedures and you present your plans at a staff meeting.

Much to your surprise, several of your colleagues object very strongly to your suggestions, stating that they do not believe in testing children in any formal way. They say that tests don't tell them anything they don't already know. They also imply that testing makes children anxious; and when parents get to know their children's results this can cause a great deal of unnecessary concern in some cases.

What are you going to do?

One obvious action would be to withdraw your plan and give in to your colleagues' arguments. However, you feel quite strongly that some monitoring of reading progress is necessary and you are prepared to argue your case.

Try to summarize the points you would make to support your suggested programme. Try also to answer the specific objections raised by your colleagues.

In general, how might the regular assessment of reading throughout the school influence the achievement levels of individual children?

Further reading

Baskwell, J. and Whitman, P. (1988) *Evaluation: Whole language: Whole child*, New York: Scholastic.

Bryant, P. and Bradley, L. (1985) *Children's Reading Problems*, Oxford: Blackwell.

Bradley, L. (1985) *Assessing Reading Difficulties* (2nd edn), London: Macmillan.

Burmeister, L.E. (1978) *Reading Strategies for Middle and Secondary School Teachers* (2nd edn), Reading, Mass: Addison-Wesley.

Cambourne, B. (1988) *The Whole Story*, Auckland: Ashton Scholastic.

Clay, M.M. (1985) *The Early Detection of Reading Difficulties* (3rd edn), Auckland: Heinemann.

Ekwall, E.E. (1986) *Teacher's Handbook on Diagnosis and Remediation in Reading* (2nd edn), Boston: Allyn & Bacon.

Gibson, L. (1989) *Through Children's Eyes*, New York: Teachers College Press.

Gillet, S. and Bernard, M. (1989) *Reading Rescue* (2nd edn), Hawthorn: ACER.

Holdaway, D. (1990) *Independence in Reading* (3rd edn), Portsmouth: Heinemann.

Johnson, T.D. and Louis, D.R. (1985) *Literacy through Literature*, Sydney: Methuen.

Kemp, M. (1987) *Watching Children Read and Write*, Melbourne: Nelson.

Pumfrey, P. and Elliott, C. (1990) *Children's Difficulties in Reading, Writing and Spelling*, London: Falmer.

Smith, C.B. (1990) 'Helping slow readers', *Reading Teacher* 43, 6: 416.

Chapter 7

Reading: making a start

Successful remediation depends upon purposeful work in realistic situations: we learn to read by reading and to write and spell by writing. It is essential that work be within the competence of students so that the process is practised and success ensured.

(Preen and Barker 1987: 3)

Following the careful assessment of a learner's abilities as suggested in the previous chapter, it should be possible to plan the appropriate starting points for intervention. Chapters 7 and 8 provide a compendium of ideas and methods from which to select, ranging from pre-reading level to post-secondary school level. These ideas may be used within or alongside the general language and reading curriculum in the regular classroom.

PRE- AND EARLY READING EXPERIENCES

For most children a carefully structured pre-reading programme is unnecessary. Once the child has adjusted to the demands of school life, instruction in reading can and should begin. For a few, however, particularly those with significant intellectual impairment or perceptual difficulties, it will be valuable to provide pre-reading experiences which prepare these children for beginning reading, to take them to the threshold of simple word recognition. Training in listening skills, encouraging a liking for stories, ensuring familiarity with language patterns – all form important parts of the programme. Indeed, aural–oral language enrichment activities form the basis of all reading readiness programmes (Sippola 1985; Williams 1986).

When the pre-reading activities involve word-to-word matching, word-to-picture matching, and letter and word copying, the child is ready to enter the next stage of development. The golden rule to remember is to make the work link as closely as possible with the educational skills and media the child needs to use at this time. For instance, in pre-reading activities, if the child needs to improve in visual discrimination it is likely to be of maximum benefit if letter and word matching are utilized, rather than the matching of pictures and geometrical shapes.

Form perception and visual discrimination

For just a very few children, particularly those with visual impairment or those with neurological problems, form perception may need to be improved. If oral language is adequate and if the child has realized that the marks on paper represent words which can be spoken, the next important skill to consider is that of form perception, which at its highest level is reflected in the fine discrimination of letters and letter sequences.

If a young or disabled child is very poor at form perception the teaching will need to begin with the fitting of hardboard shapes into inset form-boards, matching and sorting simple regular shapes and feeling these shapes hidden within a puzzle box where the child can handle but not see them. He or she then identifies the shape just handled from a set of line drawings outside the box. Later the activity can be reintroduced using small plastic letters of the alphabet in the puzzle box, these being handled and identified in the same way. This activity is useful for holding attention through active participation and enjoyment.

Other useful activities which will help to develop awareness of shape and form and encourage attention to detail include: copying regular shapes using drinking straws, drawing around templates, drawing within stencils, tracing figures, completing unfinished figures on worksheets. These activities are of particular importance to young children with impaired vision or with perceptual problems.

The sequence for training visual discrimination should follow the progression:

- Picture matching.
- Shape matching.
- Letter-like shape matching.
- Letter and word matching.

The point of entry into this sequence for a particular child will be determined from diagnostic assessment.

Word-to-picture matching is a useful activity in the beginning stages of word recognition. Colourful pictures can be cut from magazines and mail-order catalogues, or the child's own drawings and paintings can be used. Appropriate words or captions are provided on slips of card. The child places the card on or next to the picture and reads the word. The activity can be used with groups of children, particularly if a magnet-board is used to display the words and pictures.

If a child is able to sort and match word shapes and has adequate language development, he or she is ready to read through one of the various whole-word and meaning-based approaches, even though phonics readiness may not be present. The child will benefit from a language-experience or shared-book approach (see later).

Visual retention and visual sequential memory

It is helpful for some children to be trained in the careful observation of material, which they are then required to reproduce from memory in correct sequential order. This is sometimes done using picture cards (for example, cow, house, man, ball, cup), but it is more useful if letter cards are provided which can be arranged to spell simple words. The training should then require the child to write the sequence after brief exposure on a flash-card. This aids early spelling skills as well as word recognition skills for reading.

Undoubtedly, one of the most valuable activities at this level is sentence-building. At any age level, a learner who is beginning to read should be given the opportunity to construct and reconstruct meaningful sentences from word cards.

This procedure was the foundation of the approach known as 'Breakthrough to Literacy', and has been strongly advocated by Kemp (1987: 66) as both an assessment and teaching technique. A child's ability to construct, reconstruct and transform sentences reveals much about his or her language competence and memory for words. Sentence building can be incorporated into the language-experience approach described later.

Hand–eye co-ordination and motor control

Building, cutting, sticking, threading, tracing, jigsaw-making and games activities which go on in all pre-school and junior classrooms are already developing fine motor co-ordination for most children. A few will need much longer at such tasks and may benefit from specific training. Large chalkboard work using big movements is a very useful starting point. In cases of very poor control it is helpful if the teacher guides the child's hand in order to make the movements smooth and rhythmical, and to establish a correct motor pattern. Simple mazes and dot-to-dot patterns produced as worksheets are a useful extension from large-scale movements to finer control. Writing patterns can be used for both chalkboard work and practise sheets. It is vital that children who have some degree of difficulty in co-ordination are taught correct letter formation. Handwriting or printing should not be left to incidental learning. This applies particularly to children with cerebral palsy, spina bifida, hydrocephalus or with neurological dysfunction resulting in clumsiness.

Problems of laterality (that is, choice of hand for manual tasks and dominant eye in visual tasks) and poor directional sense (orientation) are sometimes found to be present in slow learners and children with specific learning difficulties. These factors are rarely the cause of a child's learning problems, but rather are another symptom of inefficient functioning. Some older American programmes stress the need to establish a strong lateral preference in a child before attempting remediation in academic skills, and suggest exercises for doing this. However, such programmes have not proved to be particularly successful and most teachers today would not deliberately set out to rectify crossed laterality or to alter hand preferences in their children with special needs.

If the child's balance and general co-ordination are very poor, teachers may need to plan specific activities for inclusion in a daily PE programme (e.g. hopping, beam-walking, small ball catching, etc.). In some schools these children may be receiving special physical education or therapy from a visiting teacher, and close liaison with this teacher will be essential if the activities are to be integrated and reinforced in the regular class programme.

Reversal probelms

Crossed laterality, lack of firmly established lateral preference and poor directional sense frequently result in a marked tendency to *reverse* shapes (e.g. letters or words in reading, numerals in arithmetic). In extreme cases, mirror-writing may be produced by the child. It is quite normal for children up to the age of six-and-a-half years to confuse letters like p, b, d and q in their reading and writing, so undue attention to this problem would be out of place below that age. However, reversal problems which continue in some cases through to the secondary school level do require attention. A few ideas for remediation are provided here.

If a child above the age of seven years is still confusing p, b, d, q or u, n, it is essential that he or she should be given a motor cue (kinaesthetic training) to establish the correct direction for these letters. Finger-tracing one of the letters until mastered is probably the most positive way to overcome the problem. First the child should close eyes or wear a blindfold, while the teacher guides the index finger of his or her preferred hand over the shape of the letter 'b' on the blackboard. The letter is simultaneously sounded or named as tracing is repeated several times. The teacher now takes the child's finger over a series of other letters and the child must indicate quickly and clearly, but still with eyes closed, each time a letter 'b' is traced. The aim here is basically to give a child a physical image against which to discriminate d and b. It is also useful to provide the child with a self-help card showing that the 'little b' is really only the bottom half of a capital B. This card can be left displayed in the classroom for some time after training. It is important to stress that if the child is given the correct motor cue for letter and numeral formation in the early stages of handwriting instruction, many of the reversal problems will not persist.

Auditory training

It has been shown conclusively (Treiman 1985; Tunmer 1990) that in the process of learning to read, auditory skills are just as important as oral language skills and visual skills. Progress beyond the stage of building up a basic sight vocabulary using whole-word recognition is dependent upon the development of phonic skills. As previously stated, the acquisition of phonic skill is in turn dependent upon adequate auditory discrimination, auditory analysis, and phoneme blending, all included in the wider term 'phonological awareness'. It is likely that these processes are also involved to some extent in spelling ability.

Auditory training need not always precede any introduction to reading, unless a child's auditory perception is markedly deficient or where a child has a known hearing loss and auditory training is recommended as part of a programme to increase the child's use of residual hearing. Usually auditory training can be provided alongside the child's early reading experiences while a basic sight vocabulary is being built up. Many of the activities which are being used to teach basic phonic knowledge are also simultaneously training listening skills. For instance, many of the games from the *Programmed Reading Kit* (Stott 1962) develop auditory discrimination, auditory analysis and auditory blending, as well as teaching the sound values of the particular symbols involved in the game.

The principal aims of auditory training are to increase awareness of sound patterns, to encourage careful attention to speech sounds and to develop the skills of listening. Brief consideration will be given to the three auditory processes referred to above.

Auditory discrimination   A teacher will find it useful to collect pictures from mail-order catalogues and colour supplements to use in games requiring auditory discrimination. The pictures may be set out in pairs and the child must quickly touch one of a pair of pictures when the word is called: for example, 'Pear' (pictures show 'bear' and 'pear'), 'Three' (pictures show 'three' and 'tree'). Worksheets can also be made with pictures of objects which the child must identify when the initial sound is given. When games like these have been played it is useful to get the child to say the name of each pictured object clearly and then to listen to his or her own voice played back on a tape recorder, thus dealing with articulation alongside auditory discrimination.

Classroom games which involve 'finding the odd one out' (for example, *b*oy, *b*ag, *h*and, *b*and) and which may involve rhyme (for example, s*and*, h*and*, feet, l*and*, b*and*) are popular. With young children, 'I spy' games using initial letter sounds rather than letter names are useful.

Auditory analysis   Some of the activities listed above have included simple levels of auditory analysis, e.g. isolating the initial letter sound. Games can be extended to listening for final sounds (for example, 'Put a line under the pictures that end like sn*ake*.' Pictures show r*ake*, bucket, *cake*, ball).

Auditory analysis (segmentation) can be taught, or at least encouraged, by spending a little time in taking words apart into their component sounds, raising the actual process to the level of awareness in the child. For example, 'What's this picture, Jackie? Yes. Good. It's a frog. Let's listen to that word FROG. Let's say it very slowly. FR–O–G. You try it.' This involves listening, not reading.

Phoneme blending   This is also referred to as speech sound blending, and is the complementary process to auditory analysis. Encourage the child to gain experience in putting speech sounds together to build a word. 'I spy with my little eye a picture of a FR–O–G.' Use the same technique while reading or telling a story to the children: 'The boy came to the wall. He couldn't get over. The door was st–u–ck....' Children quickly supply the words as the story goes on. Sound blending is also used in the early stages of word-building from print with simple consonant-vowel-consonant words (l–o–t; m–a–n). Teachers must be on the look-out for children who find this process difficult, since it is a vital subskill for reading and can be trained if necessary.

Phonemic awareness and reading achievement

Phonemic awareness appears to be important not only for development of phonic decoding skills but also as a direct aid to rapid word recognition. Studies have shown that children can be helped to increase their phonological awareness through specific training, both separate from and embedded within their reading programmes.

Olson (1990) suggests that young children should be exposed to activities which raise their awareness of speech sounds, rhymes and alliteration through daily activities in pre-school settings. She recommends as useful listening games and puzzles which require the children to clap out the number of syllables in their names, the number of words in a phrase, and later the number of sounds within a familiar word. Activities can also be introduced which require children to blend sounds or syllables together to make words.

It is often helpful to inspect young or slow learners' invented spelling in their early attempts at writing. This can reveal the extent to which they have developed phonemic awareness.

In the programme *Reading Success* (Reynolds and Dallas 1991) six aspects of phonological awareness are specifically taught, alongside the reading of texts for enjoyment and information. These six aspects are:

- Segmentation (sentences into words, words into syllables, words into separate sounds).
- Blending (sounds into syllables and words).
- Isolation (identifying the initial, final and medial sounds in a target word).
- Alliteration ('greedy green gremlins giggle').
- Exchanging (substituting a new initial sound for another sound to produce a new word: *met* becomes *pet*).
- Rhyming (listening to and saying nursery rhymes; finding words which rhyme).

Olson (1990) considers that one of the strengths of the Whole Language approach is the emphasis it places upon writing from the earliest stages. The use of invented spelling by the children may help them develop phonic awareness and an understanding of the alphabetic principle. Certainly the frequent use of rhymes and alliteration in the stories shared by the children in Whole Language classrooms could be helpful in advancing their phonological awareness.

The use of word processors for story creation may also indirectly assist the development of auditory analysis and segmentation. Jackson (1987) suggests that word processing forces both teachers and students back to a situation where they need to pay attention to the phonological and orthographic bases of language, in order to key-in correct spelling of words.

In general, research in recent years has confirmed that difficulties in learning to read are more likely to be related to problems with phonological awareness than to problems with visual perception. Students with hearing loss are obviously most at risk, since their ability to access the phonological aspects of the language around them is impaired. For them it will be helpful at first to focus more upon predominantly *visual* approaches to reading, such as flash-card work, sentence building, transformations, and written recordings for language-experience books.

Over to you

Describe the methods and resources you might use to provide a useful introduction to the first stages of reading for a student with mild intellectual disability in the early years of primary school.

Indicate how you might incorporate some of these activities within the regular classroom programme.

SELECTING AN APPROACH

Assuming that the learner has the necessary entry skills of adequate visual discrimination, phonological awareness and at least some ability to converse in simple sentences, two complementary approaches might be used: shared-book experience and language-experience reading. The two approaches are entirely compatible with modern theories of language acquisition and reading skill development. In both cases when used for remedial teaching purposes they require a much greater degree of structuring than is necessary when applied to children without learning problems. Neither method precludes the teaching of word-attack skills, as will be illustrated in the descriptions below.

Shared-book experience (Holdaway 1982)

In the shared-book approach children are brought to an enjoyment of reading through stories read by the teacher using a large-size, specially prepared book which can be seen easily by the group or class of children. Holdaway says that the book should have the same visual impact from 10 feet away as a normal book would have on the knee of the child. Stories, poems, jingles and songs which children love and which present an opportunity for them to join in, provide excellent material for the early stages. Familiarity with the language patterns involved in the stories is developed and reinforced in a natural way. Attention (on-task behaviour) is easily maintained by the teacher, who can present the material with enthusiasm and whole-hearted enjoyment. The pages of the book become a giant teaching-aid on which the teacher can develop word recognition and letter recognition skills informally, as well as convey the story. The teacher may, for example, place a hand over a word (or mask it in some other way) so that the group of children must suggest what the word is likely to be, thus helping them to develop an awareness of contextual cues, language patterns and prediction.

As a beginning-reading method the approach has proved equal or superior to other methods and produces very positive attitudes towards reading, even in the slower children. By its very nature, a shared-book session is *inclusive* of all children.

With the least able children it is likely that, in order to establish greater independence, more attention will need to be devoted to mastering letter sounds; but this too can be made enjoyable through games, rhymes and songs rather than 'drills'. For example, the *Letterland System* (Wendon 1989) developed by a very imaginative teacher, uses alliteration in the names of the key characters to help the children associate and remember a sound with a symbol. This approach could easily be integrated into the shared-book programme. The pictograms themselves are letters with pictures superimposed in such a way that they reinforce the shape of the letter, while creating a story link in the child's mind. The h is presented as the *H*airy *H*atman, who walks along in words whispering 'h, h, h, for *h*hairy *h*hat'. The w is introduced as the *W*icked *W*ater *W*itch, with her two pools of water held within the shape of the letter. More complex combinations are all covered in the scheme. For example when a (for apple) is next to w (for Water Witch) the witch casts a spell which the makes the apple taste *aw*ful.

Games and activities from Stotts' *Programmed Reading Kit* could also be used to provide a carefully structured and sequenced progression for the acquisition of phonic skills.

It should be noted that shared-book experience embodies all the basic principles of effective teaching, particularly the important elements of teacher demonstration, modelling, active participation and successful practice. The approach is also soundly based upon, and replicates, those aspects of 'the bedtime story at home' which Holdaway found to be important influences on early reading progress in school. These principles are described clearly by Johnson and Louis (1987) in their excellent book *Bringing it all Together*.

Language–experience approach

The language-experience approach uses the child's own language to produce carefully controlled amounts of reading material. It could be described as a form of 'dictated story' approach. From the viewpoint of the slow learner or failing reader, the approach combines two major advantages. There is the possibility of utilizing the child's own interests to generate material for reading and writing; and the teacher is able to work within the child's current level of language competence at all times. Moyle (1982) has stressed the tremendous value of this approach for children who are well below average in general language development. The work produced is usually relevant and motivating.

With the young child or the child of very limited ability, the starting point for the language-experience approach can be the labelling by the teacher or aide of some of the child's art work or drawings, no matter how primitive, with captions which the child suggests. 'This is my cat, Dotty', 'I can ride my bike fast.' The child and teacher together read these captions and revise them for a few minutes each day, without at this stage drawing attention to individual letters or words. If *Breakthrough to Literacy* materials are available in the classroom, the child can be encouraged to build these sentences using word-cards in a sentence holder. During this early stage of the programme the child can be helped to contribute a dictated sentence following some class excursion to the airport or a farm: 'I saw a Jumbo Jet'; 'The cow licked David on the face.' These sentences are added, along with others from the class, to the picture-map which the class has produced as part of the follow-up to the excursion. Again, they are not in any way analysed or drilled, and serve the purpose of establishing in the learner's mind the notion that 'What I say can be written down.'

After a few weeks of this introductory work the child is ready to make his or her first book. A topic is carefully selected: e.g. 'speedway'. The teacher produces some visual material which will provide the illustration for the first page, perhaps a picture of the child's favourite speedway rider from a magazine. Teacher and child talk about the rider and from the discussion they agree upon a single brief statement which can be written under the picture: 'This is Chris Copley'. The teacher writes (prints) the agreed statement for the child who then copies it carefully under the teacher's version. If the child cannot copy due to perceptual-motor or co-ordination problems, he or she can trace over the words with a coloured pencil or wax crayon. Both teacher and child then read the statement together once or twice and the child is left to paste the picture carefully into the book. Even this activity must be closely supervised with some children, in order that the page looks attractive rather than messy. With some older children they can be encouraged to type the same sentence on a sheet of paper and paste that into the book to help generalization from handwritten to typed form of the same words.

Next day the child is presented with the same statement written on a strip of card: 'This is Chris Copley'. Without reference to the book the child is encouraged to read the words. He or she may have forgotten the material, so some brief revision is needed. The child then cuts the strip of card into separate word cards. These are placed at random on the desk and the child has to arrange them in correct sequence. If the child fails, he or she must spend time matching the word cards against the original in the book until the sequencing task can be performed correctly. At this point the teacher picks up one of the cards, perhaps the word 'is', and using it as a small flash-card asks the child to pronounce the word. This is continued until the child can recognize each word out of context. The word cards are then placed in an envelope stapled in the back cover of the book, ready to be revised the following day.

Over the next week the child continues to produce a page of his or her book, with much guidance from an adult. Revision of the previous day's words ensures repetition and overlearning to the point of mastery. The teacher's control over what is written will ensure that not too much is added to the book each day, which might otherwise result in failure to master the new words. If the child is allowed to dictate too much material, this will result in failure to learn, and loss of satisfaction.

Once important sight words are mastered, these can be checked off or coloured in on a vocabulary list in the front cover of the child's book. McNally and Murray's *Key Words to Literacy List* or the Dolch sight vocabulary lists are very appropriate for this purpose. Such charting of progress in the book gives the child visual evidence of improvement and also indicates to the teacher what has been covered so far and what still needs to be taught. If certain words seem to present particular problems for the child, games and activities can be introduced to repeat and overlearn these words until mastered (e.g. word bingo). Gradually the amount written can be increased, and after some months a child will need less and less direct help in constructing his or her own sentences. The approach may sound slow and tedious but it does result in children with even the most resistant cases of reading failure making progress. It is highly structured and the growth in word recognition skills is cumulative.

At some stage in the programme the teacher must help the child to expand his or her word-attack skills. For example, perhaps the child has used the word 'crash' in writing about the speedway interest. In a separate booklet the teacher can help the child to learn the value of the blend 'cr' by collecting other cr words (crab, crook, cross, cry, etc.). Similarly they can experiment with the unit 'ash' from the word 'crash' (b-ash; d-ash; c-ash; r-ash; etc.). This incidental word study linked with meaningful material from the child's own book is important, but it will still be inadequate for developing fully functional decoding skills. It will be necessary to teach word-attack and spelling skills quite explicitly for certain students.

Once a child has made a positive start using this language-experience approach he or she can be introduced to a carefully selected 'real' book. It is wise to prepare the way for this transition by including in the child's final language-experience book most of the words which will be met in this new book.

The basic principles of the language-experience approach can be used with non-literate adults and those learning English as a second language.

Clearly the shared-book experience can operate in parallel with the individualized language-experience approach in both whole-class and remedial group situations.

Johnson and Louis (1987) have described the language-experience approach as being excellent as an introduction to literacy, since it shows that writing recreates meaning, and that speech and writing are connected. Thomas (1991) argues that language related to real experience is a vital prerequisite or precursor for any introduction to reading, and that parents have an important role in providing this enrichment in out-of-school time.

The visuo-thematic approach (Jackson 1987)

Jackson described a carefully structured variation of the language-experience approach which he had found useful in clinical settings. He called the approach 'visuo-thematic'. The learner (child or adult) is presented with a visual stimulus picture which has a number of ideas in it to generate discussion and to suggest a story, without too much imagination being required. Jackson found detailed cartoons from magazines or newspapers to be useful, and he suggests that the learner be encouraged to seek out suitable material to bring to each session. Jackson outlines the procedure in the following steps.

The child obtains a picture which he or she pastes on to a piece of cardboard, together with a matchbox in the corner. This matchbox is to house small cards containing all the words the child can think of to describe various aspects of the picture. The child is then required to have three columns ruled on a page headed 'naming words', 'describing words', and 'action words'. He or she is then asked to try to think of at least six words which can be placed in each of the above columns, thus giving a total of at least eighteen words for the picture. The words are written out at home or during the lesson in their appropriate columns and the child is then asked to put each word on a small card and place it in the box. In this way a 'library' of pictures and their associated vocabularies is built up by the child. When the child comes to the lesson the teacher or aide checks the words for accuracy and tests the child's ability to recall them. Some practice is then given in spelling the words.

The next step is for the child to construct his or her own series of questions about aspects of the picture. The child is then asked to write a story about the picture and to select a title. The story is read by the child and adult together, and any corrections are noted. After this the child is asked to rewrite the story or to type it in its final form and to paste it in the book beside the vocabulary lists. This procedure is repeated at least once a week, using on each occasion a different story but the same format and structure. Each story is filed and kept available for re-reading later.

Jackson (1991) has provided extremely useful suggestions for working individually with a student with severe reading problems in his book *Discipline: an Approach for Teachers and Parents*. His 'structured alphabet kit' is also clearly described in that text.

Over to you

Take any one of the approaches presented in the section above and discuss how it might be accommodated in a classroom where the general language arts programme is based upon Whole Language philosophy.

Reading recovery (Clay 1985)

Reading Recovery is an early intervention programme first developed in New Zealand and now used in North America, Britain and Australia. Children who are identified as having reading difficulties after one year of school are placed in the programme and receive daily intensive tuition on a one-to-one basis. They remain in the programme for approximately fifteen weeks, or until they have reached the average level of their class (De Ford 1991). The aim of the programme is to reduce substantially the number of children who experience ongoing and cumulative literacy problems. This is achieved by providing the opportunity for accelerated learning. It is claimed that Reading Recovery can be so effective that only 1 per cent of children require further, long-term assistance with reading and writing (Clay 1990). It should be noted, however, that this level of efficacy has been questioned by some observers, who believe that gains made in the programme are not always maintained (Chapman and Tunmer 1991).

A typical Reading Recovery lesson includes seven activities:

- re-reading of familiar books;
- independent reading of the book introduced the previous day;
- letter identification activities with plastic letters;
- writing of a dictated or prepared story;
- sentence-building and reconstruction from the story;
- introduction of a new book;
- guided reading of new book.

The texts selected are designed to give a high success rate; and confidence is boosted by frequent re-reading of the familiar stories. Optimum use is made of the available time and students are kept fully on-task. Some attention is given within the instructional time to listening for sounds within words and practising phonic skills; but Chapman and Tunmer (1991) suggest that even *more* attention should be given to developing the child's metalinguistic and phonological awareness within the programme.

The obvious stumbling block is the need to find time and appropriate personnel to provide daily tuition to the selected students. It is probable that volunteer helpers used within learning assistance programmes (LAP) would improve the quality and impact of their assistance if they utilized the teaching strategies from Reading Recovery under the teacher's direction.

Details of the Reading Recovery programme, including instructional strategies, practical ideas and use of time, are given in Clay's (1985) book *The Early Detection of Reading Difficulties.*

DO LEARNING DISABLED STUDENTS NEED DIFFERENT METHODS?

Children with a specific reading disability do not, in general, need a totally different approach for instruction in reading. It was stated in Chapter 1 that their priority needs are for a carefully structured and effectively taught programme, which emphasizes the functional aspects of literacy and places a clear focus upon acquiring appropriate strategies for decoding text. The methods advocated for learning-disabled students are the same as those advocated for any student, but applied with greater precision. In particular, students with a specific reading disability require the following issues to be adequately addressed.

- Having some real reason for reading, writing and spelling is essential. Establish a close interrelationship between oral language, reading and writing. There is a real danger that children with severe reading problems may receive, if tutored individually, a remedial programme which contains too many isolated skill-building drills. There is a need to apply these skills realistically as they develop.
- Many dyslexic children benefit from being taught more about the structure of language (for example, the meaning of the terms 'syllable' and 'prefix', etc.) as part of their programme.
- A structured use of the language-experience approach is widely advocated for learning-disabled children.
- The use of cognitive strategy training (see Chapter 3) will help the student gain better control over his or her reading and writing. This is particularly important in higher-order reading skills, such as comprehension.
- Emphasis usually needs to be placed upon the systematic teaching of phonic decoding skills (that is, the teaching of letter sounds and how

to blend these into words). Phonological awareness may need to be developed.

- Multisensory approaches seem to help the learning-disabled child assimilate and master particular units such as letters and words.
- Material must be selected very carefully to match the child's current ability and interest level. However, some LD students profess to *like* the books in basal reading schemes (Reetz and Hoover 1992).
- Teachers should not present too much material at once. They should determine as rapidly as possible how much a particular student can handle successfully at one sitting, and avoid tiring or frustrating the student. However, regular and intensive practice sessions are essential; and the ultimate long-term aim is to *accelerate* the rate of learning.
- Revise and review previously taught skills or concepts at frequent intervals. Practice and overlearning are vital for success.

SUMMARY

In this chapter attention has been given to appropriate pre-reading and early reading experiences, necessary for some students with learning difficulties or disabilities. It was pointed out that pre-reading activities are not routinely required by all students.

Particular attention was given to the important topic of auditory training, since phonological awareness has been identified in a number of research studies as an essential prerequisite for early reading success.

Several beginning-reading approaches were described in detail. In general, most remedial reading approaches do not differ greatly from mainstream approaches. Much useful help can be provided for many children with special needs simply by a more carefully structured use of the regular class programme. Where this is possible it is to be preferred to offering a totally different programme requiring one-to-one tuition in a withdrawal room situation. However, some children's learning difficulties are so acute, or their attitude toward reading so negative, that their needs can only be met by a carefully designed programme which requires methods and materials that differ markedly from those in regular use. The following chapter contains some additional ideas to use in such cases.

Discussion points

- Review the teaching methods presented in this chapter. Which would you find most useful in your present teaching situation?

- How would you begin to teach reading to a student from a non-English speaking background whose oral language is limited?

Further reading

Blachman, B.A. (1991) 'Early intervention for children's reading problems', *Topics in Language Disorders* 12, 1: 51–65.

Builder, P. (1991) *Exploring Reading*, Hawthorn: Australian Council for Educational Research.

Ekwall, E.E. and Shanker, J.L. (1985) *Teaching Reading in the Elementary School*, Columbus: Merrill.

Graham, S. and Johnson, L.A. (1989) 'Teaching reading to learning disabled students: a review of research supported procedures', *Focus on Exceptional Children* 21, 6: 1–12

Johns, J. (1986) *Handbook for Remediation of Reading Difficulties*, Englewood Cliffs: Prentice-Hall.

Pumfrey, P. & Elliott, C. (1990) *Children's Difficulties in Reading, Writing and Spelling*, London: Falmer.

Smith, F. (1992) 'Learning to read: the never-ending debate', *Phi Delta Kappan* 73, 6: 432–41.

Wearne, K.J. and McMonnies, C.W. (1992) 'Reversal prevalence and reading level among third graders', *Australian Journal of Remedial Education* 24, 1: 15–18.

Chapter 8

Reading: additional techniques and resources

Good teachers are committed to balanced, eclectic approaches; they provide whatever a child needs to achieve optimal growth in language and reading development.

(Mather 1992: 92)

The approaches described in the previous chapter, used selectively, are all useful for helping a student to make some initial progress in learning to read. This chapter provides some additional practical ideas which may be used alongside, or incorporated within, the general programme to provide variety, enjoyment, motivation and additional practice.

An important final section of the chapter looks at ways of improving comprehension skills in students who experience difficulty in extracting meaning from text.

TECHNIQUES AND RESOURCES

The use of comic strips

The use of picture material from children's comics and cartoons can provide an enjoyable and motivating beginning-reading approach for primary or very slow learning secondary students (Johnson and Johnson 1977).

The children select a comic strip. They number each individual picture in logical sequence and cut and paste each picture in the top half of a blank sheet of A4 paper. They can dictate their own interpretation of the 'story' to the teacher or other tutor (e.g. parent, peer, aide). The teacher prints the words for each story below the appropriate pictures, reading these back to the child and then asking the child to read them unaided. Finally the pages are secured together and a cover is made. The children can then share their small booklets with others in the class. The story dictated by a child does not have to be identical with the one intended by the artist. The teacher should accept the children's own versions.

During the process of writing down the child's dictated story the teacher can draw attention to certain single letters and letter groups in order to begin to develop some basic word-attack skills. Words which are particularly difficult but important are put on flash-cards for revision and practice. At a later stage the child copies the story into his own book. Gradually the child will be able to construct more of the story without adult help.

Another possible use of comic strips and cartoons for remedial reading and writing involves the removal of the captions or the 'speech-balloons' using some form of correcting fluid or white ink. The child then discusses with the teacher what the characters might be saying and is helped to write the words into the 'speech-balloons'. These are then read to the teacher and other children.

Audio-visual approaches

Of the various approaches which use audio-visual presentation there is one which is particularly motivating for older students, the Bowmar Reading Incentive Programme. This presents reasonably sophisticated themes like drag racing, motor cycles, hot-air balloons, etc., through the use of film strip, sound commentary on tape and a student's reading book which embodies the same language as presented in the taped commentary. The kits in this series each have a teacher's guidebook and sets of the student books. The very colourful and lively presentation, and the opportunity for the student to become familiar with the language structure and vocabulary associated with each theme before having to read it in the books, are the principal attractions. The use of the taped commentary in conjunction with the books then allows for abundant repetition and overlearning (Radlauer and Radlauer 1974).

Teachers can, of course, make their own programmes for use with a tape recorder. Indeed, this item of hardware is an indispensable aid in all remedial situations. It may be used for nothing more ambitious than pre-recording of popular stories which the children can listen to through headsets while following the text in the book. In this way material which would otherwise be at frustration level for a child can be presented in a very meaningful manner. Other uses of tape may be to programme aspects of phonic work or spelling assignments, or to set comprehension questions at literal, interpretive, critical and creative levels.

The use of popular songs on audio-tape provides repetition with enjoyment and has proved to be useful in remedial or special class situations. A zig-zag book containing the words from a current song is prepared for the child or the small group. The children follow the words in the book as the song is played from a cassette. Later the words are read without the music and some key words may be put on flash-cards to be recognized out of context.

The overhead projector is also valuable for presenting aspects of reading in a predominantly visual way. Many teachers make their own transparencies and use colour to good advantage in developing word study skills. The overhead projector is also useful in presenting cloze exercises and preparing word webs (see below).

The Bell & Howell 'Languagemaster' remains a very popular machine. Its main value lies in the fact that the child is actively engaged in the operation of the machine and is using visual, vocal and auditory channels simultaneously, while also receiving immediate corrective feedback.

The machine is in essence a tape-player and recorder that allows the simultaneous presentation of moving visual material with auditory output (or oral input from the learner). A card, with a strip of recording tape at its base, is fed into the machine in a right-to-left direction (the child therefore scans it in a left-to-right direction). The card contains space for words and/or pictures to be presented and the tape gives auditory information relating to the words or pictures. By switching to a different track the child can record his or her response to the question and can play back this answer for checking with the original.

The Languagemaster has a long history of useful service. As well as being useful for teaching and overlearning of the basic sight vocabulary, it can be used to reinforce the learning of new words in a reading scheme or in the child's language-experience book. It can also be used to teach a child certain 'self-help' skills within the reading process. For example, key words or particularly difficult vocabulary from a specific book can be put on to the Languagemaster cards, together with the recording of the word. The child reads the page in the book, guessing the difficult word, then plays the card to check or learn the pronunciation.

Games and apparatus

In almost all texts dealing with remedial or corrective reading, teachers will find abundant encouragement to use games and word-building equipment as adjuncts to their programmes. Games, it is argued, provide an opportunity for the learners to practise and overlearn essential material which might otherwise become boring and dull. Such repetition is essential for children who learn at a slow rate or who are poorly motivated. The use of games and equipment may also be seen as 'non-threatening', serving a therapeutic purpose within a group or individual teaching situation.

There can be little doubt that well-structured games and apparatus can perform a very important teaching function. Word bingo, picture-to-word matching sets, syllable jigsaws, word wheels, phonic rummy games, etc., can all help to develop word recognition, phonic knowledge and decoding skills. However, it is essential that a specific game or piece of equipment has a clearly defined purpose and that it is matched with a genuine learning need in the children who are to use it. The material should contribute to the objectives for the lesson, not detract from them. Too often, games are used in a very random way, almost to amuse the children or to keep them occupied. While this may be justified on therapeutic grounds it cannot be defended pedagogically. A study carried out by Baker, Herman and Yeh (1981) with second- and third-grade children found that the unstructured use of games, puzzles and supplementary material was *negatively* related to achievement in reading and mathematics.

It is also important that the use of games or apparatus be closely monitored by an adult, if time is not to be wasted by the children and if the material is to be used correctly.

Alphabet kits

An inexpensive but extremely useful resource to use with beginning readers of any age is a set of plastic letters. For many years their use with dyslexic students has been strongly advocated for word-building and spelling practice. Jackson (1991) includes them as an important component in his approach for students with severe reading disability, and he devised a 'structured alphabet kit' to be used in individual tutorial sessions. The use of plastic letters also forms an essential part of Bryant and Bradley's (1985) programme to assist children to categorize and identify sounds. These writers suggest that the use of groups of letters, arranged to spell simple words in front of the child, allows for the removal of a particular letter while still leaving the rest of the word visually intact. The child can then substitute other letters to make new words, and in doing so develop valuable insight into word structure and sound–symbol relationships. Plastic letters are used for precisely this purpose in the Reading Success programme (Reynolds and Dallas 1991).

It can be argued that the use of plastic letters adds a 'concrete' level of representation which some students may cope with more successfully than the purely auditory or purely graphic. Cashdan and Wright (1990) strongly support the use of such aids in not only helping the development of an awareness of the written language system, but also adding to the interest and enjoyment of the teaching session.

Multisensory or multimodal approaches

The names Fernald, Gillingham, Stillman and Orton usually come to mind when multisensory approaches are mentioned. Basically all of these educators advocated methods which use as many channels of input to the learner as possible. The methods usually involve the learner finger-tracing over the letter-shape or word-shape to be mastered, while at the same time saying and hearing the auditory component and seeing the visual component.

The Fernald approach involves four stages:

1   First the learner selects a particular word which he or she wants to learn. The teacher writes the word in blackboard-size writing (cursive) on a card. The child then finger-traces the word, saying each syllable as it is traced. This is repeated until the learner feels capable of writing the word from memory. As new words are mastered they are filed away in a card index for later revision. As soon as the learner knows a few words these are used for constructing simple sentences.

2   The second stage involves the elimination of direct finger-tracing and the child is encouraged to learn the words through studying their visual appearance and then writing them from memory. This stage improves visual imagery and may thus be used also for remedial instruction in the correct spelling of irregular words. The words are still stored on card and used for frequent revision. The material is usually consolidated by the child producing his or her own small books.

3   The third stage continues to develop visual word-study techniques and encourages a more rapid memorization of the words, followed by swift writing. The word-card drill is usually retained only for particular words which give difficulty. At this stage the child also begins to attempt to read new material prepared by the teacher.

4   The final stage involves the child becoming almost entirely independent in his or her reading skill, having generalized an understanding of word structure and having been helped to make use of contextual cues.

The Gillingham and Stillman approach and the Orton approach are basically the same as the Fernald approach, employing a Visual-Auditory-

Kinaesthetic-Tactile (VAKT) method. The only significant difference is the emphasis given to sounding-out rather than slowly pronouncing the word during the finger-tracing stages. More attention is given to learning the letter sounds and applying these in word-attack.

It can be argued that multisensory approaches using several channels of input simultaneously help a child to integrate, at a neurological level, what is seen with what is heard, whether it be a letter or a word. On the other hand VAKT approaches may well succeed where other methods have failed because they cause the learner to focus more intently on the learning task. Whatever the reason, this teaching approach, which brings vision, hearing, articulation and movement into play, does appear to result in improved assimilation and retention. It is obviously easier to apply this approach with younger children; but in a one-to-one remedial situation it is still a viable proposition with older students.

Bryant and Bradley (1985) provide a very well-argued rationale for the inclusion of multisensory teaching in their book *Children's Reading Problems*.

Cloze procedure

Cloze procedure is a simple approach designed to make a reader more aware of context cues and meaning as aids to guessing unfamiliar words. The procedure merely requires that certain words in a sentence or paragraph be deleted and the reader asked to read the paragraph and supply the possible words which might fill the gaps:

> It was Monday morning and Leanne should have been going to sch......... She was still in........... She was hot and her throat was...............
>
> 'I think I had better send for the d............,' said her................. 'No school for you...................'

Variations on the cloze technique involve leaving the initial letter of the deleted word to provide a clue; or at the other extreme, deleting several consecutive words, thus requiring the student to provide a phrase which might be appropriate. The use of the cloze procedure can be integrated as part of the shared-book experiences already described.

These cloze activities can involve group work. The prepared paragraphs are duplicated on sheets for the children or displayed on the overhead projector. As a group the children discuss the best alternative and then present these to the teacher. Reading, vocabulary and comprehension are all being developed by a closer attention to logical sentence structure and meaning.

Rebus reading approaches

Any approach which uses a picture or symbol in place of a particular word may be described as a 'rebus' approach. The method allows a child to feel that he or she is reading at a functional level by replacing difficult nouns or concepts with a picture or symbol. Figure 3 is a simple illustration of this principle, from a series called *Truckin' with Kenny* (Rogers 1982).

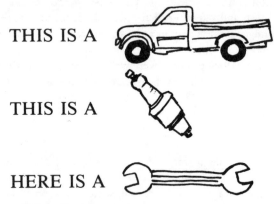

Figure 3 The rebus approach

It is an approach which can serve to boost confidence in the early stages and can allow a story-line to be developed without tight constraints of vocabulary control.

Rebus approach can also be adapted as a group activity, where children work together to construct the story, and then read it aloud to others. This provides opportunities for children at all levels of ability to contribute, and is a useful example of inclusive practice. Figure 4 was collected from a group of primary students.

The Impress Method (also known as the 'Neurological Impress Method' and the 'Read-Along Approach'

The Impress reading method is a unison reading procedure in which the student and the teacher read aloud together at a natural rate. The student

Figure 4 Example of a group rebus approach

is permitted to use the index finger to keep the place on the page, and may even be physically guided to do so by the teacher.

The Impress Method is particularly useful when a child has developed some word recognition skill but is lacking in fluency and expression. It is recommended that sessions should last roughly fifteen minutes and be provided on a very regular basis for several months. It may be necessary to repeat the same sentences or paragraphs several times until the student becomes fluent at reading the material alone.

The Impress Method is very appropriate for use in peer-tutoring, where one child who is a better reader provides assistance for a less able friend. In such cases the 'tutor' usually needs to be shown how to act effectively as a helper.

Eldredge (1990) has had good success using a variation of read-along with a group of poor readers. He uses the term 'group-assisted reading' to describe an approach which uses reading in unison to emphasize correct phrasing, intonation and pitch. The decoding burden is removed, allowing students to concentrate upon meaning. Eldredge's system involves reading a challenging text several times with the students while each student follows or tracks the print in the book. Students then practise the reading in pairs without teacher assistance. Significant achievement gains in reading comprehension and vocabulary were reported.

A similar approach which requires non-fluent readers to repeatedly read a short passage aloud until fluent has also been found useful in building confidence and increasing skills (Bowd 1990).

Word processors

Microcomputers and word processors can be used most effectively to help students acquire confidence in creating their own stories. Wray and Medwell (1989) have suggested that the use of word processors for desk-top publishing adds a valuable new dimension to the language programme in any classroom. Creating and printing one's own stories can enhance a child's interest in books, and at the same time develop skills in composing, editing, proof-reading and design.

At a more basic level, computer programmes exist which will help students to improve their word recognition, decoding, sentence completion, and spelling skills. For example, a target word may be displayed on the screen and the student required to copy it using the keyboard. The word is then embedded in a sentence for the student to read and copy. The word is presented again with the initial letter missing and student is required to complete it. Gradually the cues are removed until the student is reading and writing the word correctly with a high degree of automaticity.

Computer programmes can also be used to improve comprehension skills (Anderson 1990); and programmes can be devised to provide additional study material related to texts and novels being used by the class (Wepner 1991).

In general, word processors are valuable because they integrate reading with writing and require the student to *interact* with the text which is being presented. Computers are infinitely patient, allow for self-pacing by the student, present material in carefully sequenced steps and provide immediate feedback (Au and Bruce 1990). Students are required to be active throughout the learning session and are found to have higher levels of motivation when working at the keyboard (Loughrey 1991). Whether used by one student alone, or by students working together, the computer is an excellent tool within the regular classroom.

In the home situation the computer can aid literacy development. Children can work with a parent on early reading skills, such as word recognition, simple spelling and following instructions (Rickleman and Henk 1991).

LISTENING TO CHILDREN READ

Regardless of which approach or blend of approaches a teacher decides to use in working with individual children, listening to the child read aloud should be an essential part of the programme. It permits the teacher to monitor such features as self-correcting behaviour, use of context, word-attack skill, fluency and phrasing. This writer has found it valuable to use such time as a 'reading together' experience, rather than merely listening to the child read. Having selected an appropriate book the session may take the following form:

- You (the teacher) volunteer to read the first page or two while the child follows in his or her copy of the book. The teacher's fluent reading of the text serves not only to model appropriate expression and rate but allows the child to get the flavour of the story. Names of characters will have cropped up and topic-specific terms will have been encountered by the time the child's turn comes to read. Allow the child to finger-point to keep the place in the text if necessary, rather than become lost and left behind in the story.
- Now invite the child to read the next page or half-page. As you listen to the performance, anticipate any difficult words and simply provide them to maintain, at this stage, continuity and meaning.
- Praise the child briefly for the reading, then continue yourself with the next page.
- Again invite the child to read the next page, providing help only when necessary. Don't destroy continuity by suggesting that the child sound-out a word. You might, however, suggest that the child read the rest of the sentence if he or she can't recognize a word. This will usually enable the reader to self-correct or make a contextual guess.
- After reading at least four or five pages together in this way, the child will feel that a significant part of the story has been read. Indeed the story content (plot) will be emerging and a few minutes may be spent in talking about the key points so far to aid recall and comprehension. (This approach might be contrasted with the typical classroom ritual of hearing a child read one page, then marking his or her card and putting the book away until the next day or later in the week. So little of the actual story is covered each day that it is almost impossible

for the child to understand what it is really about. The least able readers suffer most in this system.)

- In later sessions the amount that you read is gradually reduced, allowing the child more time to perform independently. It is at this stage that you can gain insights into the child's skills by attending to the nature of miscues which may occur from time to time.
- It is important that a child be helped to read a significant amount at each session. By breaking into the vicious circle of 'I can't read well – so I avoid reading – so I don't get much practice – so I don't improve', you are able to prove to the child that he or she is, indeed, making progress. Some form of daily charting of pages read can be very useful here.

It is important to aim to make the child an *independent* reader. The amount of correction and feedback given to a low ability reader may tend to maintain that child's dependence on adult support and guidance. Frequently the feedback tends to be drawing the child's attention to the phonic properties of a word, or simply supplying the word, rather than helping the reader to pick up cues from context and thus become more independent in performance. Less frequent and less direct support seems to provide more opportunity for the child to self-correct and maintain attention to meaning (McNaughton 1981). In particular, teachers should pause longer before prompting a student.

IMPROVING COMPREHENSION

As long ago as 1969 Nila Banton Smith identified four levels of comprehension, each level containing a cluster of component skills and each being dependent upon competence at the previous levels. The most basic level is referred to as 'Literal Comprehension' (understanding, at least superficially, the basic information which is being presented). This level is dependent upon such subskills as recognition of main idea, grasp of sequence and order of detail, and recognition of cause and effect relationships when these are stated in the text. To a large extent even this level depends upon the learner's own previous knowledge and experience. If the concepts being presented are very new, even literal comprehension and recall will be difficult. This raises the question, 'Is reading a text the best way of introducing a new and unfamiliar topic?' For some learners the answer is certainly 'No.'

The second level of comprehension is 'Interpretation'. This involves going beyond what is actually presented in the text, inferring and reading between the lines and drawing conclusions. Subskills at this level include making generalizations, predicting outcomes, reasoning cause–effect when these are not stated, and discovering relationships.

The third level of comprehension is 'Critical Reading'. This involves judgement of the quality, value, accuracy and truthfulness of what is read, detecting bias or over-statement.

The final level is referred to as 'Creative Reading'. At this level the reader goes beyond the writer's material and generates new ideas or develops new insights which were not explicit in the text.

It is argued that in many classrooms comprehension exercises rarely demand responses other than at the literal (factual recall) level. While this level *is* important, since it is basic to the other three levels, a programme which sets out to develop comprehension skills in children should include questions (oral and written) which demand some thinking at the interpretive, critical and creative levels. For example, following a short story about the crash of a passenger aircraft, these questions might be posed:

- How many passengers escaped the crash? (Literal)
- Why did the failure of cabin pressure lead to the crash? (Interpretive)
- From the way he behaved before the crash, what kind of man do you think the pilot was, and could his judgement be trusted? (Critical)
- Many air crashes involving loss of life occur each year. How might flight be made a safer method of transport? (Creative)

If a child has difficulties in comprehending what is read, particularly at the first two levels, it is worth considering whether there is a serious mismatch between his or her own vocabulary knowledge and the words being used to convey the information in the text. A child may be able to read a word correctly but not know (or may misunderstand) its meaning. In such cases there is a need to devote more time to word study and vocabulary building when comprehension activities are used in classroom.

Children who read very slowly or much too fast often comprehend poorly. Attention to rate of reading is thus indicated as a specific intervention in some cases.

For some children, the actual recall of information is poor. Recall is dependent upon attention, vividness of content, intention to remember, rehearsal, and any connections with the reader's previous experience. These factors may help to identify why a particular child is having problems.

According to Dole *et al.* (1991) there are five key components to successful comprehension of text: locating the main idea, drawing inferences, generating questions, monitoring one's own understanding, and making a summary. Research has indicated that these aspects of comprehension can be improved if given due attention and if taught explicitly. In particular, students with reading difficulties benefit from specific training in self-monitoring and in summarizing (Malone and Mastropieri 1992).

Cole and Chan (1990) have reviewed the classroom-based research on what is known as 'reciprocal teaching'. In this approach to the improvement of study skills, teachers and students work together in the initial stages, sharing ideas, generating questions which may be answered by a specific text, predicting answers, checking for meaning and finally collaborating on a summary. The teacher's role is one of demonstrating effective ways of gaining meaning from text; but the long-term aim is to have the students internalize these strategies for themselves. (See also the PQRS strategy described in Chapter 3.)

Some suggestions for improving comprehension are summarized below. See also the chapter 'Promoting Comprehension' in Johns' (1986) text; and problems with study technique in Preen and Barker (1987). Cole and Chan (1990) provide an excellent coverage of metacognitive instruction related to reading comprehension in their Chapter 9. Lovitt (1991) presents useful advice for linking visual imagery with reading comprehension, and on self-questioning to improve understanding.

Improving comprehension

The following additional suggestions may help to improve comprehension:

- Ensure that the material presented is interesting to the child and at an appropriate readability level.
- Always apply comprehension strategy training to real texts and read the texts for some genuine purpose. Don't rely upon contrived comprehension exercises used in isolation.
- Prepare for entry into the printed material. Ask, 'What might we find in this chapter? What do the illustrations tell us? What does this word mean? Let's read the subheadings before we begin', etc.
- Encourage students to set comprehension questions for each other; then use these questions to discuss what is meant by critical reading, inferring, predicting, etc.
- Read through any comprehension questions *before* the story or passage is read, so that the child enters the material knowing what to look for.

- Use daily newspapers and magazine articles as the basis for some classroom discussion and comprehension activity. Highlighter pens can be used to focus upon key ideas, important terms, facts to remember, etc.
- For the more limited readers, make frequent use of instruction sheets which the student must read, interpret and act upon. For example, instructions for a simple science experiment; following a recipe; making a model.
- Making a summary is an excellent way of ensuring that students have identified main ideas.
- In general, make sure that students are aware of the goal in reading a particular text. Teach them how to make use of strategies which will help them to extract meaning from what is read. Don't simply test comprehension, teach it!

Word webs

Another useful activity which aids comprehension and study skills and in which all students can make a contribution is that of 'word webbing' or the use of 'graphic organizers'. Word webbing is advocated as a way of preparing for entry into a text or for organizing ideas prior to writing on a new theme (Johnson and Louis 1987; Hickerson 1992).

Whitehead states, 'Before children read they need to plan' (1990: 3). Word webs, or graphic outlines, help to formalize this planning. Charts containing key words to be encountered in the text are prepared in advance by the teacher, or the teacher and students together brainstorm ideas and write key words on the blackboard. Tentative connections are made between some of the words, and these connections are discussed. As the reading of the text proceeds, new connections are made and additional important words added to the web.

Word webs help students to organize their thoughts and to link new ideas with what they already know. The final chart serves as a useful aid for students when they begin to write a summary for the topic studied. Hickerson (1992) describes webbing as a comprehension-monitoring technique combined with a note-taking strategy, and considers it applicable for primary, secondary and post-secondary settings. In many ways, this technique is similar to the brainstorming of words associated with a theme previously described under Jackson's 'visuo-thematic approach'.

When students have become proficient at word webbing they may use the technique as individuals or collaboratively in groups.

Figure 5 is a word web relating to a magazine article which has an illustration of a woman changing the tyre on her car on a country road.

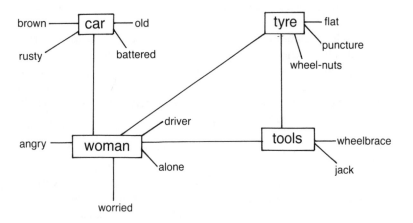

Figure 5 A word web

Johnson and Louis (1987) provide the most comprehensive coverage of word webbing in their text *Bringing it all Together*.

Over to you

In their book *Teaching Reading in the Elementary School*, Ekwall and Shanker comment that 'Many teachers spend too little time teaching comprehension because they do not know how to teach it' (1985: 211).

Read through the sections in this chapter dealing with comprehension, and also read again the appropriate sections of Chapter 3.

(Continued...)

Select a novel, a magazine article or a subject textbook which is suitable for the students you teach. Devise a procedure which you could use with the students to study and extract meaning from the material you have selected.

Don't forget the importance of your own modelling of important strategies.

How might you extend the activity into independent practice for the students?

How will you attempt to provide for generalization of the new strategies to other reading materials?

SUMMARY

This chapter provided some additional ideas for teachers to use when adapting a reading approach for individual students' needs. Many of the techniques mentioned are not, in themselves, total approaches to reading; they can be used to complement and extend existing approaches. The majority of students will not require this degree of adaptation to their programmes, but where appropriate, these suggestions may help to maintain a student's interest and enjoyment while at the same time providing successful practice of essential skills.

When programming for special assistance in reading, the teacher must constantly keep in mind that the long-term goal is to help the learner become an independent reader, capable of reading for pleasure and for information; or in the case of the student with intellectual disability, reading for social survival. The teaching of phonic skills, word-attack and so forth must never become an end in itself, but must be recognized as a step on the ladder to fully functional reading ability.

All teachers, and all helpers in learning assistance programmes, should develop skills in listening to children read and providing appropriate support and feedback. Advice on this issue was provided in this chapter.

The suggestions for improving comprehension skills presented above have wide application and should readily find a place in the whole class programme.

Discussion points

- Which of the techniques or approaches described in this chapter could be used with adults who have literacy problems?

- 'If you gave me a pencil and paper, or a blackboard and chalk, I could teach a child to read.' Give your views on this statement.
- Discuss some of the difficulties a teacher might encounter in trying to apply some of the strategies and techniques described in this chapter. How might these problems be minimized?

Further reading

Armbruster, B., Anderson, T., and Meyer, J. (1991) 'Improving content-area reading using instructional graphics', *Reading Research Quarterly* 26, 4: 394–416.

Behrmann, M.M. (ed.) (1988) *Integrating Computers into the Curriculum: a Handbook for Special Educators*, Boston: College-Hill.

Billingsley, B.S. and Wildman, T.M. (1990) 'Facilitating reading comprehension in learning disabled students', *Remedial and Special Education* 11, 2: 18–31.

Church, G. and Bender, M. (1989) *Teaching with Computers: a Curriculum for Special Educators*, Boston: College-Hill.

Fuchs, L. (1987) *Teaching Reading in the Secondary School*, Bloomington: Phi Delta Kappa Foundation.

Palinscar, A.S. and Klenk, L. (1992) 'Fostering literacy learning in supportive contexts', *Journal of Learning Disabilities* 25, 4: 211–25.

Preen, B. and Barker, D. (1987) *Literacy Development*, Sydney: Harcourt Brace Jovanovich.

Schunk, D.H. and Rice, J.M. (1992) 'Influence of reading comprehension strategy information on children's achievement outcomes', *Learning Disability Quarterly* 15, 1: 51–64.

Van Daal, V.H. and Van der Leij, A. (1992) 'Computer-based reading and spelling practice for children with learning disabilities', *Journal of Learning Disabilities* 25, 3: 186–95.

Chapter 9

Fostering development in writing and spelling

> The ability to communicate well in writing is a prerequisite for success in school. Students with learning disabilities typically have a hard time meeting the writing demands of school because they have problems related to mastery of the more mechanical aspects of written expression such as spelling, handwriting and punctuation, as well as the higher level skills of composing.
>
> (Vallecorsa, Ledford and Parnell 1991: 52)

Perhaps more than any other area of the curriculum, creative writing presents problems for the slower learning child, the unmotivated child and the child with a learning disability. Certainly it is the most demanding of the language skills. Contemporary approaches to the teaching of writing (e.g. Harste, Short and Burke 1988) have done much to alleviate the anxiety and frustration which, in years gone by, many slower students must have experienced whenever 'writing' or 'composition' appeared on the timetable. To them it meant a silent period of sustained writing, with little or no opportunity to discuss work or ask for assistance. Great importance was placed on accuracy and neatness at the first attempt, and many children must have felt extremely inhibited. Even when the teacher wasn't a severe judge of the product, the children themselves sometimes carried out self-assessment and decided that they couldn't write, because their product was not perfect. This view was often reinforced by their parents. An attitude quickly developed in the child: 'I can't write', and a failure cycle was established.

What is the change which has come about in recent years which now enables more children to express themselves through the medium of writing? The change has been one of a shift of emphasis from finished product to the actual process of composing and revising. The method is represented best in the 'process-conference approach' of Donald Graves

(1983), which will be described in a moment. It seems that the impact which this educator and his colleagues have had upon classroom practice in a very short space of time is quite dramatic when compared with the usual changes or innovations in education, which commonly take up to ten years before they influence teaching behaviour. Graves *et al.* were researching in 1978–80 and publishing in 1981. By 1982 a very high percentage of primary teachers appeared not only to know of the process-conference approach, but were actually implementing it in their classrooms. It is likely that part of its ready acceptance was due to the way in which it neatly complemented contemporary psycholinguistic views on the teaching of reading (i.e. children learn to read mainly by reading for meaning; and children learn to write by writing for some real purpose). The ability of Graves to spell out the practical implications of his research in terms which teachers could readily apply was also a very important feature: teachers could immediately use his ideas.

THE PROCESS-CONFERENCE APPROACH

Briefly, the process-conference approach embodies the following principles:

- Writing, as a process, usually involves a number of separate stages, from the initial hazy formulation of ideas to the first written draft, through subsequent revision and editing to a final product (although not *all* writing should be forced to pass through all stages) (Lewis and Doorlag 1991).
- The choice of topic should usually be made by the writer. Personal narrative is likely to result in the most lively and relevant communications.
- A child writing in a classroom has a potential audience in not only the teacher but also the peer group. A friend or partner can be used as a sounding board for ideas and can read, discuss and make suggestions for written drafts.

  > Teachers who enable children to help each other, provide not only important service in immediate child help, but a unique chance to learn more about writing by helping another person. Children in this situation are able to use language to talk about writing more specifically.
  >
  > (Graves 1981: 203)

- The teacher should confer with each and every child about the writing being produced. This involves far more than the automatic dispensation of praise and encouragement: and it will involve quite different amounts of time and advice according to individual needs and abilities.

- Teachers themselves should write in the classroom and thus demonstrate the composing, editing and publishing stages in action.
- When possible and appropriate, children's work should be 'published' for a wider audience (class book, display board, school library, etc.).
- Use of the process approach has proved to be effective in helping students with learning problems to improve the quality and quantity of their writing (Bos 1988). The results appear to be particularly encouraging when the process approach is combined with use of a word processor (Vallecorsa, Ledford and Parnell 1991).
- It should be noted that the process-conference approach can certainly be regarded as an inclusive practice, as it involves collaboration between children and between teachers and children. Each and every child can be helped to produce and share something of personal worth in the form of a written recording. Clearly the approach also allows for much 'personalization' through the topic chosen, amount of assistance given, individual word-lists generated, number of pages produced, etc.

PROVIDING SPECIAL ASSISTANCE

General principles

According to Vallecorsa, Ledford and Parnell (1991) the first important step in improving writing skills is to allocate sufficient time for writing within the school day. It seems that writing is often seen as an adjunct to other subjects, rather than something which needs to have specific time devoted to it (Isaacson 1987). If writing occurs daily there is much greater likelihood that motivation, confidence and actual writing skills will improve.

It is also essential to give students an adequate stimulus for writing. The topic must be interesting and relevant, and students must see a purpose in the activity of transferring ideas to paper. Regardless of whether the activity involves writing a letter to a friend or composing a science-fiction fantasy story, the students should perceive the task as enjoyable and worthwhile.

Students with writing difficulties need to be given a clear structure which they can use whenever they write (Lewis and Doorlag 1991). They need to be given ideas about how to begin, how to continue, and how to complete the task. Examples of such guidance will be provided later in the chapter, but in general it follows the three basic stages of planning to write, writing a first draft, and revising and polishing a final product. At each stage teachers need to provide abundant guided practice and positive encouragement. The teaching of writing should embody the basic principles of effective instruction – modelling, guided practice, feedback (mainly via the conference process between teacher and student) and independent practice. The teaching approach should also include self-instruction strategy training, such as that discussed in Chapter 3. In this context the student would be taught a set of questions or prompts which would facilitate the generation of ideas for writing and would assist with the organization and presentation of the material across different writing genres. Graham and Harris (1989) report very positive effects of such strategy training with learning disabled students in primary school.

It is important, particularly at secondary school level, to have all subject specialists participate in assisting children to develop writing skills (Sewell: 1982). Composing and revising should not be confined to lessons marked as 'English' on the timetable, but should be recognized as a whole-school responsibility.

Slower learners and reluctant writers

Children who exhibit difficulties in written expression fall into one of two groups. The groups are not mutually exclusive and there is some overlap in terms of instructional needs. The first group comprises those children of any age level who have general difficulties in learning to read, write and spell because either they are slower learners (perhaps even mildly intellectually disabled), or they are of normal intelligence but have a genuine disability when dealing with language in written or printed form. In both cases a lack of ability accounts for their current problems and the teacher needs to make any writing task clear and simple enough to ensure success when the child is given additional help and guidance. The second group comprises those children of any age who can write but don't, the reluctant and unmotivated students. These children appear not to see the relevance of writing, or have not experienced the excitement of written communication and get no satisfaction from it. Some of these students may have encountered negative or unrewarding experiences during the early stages of becoming writers and thus have acquired what has been termed 'writing apprehension', which now causes them to avoid the task whenever possible (Auten 1983). Their problem is one of poor motivation leading to habitually low levels of productivity. Here the teacher must regain lost interest and build confidence.

The classroom atmosphere which encourages all children to experiment and take risks in their writing without fear of criticism or ridicule is a very necessary (but in itself insufficient) condition for the least able students. In many cases, particularly with the upper primary or secondary student with a history of bad experiences in writing, simply creating the atmosphere is not enough; more than the ordinary amount of guidance and encouragement from the teacher will also be needed. Indeed, Graves (1983) describes some such children in his chapters entitled 'How to help children catch up' and 'How to help children with special problems of potential'. His study (1981) of the ways in which very young children begin to write and compose throws some light on the performance and needs of older children with difficulties in writing. In particular these studies indicate how important it is to view a child's writing attempts *diagnostically* to determine how much a child can achieve unaided, and to observe the strategies he or she brings to the planning, composing, spelling and revising stages.

With some slow-learning children, the initial stimulus for writing may have to come from the teacher rather than from free choice. The notion of a teacher setting a topic is *not* against the philosophy of Graves. On the other hand, some children will have interests and experiences about which they can talk freely and can then be helped to write. The link here with the language-experience approach to reading for such children should be obvious: 'What I know about I can talk about. What I can talk about someone can help me to write. What I have written I can read'.

Graves (1983) suggests the following possible sequence in assisting a child with difficulties to produce something satisfying. In addition he says that such children need to be helped daily, usually during the first ten minutes of the lesson:

- Initial 'warm up' – perhaps a few minutes spent with handwriting patterns or letter formation.
- Copying of something previously written.
- Discussion of new topic for writing.
- Drawing the topic.
- Further discussion with teacher.
- Composing one or two sentences.
- Feedback from the teacher.

With children of limited ability or those lacking in confidence, the teacher may have to structure very tightly the discussion at various stages, even to the extent of writing down key vocabulary and possible sentence beginnings for the child to use. Graves advises teachers not to be afraid of saying, at times, 'Try doing it this way.' Teachers are still permitted to teach! However, during the discussion and feedback stages (the 'conferring') the teacher should not over-correct, but rather encourage the child to talk and to think. The main aim is to help the child generate ideas and then to sort these into an optimum sequence.

In the early stages it is important not to place undue stress upon accuracy of spelling since this can stifle the child's attempts at communicating ideas freely. Invented spelling gives children the freedom to write with attention to content and sequence. Charles Cripps makes an excellent point when he says, 'it is essential that a misspelling is never referred to as something "wrong" but instead as something nearly right' (1983: 22). As the child becomes more confident and productive, the teacher, while still remaining supportive, will make the conferring stage rather less structured. Enabling-type questions are still used to extend the child's thinking and to build upon the writing so far produced. Searle (1984) uses the term 'scaffolding' to suggest this surreptitious support which can be reduced gradually. In the case of the least able children, particularly in upper primary and secondary classes, it will be mainly the teacher who monitors the child's work-in-progress and who has most to offer when they confer. Extreme care must be exercised in using peers to read and comment upon the writing of other children with difficulties. In some classrooms able children will have a sufficiently positive attitude towards children who are less able and can offer very useful assistance in a peer-tutoring role. In other classrooms, or in some individual cases, the able writer may be inclined to ridicule any naive contributions and thus rapidly undermine the confidence and motivation of the slower child. Peer critiquing is often written about and talked about as if it is a simple strategy to employ in the classroom, but actually it needs to be done with great sensitivity. Teachers must spend time in modelling the critiquing process before expecting children to implement it skilfully: e.g. how to highlight the good points, how to detect what is not clear, how to help with the generation of new ideas, how to assist with adding or deleting material and polishing the work.

Many of the less able children have, in the past, written very little during times set aside for writing. This is part of the vicious circle which might be described thus: 'I don't like writing so I don't write much, so I don't get much practice, so I don't write much – etc.' Humes (1983) has advocated frequent writing practice (daily) and even to the extent of using 'speed writing' against a time limit (e.g. for five minutes), with children copying existing material as rapidly as possible to convince them that they can indeed 'write a lot' when style and accuracy are not to be judged. A modified form of precision teaching can be used to increase the output of some students. The number of words written or sentences completed in the allotted time during writing lessons can be counted and charted each day (Lindsley 1992). Again, even this rather formal imposition is not condemned by Graves (see Graves 1983: 208).

Small booklets are usually better than exercise books for slower children. The opportunity to make a fresh start almost every week is far better than being faced with the accumulation of evidence of past failures which can accrue in an exercise book. For students of all ages a loose-leaf folder may be very useful as a replacement for the traditional exercise book. There is a place for the daily diary, journal or news book; but teachers should avoid such writing becoming merely habitual, repetitive and at times poorly constructed 'garbage' (Auten: 1983). There is a danger of this being the case even with children who can write well.

Leading from the points above it is obvious that our notion of 'free writing' for the least able students should be interpreted as 'freely guided writing' in the early stages. Quite original ideas may be there, but the process of organizing them before getting them down on paper needs to be teacher-supported. As confidence and proficiency increase with the passage of time, the amount of direct help can be greatly reduced for most students.

Since the foundation of the process-conference approach depends so much upon the child-writer having someone with whom to confer, it is important to consider other possible sources of assistance in the classroom. In addition to the teacher and the peer group, help may also be provided by teacher aides, older students (cross-age tutoring), college and university students on field placements, and parent volunteers. In all cases these helpers must know what their role is and will require some informal training by the teacher if they are not to adopt an approach which is too demanding of perfection.

Over to you

Assume that you need to provide some in-service training for a group of parents who have offered to help children write within a school-based learning assistance programme.

- List the basic principles you would wish them to apply when they work with the children.
- Add to your list as you move through the remaining sections of this chapter.

SOME SPECIFIC STRATEGIES

Providing a framework

In helping children generate ideas and compose in writing, Graham, Harris and Sawyer (1987) and Humes (1983) suggest that they be taught a framework of questions which can be used if necessary during the initial stages of planning – e.g. 'What happened first?', 'Where did it happen?', 'To whom did it happen?', 'What happened next?' Self-directed questions such as 'What does it look like?, 'What does it feel like?' will help children become more descriptive in their writing. These temporary props are very useful for slower children, but they must not be allowed to become utterly dependent upon such starting points.

Another strategy suggested by Humes (1983) is that of 'shuffling ideas'. As ideas for writing are generated, each is written quickly on a separate card and finally the cards are re-ordered until the most suitable and appealing sequence is obtained. The sequence can become the focal point for discussion between teacher and child, or between two children. The procedure avoids the problem which sometimes occurs when a child is asked to revise a draft written in full on a single page, and it does help to establish the idea of planning and revising. 'When students overcome the idea that the first draft is the only draft, they become revisers' (Humes 1983: 13).

To assist with the development of revising and editing skills Humes suggests that the whole class (or a small group of students) might look at a duplicated essay or one displayed on an overhead projector and make suitable alterations and improvements to it after discussion.

Another useful related activity is that of 'sentence combining'. Often the slower students will tend to write very short sentences, lacking fluency and variety:

I saw Norwood play on Saturday.
They beat the Panthers by 16 points.
Button got injured.
It was in the first quarter.

These sentences can be combined in various ways, e.g.:

On Saturday I saw Norwood beat the Panthers by 16 points.
The only bad part was in the first quarter when Button was injured.

Suitable exercises can be devised to help children develop skills in combining sentences.

Word webs, referred to in Chapter 8, also provide a useful starting point from which to generate sentences which can be elaborated and extended into paragraphs.

A procedure for helping students to prepare a simple essay[†]

The teacher demonstrates this procedure, incorporating ideas from the class. Students are then given guided practice and further modelling over a series of lessons, each time using a different theme.

- Begin by writing a short, declarative sentence that makes one statement:

We have too many cars coming into our school parking area.

- Next, write two or three sentences which add information to, or are connected with, the first sentence. Leave two lines below each new sentence.

We have too many cars coming into our school parking area.
The noise they make often disturbs our lessons.

The cars travel fast and could knock someone down.

What can we do about this problem?

- Now write two more sentences in each space.

We have too many cars coming into our school parking area. The noise they make often disturbs our lessons. The drivers sound their horns and rev the engines. Sometimes I can't even hear the teacher speak. The cars travel fast and could knock someone down. I saw a girl step out behind one yesterday. She screamed when it reversed suddenly. What can we do about this problem? Perhaps there should be a sign saying 'NO CARS ALLOWED'. They might build some speed humps or set a speed limit.

- Edit sentences into appropriate paragraphs. Combine some short statements into longer, complex sentences.
- Edit for style.
- Use of a word processor makes each of these steps much faster and makes the process of editing and checking spelling easier.

† Based on an intervention procedure described by Doorlag 1989: 42–4.

Writing a summary

The complementary skills of reading and writing come together in the task of writing a summary or precis of a passage, a chapter or a book. Casazza (1992) suggests that summarizing text helps students to focus on key points and to sequence these in writing in a coherent way. She presents three basic rules for preparing a summary, and states that students should be taught these rules explicitly and trained to use them independently. First they must identify the main idea and generate a statement which embodies the main idea. Then they identify minor or irrelevant detail and redundant information. They must combine statements or ideas which have similar information, and link these to the main idea statement. By using an overhead projector the teacher can model the application of the three rules to several different pieces of text. Students are then given guided practice and feedback. Casazza (1992) also advocates having students evaluate the summaries of their peers and of the teacher. A check-list can be used with a rating scale to allow for appraisal using such descriptions as: 'identifies topic clearly'; 'identifies main idea correctly'; 'paraphrases accurately'; 'omits irrelevant detail'; 'combines similar ideas coherently'; 'stays within required word-length'.

Even this degree of direct guidance in summary writing is insufficient for some students. They need to have the task broken down into much more manageable steps. One or more of the following procedures can be helpful to such students:

- The teacher provides a set of statements, true and false, based on the text just read. The statements are presented on the sheet in random order. The student must read each statement and place a tick against those which are true. The student then decides the most logical sequence in which to arrange the true statements. When written out, these statements provide a good summary of the text.
- Provide some sentence beginnings, in a sequence which will provide a framework for the summary. The student completes the unfinished sentences and writes the summary.
- Provide a summary with key words or phrases omitted. The words may be presented below the passage in random order, or clues may be given in terms of initial letters of word required, or dashes to represent each letter of the word. The student completes the passage by supplying the missing words.
- Simple multiple-choice questions can be presented. The questions may deal with main ideas from the text and with supporting detail.

In selecting the appropriate responses and writing these down, the student creates a summary.

Self-regulation in writing

According to Isaacson (1987), writers eventually need to learn ways of organizing and monitoring their own writing processes. As they become a little more confident and competent, they need to use checking strategies when editing their work for clarity, consistency, accuracy and interest. This degree of self-regulation can only be developed if teachers often demonstrate and verbalize the necessary strategies and then provide opportunities for students to apply them. At a metacognitive level, students should be encouraged to ask themselves questions, such as 'Did I write a good story? Can I make it even better? Should I change this word? Could I say that in a different way? What would someone else think of this story?' Lewis and Doorlag (1991) describe a 'self-edit think sheet' which requires student writers to read over their work and place a star against the part they like best, a question mark against any part that might not be clear to others, and to lightly circle any words which might need attention to spelling or meaning.

Word processors

Undoubtedly, the arrival of word processors in the classroom heralded a new opportunity for students of all levels of ability to enter the realm of writing and composing with enthusiasm and enjoyment. In particular, students with learning difficulties can gain confidence in creating, editing, erasing and publishing their own unique material through a medium which holds attention and is infinitely patient (Kerin 1990; Newman 1984).

In the previous chapter the use of word processors for developing lower-order skills such as word recognition and phonic decoding was discussed. Their use, however, is not confined to such drill and practice procedures, and higher-order reading comprehension and writing skills can be enhanced through word processing (Au and Bruce 1990; Lewis and Doorlag 1991).

The present writer has found that slower learning students need first to develop at least some modest keyboard skills if the word processing is to be achieved without frustration. It is usually necessary to teach only the most essential skills to enable the student to access the programme, type the work and save the material at regular intervals. Even this simple level of operation can give certain students a tremendous boost to confidence and can encourage risk-taking in writing and composing (Cole and Chan 1990). Printing can be left to the teacher or classroom aide in the beginning stages. (See also Hasselbring and Goin 1989.)

By combining the conference approach to writing with the use of a word processor, the student's story in first draft form can be printed, without using the in-built spelling check. Student and partner, or student and teacher can then go over the print-out and discuss good features of the story, and identify sentences or phrases or particular words that might be improved. It is useful for the teacher to note which words the student can self-correct in terms of spelling, and which misspelt words are not detected without assistance. A second draft of the story can then be made after the student does the necessary revisions and uses the spell-check.

Lewis and Doorlag (1991) reviewed research evidence on the benefits of using word processors with learning disabled students. Among their conclusions were that word processing seems to be of great benefit to students who don't usually write very much, and to those with the most severe spelling problems.

A procedure for helping students improve their own essays was described by Graham and MacArthur (1988). They taught the students to work through the following six steps when revising and extending their work on the word processor.

1   Read your essay carefully.
2   Find the sentence which is telling you the main point.
3   Add two more sentences which tell you more about that point.
4   Scan each sentence. Does it make sense? Do I need to change it? Can I make it more interesting?
5   Make the changes on the computer.
6   Re-read the essay and make any final changes.

(Compare this strategy with that given on p. 131.)

STARTING POINTS

Book production

Extending the earlier suggestion of small booklets, it is useful to have the students prepare somewhat more ambitious products. The following topics are particularly motivating for reluctant writers.

'**A book about myself**' My family. Where I live. What I do. Things I like. Things I hate. My friends. The book can also include factual material: e.g. height, weight, pulse rate, etc.

'**A book about this school**' Descriptions. Photos. Plans. Interviews with teachers.

'**A book about my class**' Descriptions. Photos. Interviews.

'**Our book of jokes**' Don't forget to censor these before parent evening!

'**Our neighbourhood**' Location. Personalities. Shops. Industries. Entertainment.

'**Our visit to...**' Impressions and summaries following field trips and excursions. (Don't make this a regular feature of every trip or you will find yourself in the position of the old joke where a class was on an excursion and two children saw a flying saucer land in a field. 'Sir! Sir!', one child began. 'Shut up you fool!' said the other 'We'll only have to write about it.')

'**A Visitor's Guide to Planet Zargok**' Sections describing the people, the cities, the food, the transport, the animals and plants. A dictionary section to translate the planet's vocabulary into English.

Video or film scripts

Much use is made of improvised drama in both primary and secondary classrooms, drama requiring no scripts. A useful variation is to get the students, particularly the reluctant writers, to prepare a script in detail and then film or record the action after rehearsal. The combination of practical work, writing and production of something which can then be seen and discussed is usually adequate stimulus for even the most reluctant student.

You write the rest: an anecdote

One technique which I used when teaching in special classes was to prepare a story about a popular character currently appearing on children's television. The story is told or read to the class for enjoyment; but just when it gets to a cliff-hanger climax the story stops. What happens next? Individuals can write their own episode, or you can brainstorm ideas from the group.

I found it particularly useful to type a simplified version of the story I had read to the children, spreading this over several half-pages of a small booklet and providing a frame for an illustration above each passage of print. The children, who were not proficient readers, could cope with the simplified material since it dealt with a story just read to them; the plot was familiar. The second half of the booklet was blank to allow the children to write their own endings and provide illustrations.

This example is from a *Doctor Who* story. The teacher's story ends with this paragraph:

> He was in for a shock when he switched on the televiewer. The giant spiders were spinning a web over the Tardis. The strands looked as strong as rope. Suddenly the lights went out. He dashed to the controls and frantically flicked the switches. Nothing happened. The Tardis refused to move. They were trapped!!!

Patricia's story continues:

> Dr Who was cross. The spiders sat on the Tardis and sang a jungle song. Dr Who took the plants he had collected and did an experiment on them. The plants turned into little people. The doctor put the little people outside and they began to chew through the web. Soon the wind came and the web blew away. The Tardis was free again.

> (Westwood 1985)

Letter writing and project exchange between schools

It is very useful indeed to set up an exchange-system between schools, particularly if one school is in the city and one is in the country. It may start as a 'pen pal' scheme but can extend to exchange of class books, project materials, etc., and could even result in visits between schools.

Comic strips

Comics and cartoons can be useful for getting intellectually disabled or emotionally disturbed children to write short assignments. They are pleased with the quick, tangible results.

The most popular comic strips from the newspaper can be utilized, since these tend to have no more than four or five frames of information. Using correcting fluid the teacher can white-out the original words in the 'speech balloons'. After brief discussion with an adult or peer the child can suggest suitable comments which each character might be making, and can be helped to write these in the spaces. A number of such cartoon strips can be pasted into a class book for general use.

Other ideas for writing themes are provided in Chapter 11 in Polloway *et al.* (1989).

SPELLING

For many low-achieving students, spelling continues to present a problem long after reading skills have improved. This is sometimes due to the fact that spelling (encoding of words) is not made an integral part of the reading programme. Too much emphasis may have been devoted to word recognition and reading for meaning, and too little given to writing.

Spelling instruction: some basic principles[†]

- Provide purposeful and varied writing experiences.
- Model and practise effective strategies for attempting to spell words.
- Encourage students to experiment with words, and to invent spellings if necessary.
- Develop an *interest* in words – their meanings, their structure, their origins, their uses. Be enthusiastic yourself about words and word study.
- Generate weekly word-lists from topics and themes studied across the curriculum.
- Subject specialists (e.g. science, geography, maths) should teach the terms related to their areas.
- Monitor and evaluate children's progress in spelling and provide individual guidance where necessary.
- Observe the strategies used by individual students.
- Use good spellers to assist those with spelling difficulties.
- Ensure that students develop techniques for self-evaluation and self-help (e.g. proof-reading, use of dictionary, etc.).
- Where possible, teach spelling and handwriting together.
- Recognize that students go through distinct stages of development on the road to becoming proficient spellers. Don't hold expectations concerning accuracy which ignore these developmental stages.

[†]   Based upon ideas from Reason and Boote (1986), Clutterbuck (1990), Bentley (1990), and Barone (1992).

- Set aside time each week for spelling study, otherwise it may never receive the systematic attention it deserves. However, avoid making it separate from the general classroom curriculum. Words taught in isolation have little relevance to the real writing situation.
- Don't use 'spelling aloud' in class. Spelling is essentially a writing activity.

Developmental stages

It is important for teachers and parents to be aware of the stages of development through which children pass on their way to becoming proficient spellers. Students pass through these stages at different rates (Bentley 1990), and it is unrealistic to expect a student to achieve a level of independence or accuracy in spelling which is beyond his or her current developmental level. The stages have been described in the following way:

Stage 1 (Pre-phonetic)   The child has no functional awareness of the significance of letters or words when written or printed. May scribble on paper, but letters are not representational.

Stage 2   Emerging knowledge of letter-sound correspondences, usually picked up from incidental learning. A pre-school child may write R U HP ('Are you happy?')

Stage 3   Further development of insight into word structure. Invented spellings becoming more recognizable, as they obey basic phonic principles.

Stage 4 (usually ages seven to ten years)   Evidence of attention being given to the sound values of specific letter clusters (-ight; – ough; – tion; – ing: etc.). Some self-correction and self-checking occurs.

Stage 5 (usually ages ten to eighteen years)   Growing mastery of quite complex grapho-phonic relationships; knowledge of basic spelling rules; awareness of word-structures and irregularities; increase in independence in word study.

Individual differences among spellers

Four types of imagery are used in learning to spell a word:

- Visual – or the way the word looks.
- Auditory – or the way the word sounds.
- Speech-motor – or the way the word feels when spoken.
- Hand-motor – or the way the word feels when written.

Some students rely more heavily on one type of imagery than on another, and perhaps need to be taught to use as many types of imagery as possible. It seems that dyslexic students are particularly weak in phonological skills (auditory discrimination, segmentation and blending of phonemes), which may account for the unusual types of spelling error said to be characteristic of students with this disability (Miles and Miles 1990). Training in phonemic awareness and basic phonic knowledge appears to have a positive effect on spelling ability (Ball and Blachman 1991).

Examination of children's written work can reveal a great deal about their current skills and specific needs in spelling (Anderson 1985). One of the most common problems in spelling is the tendency of the child to be over-dependent on phonic knowledge and therefore to write irregular words as if they are regular (e.g. *sed* = said; *becos* = because; *stayshun* = station; *thay* = they). Close examination of a child's exercise books, or the use of dictated word-lists, will quickly reveal the extent to which a child has this problem. The children producing these errors seem to lack the necessary strategies for carefully checking the visual appearance of a word, and even when encouraged to proof-read their material will fail to identify the errors. However, examination of the invented spellings in children's writing can provide some useful indication of their phonological awareness and knowledge of the alphabetic code (Goswami and Bryant 1990).

TEACHING STRATEGIES

Visual aspects

Visual perception of word forms is a vital element in the acquisition of spelling ability. Research has shown that children can be trained to focus more attentively on a word and to improve their visual imagery for letter sequences (Sears and Johnson 1986). One of the easiest aids to make and use is the flash-card. These are particularly useful for teaching irregular words and for the student who needs to be weaned away from a predominantly phonetic approach to spelling. The words are introduced to the student on cards about 30cm × 10cm. The word is pronounced clearly. Particular visual aspects or hard spots are stressed. The child is encouraged to make a 'mental picture' of the word, and examine it. After a few seconds' exposure, the student writes the word from memory, articulating it clearly as he or she writes. The word is then checked against the flash-card. The writing of the whole word avoids the inefficient letter-by-letter copying habit which some students have developed.

The general 'Look–Cover–Write–Check' approach advocated by Peters (1985) is based on the same principles. It involves the following steps:

- Look very carefully at the word in the list. Try to remember every detail.
- Cover the word so that it cannot be seen.
- Write the word from memory, pronouncing it quietly as you write.
- Check your version of the word with the original. If it is not correct, go back through the three steps again until you can produce the word accurately.
- Teachers should check for recall several days and weeks later.

For some students, finger-tracing over the word may help with assimilation and retention of the letter sequence. Lynch and Jones (1989) reviewed a number of teaching approaches for spelling, and describe a five-step strategy very similar to that of Peters (1985), but incorporating tracing. The strategy involves saying the word, writing and saying the word, checking the word, tracing and saying the word, and writing the word from memory.

These approaches are far better than any rote-learning and recitation procedure. They give the student an independent system which can be applied to the study of words set for homework, to corrections or omissions from free writing and to words necessary for a particular subject area. Children can work in pairs where appropriate, to check that the procedure is being followed by the partner (Hewson 1990).

Several computer programmes designed to develop spelling skills have come on to the market. Teachers should ensure that the way in which the words are presented on the screen causes the students to attend carefully to the sequence of letters, to identify these letter strings within words, and to type out the words from memory (Peters 1985). Programmes which focus too much attention on spelling letter by letter are far less effective.

Auditory aspects

A problem said to be particularly characteristic of dyslexic students, is the failure to attend sufficiently to the auditory information provided by sounds within a word and therefore to misspell even phonemically regular words, through transposition of letters or the omission of sounds or syllables (*pelop*

= people; *siad* = said; *litgh* = light; *rember* = remember). The child appears to have no strategy for checking that the word 'sounds right'. For such children much more time will need to be devoted to training careful attention to sounds within words (segmentation) and the writing and checking of these sounds in the logical sequence. The child's confidence can be boosted by compiling lists of long but phonemically regular words which, if the child listens carefully to each syllable, can be written correctly. Phonic dictation can be given regularly using passages containing mainly regular words, the teacher stressing the syllables as the dictation is given.

Strategic aspects

All spellers should be taught to decide whether a word is irregular (and thus needs the Look–Cover–Write–Check approach), or regular (and therefore can be written as it sounds). This takes the load off rote-learning and places emphasis on the ability to study words rationally.

Many individuals need to be taught how to learn material. Some students, left to their own devices, fail to develop any systematic approach. They may just look at the word. They may recite the spelling alphabetically. They may copy letter-by-letter rather than writing the whole word. They may use no particular strategy at all, believing that learning to spell is beyond them. Part of any serious attempt at helping children with spelling difficulties is to determine *how* they set about learning a word or group of words. Where a child has no systematic approach, it is essential that he or she be taught one.

Attention has been devoted to cognitive and metacognitive approaches to spelling instruction (Wong 1986). Students are taught specific self-regulatory strategies to use when learning new words or checking the accuracy of spelling at the proof-reading stage of writing. For example, they are taught to ask themselves, 'Is this word correct? How many syllables do I hear in the word? I'll try the word now [writes]. Do I have the right number of syllables? I'll try it again. That looks better!', etc. According to Wong, 'Effective spelling instruction appears to contain two components: knowledge of phonics and knowledge of spelling strategies' (1986: 172). In particular, spelling strategies must include steps which cause students to check for accuracy without being constantly reminded to do so.

Word study

Word study is regarded by Barone (1992) as an essential aspect of any spelling programme. She advocates that students be helped to analyse the structure of words they can already read easily, and be made aware of the simple rules and logic which apply to them. Within any mixed-ability class this would be done at different levels of complexity according to their levels of proficiency in reading and writing. The advantage claimed for the word-study approach is that it provides knowledge which can be generalized to the spelling of other words. The importance of teaching for generalization is stressed by Dixon (1991), who criticizes approaches which rely purely on memorization. Dixon's own approach embodies the careful teaching of basic morphology – the understanding of the meaningful units (prefixes, suffixes and word bases) from which words are constructed.

Students should not be expected to spell correctly every word they meet in the reading programme; but when certain words within a group have visual or auditory similarity it is reasonable to require the children to write them as well as read them:

cat	stack	light
rat	stick	fight
bat	stock	sight
sat	stuck	right

The common letter clusters in such word groups might be underlined in colour to draw attention to their importance. Weak spellers need to be made aware of the common sequence of letters which are typical of English spelling patterns. Good spellers seem to develop this knowledge for themselves.

A corrective procedure

Lyndon (1989) has identified the psychological construct of 'proactive inhibition' as a possible reason for the failure of many conventional remedial methods to actually help a student to 'unlearn' incorrect responses, such as habitual errors in spelling. Proactive inhibition (or proactive interference) is the term used to describe the situation where previously learned information interferes with one's ability to remember new information or to acquire a new response. What the individual already knows is protected from change. Lyndon's approach, called 'Old Way: New Way', uses the student's error as the starting point for change. A memory of the old way of spelling of the word is used to activate later an awareness of the new (correct) way of spelling the word. The following steps and procedures are used in Old Way: New Way:

- Student writes the word in the usual (incorrect) form.
- Teacher and student agree to call this the 'old way' of spelling that word.
- Teacher shows student a 'new way' of spelling the word (the correct way).
- Attention is drawn to the similarities and differences between the old and the new.
- Student writes word again in the old way.
- Student writes word in the new way, and points out the differences.
- Repeat five such writings of old way, new way and articulation of differences.
- Write the word the new way six times, using different coloured pens or in different styles. Older students may be asked to write six different simple sentences using the word in its new form.
- Revise the word or words taught after a two-week interval; and if necessary repeat this procedure every two weeks until the new response is fully established.

Spelling rules

Some experts advocate teaching spelling rules to children. The present writer found it difficult to teach spelling rules to slow learners. It is easier to teach them the words they genuinely need for their writing purposes and the strategies to use when attempting to learn them. This comment is not meant to deter all teachers from teaching spelling rules. Rules may be of some value for some children, particularly those of average intelligence who have a specific learning disability. (You *need* above average intelligence to deal with such rules as, 'If a word of more than one syllable ends in a 't' preceded by a single vowel and has accent on the last syllable, double the final consonant when changing to past tense.') Cripps has said that because rules are often more complex than the word itself, they are not recommended (Cripps 1978). Rules which are simple and have few exceptions, however, are obviously of value and should be taught (e.g. 'i' before 'e' except after 'c') (Peters 1985).

Some highly successful published spelling programmes (e.g. Dixon 1976) are based on a thorough teaching of rules.

Dictation

One form of dictation, phonic dictation, has been recommended above for a specific remedial purpose; but is the general use of dictation of any value?

Dictation has traditionally been used for testing children. However, unless the results are to be used for diagnostic purposes, e.g. the analysis of errors, there is little to support the continued use of dictation exercises.

It is sometimes suggested that dictation develops listening skills and concentration, and at the same time gives students experience of words in context. It is recommended under this system that the material be presented in written form for the children to study before it is dictated. In this way there is an opportunity to point out any particularly difficult words.

Dictation would have more value if approached in a slightly different manner. Cripps (1978) suggests that an unseen passage at an appropriate level of difficulty be dictated for students to write. They are then given a period of time to check and alter any words which they think are incorrect, perhaps using a different coloured pen. The teacher then checks the work and can observe two aspects of the child's performance. First, it is useful to look at the words the child has been able to correct (or at least knows to be wrong). Second, the teacher can record words which were in fact wrong but not noticed by the child. If, based on their level of difficulty, these words should be known by the child, the teacher must make every effort to teach their correct spelling since they have become incorrect habits.

Should spelling lists be used?

The notion that lists can be compiled which contain words which *all* children should know and use at a particular year or grade level has, to some extent, been abandoned. However, spelling lists continue to form the core of many classroom spelling programmes. The question most often asked by teachers is, 'Do children learn to spell best from lists?' If the question refers to lists of words which individual children actually use and need in their writing, the answer is certainly 'yes'. If the lists are based on other criteria, e.g. words grouped according to visual or phonemic similarity, the decision to use such a list with a particular student or group of students must be made in the light of their specific learning needs as indicated above. There is some evidence to suggest that teachers using a process approach to writing sometimes feel unsure about the place of spelling instruction in their programmes. They tend to produce word-lists in order to feel that spelling is being covered adequately, but then employ mainly rote memorization techniques for the children to learn the words. This is of doubtful value (Barone 1992).

The value of lists or word groups is that they may help the student to establish an awareness of common letter sequences, e.g. -ight; -ought. This awareness may help a student take a more rational approach to tackling an unfamiliar word. The limitation of formal lists is that they always fail to supply a particular word a student needs at the appropriate time. The most useful list from the point of view of the weakest spellers will be one compiled according to personal needs and common errors. The list might be given the unofficial title 'Words I find difficult'. A copy of this list can be kept in the back of the student's exercise book and used when he or she is writing a rough draft or proof-reading a final draft of a piece of work.

SOME FINAL POINTS

When planning an individualized programme in spelling, the following points should be kept in mind:

- For the least able spellers, daily attention will be needed, with weekly revision and testing for mastery.
- Over a period of time, collect a list of words frequently needed by children to whom you are giving special help. Use this list for regular review and assessment.
- Once a special programme is established, students should always work on specific words misspelled in free writing lessons, as well as on more general word-lists or word families in order to develop insight into word structure.
- Since repetition and overlearning are important, it is useful to have a range of games and word puzzles available to reinforce the spelling of important words. The games must be closely matched to the objectives of the programme, or they may simply keep children amused without leading to mastery.
- Teachers in secondary schools should try to give students help in spelling words from specific subject areas: e.g. ingredients, temperature, chisel, theory, etc.
- Use some form of visual record of improvement – an individual progress chart or simple graph – to indicate the number of new words mastered each week. Employ any gimmick which reinforces a student's awareness of the real progress being made.

- When making a correction to a word, a student should rewrite the whole word, not merely erase the incorrect letters. (See also 'Old Way: New Way' approach above.)
- The value of having students spell words aloud is very questionable where alphabet names rather than the sounds are used. Spelling is essentially a writing activity. The visual appearance and the flow of the sequence of written letters provide important clues to the speller which are absent when the word is spelled aloud.
- Margaret Peters is adamant that a neat, careful style of handwriting which can be executed swiftly and easily by the student is an important factor associated with spelling ability. It cannot be inferred that good handwriting *per se* causes good spelling; but laboured handwriting and uncertain letter formation almost certainly inhibit the easy development of spelling habits at an automatic response level (Peters 1967). Some evidence exists to support the notion that the teaching of joined writing from the beginning, rather than print script, helps children to acquire an awareness of common letter strings and to become more confident and proficient spellers (Cripps 1990).

Over to you

Write a brief article for a parents' magazine indicating ways in which spelling can be taught in a mixed-ability class of children in the age range seven years to nine years. Also suggest strategies parents might use to assist their children to improve spelling skills.

SUMMARY

This chapter has provided practical suggestions for helping poorly motivated and slower learning students to write and to spell. Most of the techniques can be used within the normal classroom setting and require only minor modifications to the mainstream language arts programme.

The reader will have noted in this and earlier chapters the importance placed upon the teacher modelling effective ways of approaching a task, whether it be composing and editing a story or attempting to learn how to spell a new word. Students should be helped to develop and use effective task-approach skills for themselves, and in doing so, to feel good about the work they produce and the improvements they make.

Discussion points

- How might a classroom teacher develop a core list of words most commonly needed by students in their daily writing? How might such a list be used within the language arts curriculum in that class?
- List some stimulating 'opening lines' for stories which the students can be asked to complete.
- Devise a set of notes and prompts which could be used by a student to help him or her write a brief summary from a passage of text.
- Discuss ideas for writing which you have found useful in getting even the least motivated student to participate.
- Examine and evaluate some computer programmes designed to increase spelling ability.

Further reading

Bentley, D. (1990) *Teaching Spelling: Some Questions Answered*, Earley: University of Reading.

Cheetham, J.S. (1990) *Teach your Child to Spell*, Melbourne: Hyland House.

Donovan, T.R. and McClelland, B.W. (1980), *Eight Approaches to Teaching Composition*, Urbana: National Council for Teachers of English.

Dykes, B. and Thomas, C. (1989) *Spelling Made Easy*, Sydney: Hale & Iremonger.

Englert, C.S. and Mariage, T.V. (1991) 'Shared understandings: structuring the writing experience through dialogue', *Journal of Learning Disabilities* 24, 6: 330–42.

Fehring, H. and Thomas, V. (1989) *Spelling Companion for Writers*, Sydney: Horwitz Grahame.

Fasnot, C.T. (1989) *Enquiring Teachers, Enquiring Learners*, New York: Teachers College Press.

Graham, S. and Harris, K. (1989) 'Improving learning disabled students' skills at composing essays', *Exceptional Children* 56, 3: 201–14.

Harste, J.C., Short, K.G. and Burke, C. (1988) *Creating Classroom Authors*, Portsmouth: Heinemann.

Peters, M.L. (1985) *Spelling: Caught or Taught? A New Look* (2nd edn), London: Routledge.

Pumfrey, P. and Elliott, C. (1990) *Children's Difficulties in Reading, Writing and Spelling*, London: Falmer.

Strickland, D. and Morrow, L. (1989) *Emerging Literacy: Young Children Learn to Read and Write*, Newark: International Reading Association.

Chapter 10

Developing numeracy skills

Children and adolescents who have difficulties in maths have two
fundamental needs which instruction must address: they need to
become competent in carrying out basic numerical operations, and they
need to learn how to apply these operations to solve everyday problems.

(Bowd 1990: 40)

Many children with learning disabilities and learning problems experience
difficulty in acquiring number concepts and coping with the demands of
calculation and problem-solving. For example, in the case of some physically disabled children, perceptual difficulties, poor manipulative skills and
restricted concrete experiences are frequently given as reasons for their
weakness in arithmetic. Children with restricted life experiences who
develop and learn at a slow rate may fail to develop an informal awareness
of the number system prior to school entry, something most children have
achieved by the age of four years (Ginsburg and Baroody 1983; Stoessiger
and Wilkinson 1991). To this one must add that many of these children,
e.g. those with spina bifida and hydrocephalus, may spend very frequent
periods of time in hospital for treatment or surgery and thus lose the
continuity of learning in what is the most hierarchical subject in the
curriculum. Almost all intellectually disabled children experience great
difficulty in coping with the most basic arithmetic, due to the abstract
symbolic nature of the recording required for even simple operations.
When attempting to carry out problem-solving they may select totally
inappropriate operations to perform, being unable to determine whether
to add or subtract, multiply or divide. The mildly intellectually disabled
individuals may remain at a concrete level of reasoning into their adult life.
The moderately disabled may never progress beyond a pre-operational
cognitive level, although Gumblatt and McClennen (1991) suggest that
simple functional arithmetic skills can be taught to students with moderate

to severe disabilities. Even slower learners (who are not usually regarded as intellectually disabled) may remain at a concrete operational level until the later years of secondary schooling (Richards 1982). Evidence of this may be seen in their tendency to finger-count or to use tally marks when performing calculations. This writer observed a first-year secondary school student who, when faced with the problem $73 - 29 = ?$, drew 73 tally marks in the margin of his page, then crossed off 29 and counted those remaining; an effective but inappropriate strategy in terms of time and effort.

Any children with language problems (e.g. hearing-impaired children) will also experience difficulties in solving word problems where the specific mathematical terminology may be misunderstood. These children may cope adequately with arithmetic while it remains at a visual and concrete level. 'Mathematics teachers, generally well-versed in the language of mathematics, often fail to understand the confusion and frustration experienced by pupils trying to use this language' (Munro 1977: 28). It is essential that teachers analyse the actual vocabulary which is to be used in teaching a new concept, and simplify where possible. New terms which must be introduced should be taught thoroughly, and not left to incidental learning. Students should also be taught to *read* mathematical terms (Dickson, Brown and Gibson 1984).

QUALITY OF INSTRUCTION

Not infrequently the instruction given in mathematics is poor, in that it does not match the current aptitude or learning rate of the slower children. For example, the following factors are indicative of poor-quality instruction:

- At some stage in the children's schooling the teacher's pacing of the work has outstripped their ability to assimilate the concepts and skills, and they have been left hopelessly behind.
- There was so little structuring of a 'discovery learning' or 'process maths' situation that they failed to abstract or remember anything from it. One report (Cockcroft 1982) indicates that for many children the value of experiential learning will be lost unless the follow-up is carefully structured and consolidated.
- The teacher's use of language in explaining mathematical relationships or posing questions may not have matched the children's level of comprehension.

- Abstract symbols may have been introduced too early in the absence of concrete materials or real-life examples; or concrete aids may have been removed too soon for some children; or semi-concrete aids may have been used inappropriately and have created confusion rather than clarity (Gagne 1983). There is a danger in forcing abstraction on children in advance of their understanding and experience. The children will either assimilate this with distortion or turn away from it in distaste. It is only too easy to make children hate mathematics!
- The children with reading difficulties may have been condemned to a diet of 'pure arithmetic' because they couldn't read the problems in the textbook. Teaching only a set of computational tricks does not amount to efficient teaching (Cockcroft 1982). Such tricks are usually rapidly forgotten, since they do not constitute meaningful learning.
- The children's grasp of simple relationships in number may not have been fully developed before larger numbers involving complications of place-value were introduced.
- The curriculum may have been presented in a linear sequence, with only a few lessons devoted to one topic before moving on to the next topic. Mathematics should be taught via a *spiral* method of presentation, with key concepts and processes revisited at very regular intervals in order to revise them and apply them to new situations. Regular revision is crucial for long-term retention and mastery of knowledge and skills (Dempster 1991).

The value of regular revision

In an article in the journal *Educational Leadership* (Vol 4, No.7, 1991), Dempster provided a review of research on the use of revision and testing as part of the teaching–learning process. His conclusions included the following statements with significance for teaching mathematics:

- The effectiveness of revision depends on a number of factors, including time interval between repetitions, the frequency of repetition, and the form of the repetition.
- Spaced reviews, say at weekly intervals, yield better learning than massed reviews in a short space of time.
- More frequent use of properly spaced reviews and tests in the classroom can dramatically improve classroom learning and retention.

- Spaced repetitions can foster time-on-task and help students sustain positive attitudes toward school and learning. It is helpful for students to experience the feeling of competence which frequent successful application and practice can create.
- Spaced repetitions appear to result in a richer, more elaborate understanding of the topic.
- Massed repetitions, or only a single session of repetitions, seem to evoke shallow, effortless processing with little long-term gain. 'Massed repetitions, because there is not much time between them, tend to inspire a false sense of knowing or confidence' (Dempster 1991: 73).
- A well-designed mathematics textbook will make use of spaced practice and regular review.

Rosenshine (1986) indicates that less effective teaching of mathematics is characterized by infrequent review and revision, demonstrations which are too brief or unclear, insufficient guided practice, and too little corrective feedback.

Effective teachers of mathematics are good at constructing series of lessons that successfully transmit the curriculum content to the learner. Their lessons are typically clear, accurate and rich in examples and demonstrations of a particular concept, process or strategy (Leinhardt 1986). Slower students need more frequent review, less verbal elaboration, much more guided practice and application to ensure mastery (Rosenshine 1986). In general, research on teacher effectiveness in the area of mathematics supports the use of a structured approach within a carefully sequenced programme. Evidence seems to prove that effective teachers can provide systematic instruction in mathematics in such a way that understanding can accompany the mastery of number skills and problem-solving strategies with a minimum of confusion. Within such an approach the use of practical work, collaborative group activities, and open discussion will always have a vital role in developing understanding and positive attitudes in the learners (Sutton 1992). In recent years the value of integrating mathematics with other subjects, and particularly of using *writing* in mathematics, has been recognized (LeGere 1991; Fennell 1991). An integrated approach appears to enhance student motivation and involvement, and reduce the 'maths anxiety' which is said to be present in certain students.

There exists a variety of reasons to account for some children experiencing difficulty in mastering the facts, concepts and operations in arithmetic and applying these successfully to problem-solving. While this information helps us to appreciate why a child has difficulties, it is not particularly helpful to spend a great deal of time in attempting to track down the specific causal factors in individual cases; rarely will these indicate what should be done to assist the child. As with reading, writing and spelling, the most practical approach, regardless of the child's disability, is to ascertain what he or she can already do in this area of the curriculum, to locate any specific gaps which may exist and to determine what he or she needs to be taught next. In other words, the diagnostic model presented in an earlier chapter can be applied to the assessment of skills in arithmetic and can guide programme planning in mathematics.

A DIAGNOSTIC APPROACH

With any approach to the teaching of mathematics, there is an ongoing need for regular assessment of individual progress. Periodic checks on the child's understanding of new work are essential; and such checks must usually involve working directly with the child to detect strengths and weaknesses in performance. Without this the teacher has little idea whether the pupil carries out an activity in rote fashion, through the help of other children, or with partial or complete understanding. Keeping a record of children's progress along different paths in mathematics is a constant challenge to the teacher.

The first step in the diagnostic evaluation of mathematical skills might involve formal testing of the child using published standardized tests to determine the level at which the child is functioning. However, standardized tests are of rather limited value, since they do not yield a comprehensive picture of a student's broad range of knowledge and skills (Kamii and Lewis 1991). Far more useful information can be obtained from teacher-made tests which reflect the true content of the curriculum being taught in that classroom. Curriculum-based assessment is now widely acknowledged as the most direct method for teachers to link assessment with instructional design (Gable, Enright and Hendrickson 1991). Teacher-made tests can be supplemented with information gleaned from an examination of the student's exercise books and worksheets. The nature of a student's errors can be appraised, and follow-up diagnostic tests which assess proficiency in particular processes can be used. Clarke (1992) advocates combining information from anecdotal records, examination of workbooks, practical tests and student self-assessment to obtain a valid picture of a student's current ability.

A task-analytic approach may be taken when attempting to find the point of failure or misunderstanding in basic arithmetical processes. Several of the diagnostic number tests which have been used in schools for many years are still valid and actually adopt this approach. By carefully grading the various steps involved in, say, long division, and providing test items to sample the child's competence at each stage, the teacher can detect the precise point of breakdown in computational skills or understanding. An analysis of the actual errors made by the child can then further pinpoint the teaching which needs to be done (Engelhardt 1982; Sowder, Moyer and Moyer 1986).

Reisman (1972) strongly advocated that teachers construct their own informal mathematical skills inventory containing test items covering key concepts, knowledge and skills presented in earlier years, together with essential material from the current year. Such an inventory can indicate very conveniently precisely what the child can and cannot do and will assist with the ordering of priorities for teaching.

There are various levels of abstraction involved in diagnostic work in mathematics (Underhill, Uprichard and Heddens 1980). To a large extent, identification of these levels will help a teacher to answer the question, 'What can the child do in mathematics if given a little help and guidance?'. The levels are concrete, semi-concrete, and abstract. At the concrete level the child may be able to solve a problem or complete a process correctly if permitted to manipulate real objects. At the semi-concrete level, pictorial representations of the objects, together with the symbols, are sufficient visual information to ensure success. At the abstract level the child must work with the symbols only, either in printed form or as orally dictated by the teacher. During the diagnostic work with the child the teacher may move up or down within this hierarchy from abstract to concrete, in an attempt to discover the level at which the child can succeed. The text *Towards a Good Beginning* (Burton 1985) contains a useful 'readiness assessment' for use with students who may even be at a pre-number stage of development.

It may be helpful to keep the following thoughts in mind when attempting to discover the child's present functional level. Referring to any items which a child fails to solve in a test or during deskwork following a period of instruction, ask yourself these questions:

- *Why* did the child get this item wrong?
- Can he or she carry out the process if allowed to use concrete aids or count on fingers or use a number line, etc.?
- Can he or she explain to me what to do? Ask the child to work through the example step by step. At what point does the child obviously misunderstand?

The value of this last procedure cannot be over-stressed. If a child explains to you how he or she tackles the problem, you are likely to pick up at once the exact point of confusion and can teach from there (Richards 1982). Too often we jump in and reteach the whole process, but still fail to help the child to recognize and overcome the precise difficulty.

Howell and Morehead (1987) advocate close investigation of the actual strategies used by a student in carrying out a computation or solving a problem. A discussion between teacher and student can reveal much about the student's level of confidence, flexibility of thinking and underlying knowledge. According to Salvia and Hughes (1990), teachers should probe for understanding in the following areas when appraising a student's problem solving abilities: detecting what is called for in a problem; identifying relevant information; selecting correct procedure; estimating an approximate answer; computing the answer; and checking the answer. In many ways, assessing problem-solving skills in mathematics has much in common with assessing comprehension in reading.

Teachers must recognize that the main goal in teaching mathematics to *all* students is the development of everyday problem-solving skills (Cawley, Baker-Kroczynski and Urban 1992); and diagnosis of a student's current ability in this domain should have high priority (Howell and Barnhart 1992).

Three levels of assessment

The following three levels of assessment may help the teacher to design appropriate assessment materials. It is likely that the first two levels will be the most applicable for children with learning difficulties.

Level 1

If the child's performance in basic numbers is very poor, consider the following points. At this stage almost all the assessments will need to be made at an individual level, using appropriate concrete materials, toys, pictures, number cards, etc.

- Check the child's grasp of vocabulary associated with number relationships (e.g. 'bigger than', 'altogether', 'less', 'share', etc.).
- Check the child's conservation of number.

Then check the following knowledge and skills in this order. Can the child:

- Sort objects given one attribute (colour, size, shape, etc.)?

- Sort objects given two attributes?
- Produce equal sets of objects by one-to-one matching?
- Count correctly objects to ten? To twenty?
- Recognize numerals to ten? To twenty?
- Place number symbols in correct sequence to ten? To twenty?
- Write numerals correctly from dictation to ten? To twenty?
- Understand ordinal values (fifth, tenth, second, etc.)?
- Perform simple addition with numbers below ten in written form (e.g. $3 + 5 =$)? With or without apparatus?
- Perform subtraction with numbers below ten in written form?
- Count-on in a simple addition problem?
- Answer simple oral problems involving addition or subtraction with numbers below ten?
- Recognize coins and paper money?

Level 2

If the child's performance in mathematics is slightly better than Level 1, consider the following areas. Can the child:

- Carry out simple mental addition with numbers below twenty?
- Carry out simple mental problem-solving without use of finger-counting or tally marks?
- Carry out simple subtraction mentally as above? Is there a marked difference between performance in addition and subtraction?
- Perform both vertical and horizontal forms of simple addition?

    (3 and $3 + 5 =$).
    $\underline{+5}$

- Understand the commutative law in addition (i.e. that the order of items to be totalled does not matter)? Does the child see, for example, that $5 + 3$ and $3 + 5$ are bound to give the same total? When counting on to obtain a total in such problems, does the child always count the smaller number on to the larger; or are these problems always solved from left to right regardless? ($2 + 8 =$ $12 + 5 =$).
- Understand additive composition (i.e. all the possible ways of producing a given set or total)? For example, 5 is $4 + 1$, $3 + 2$, $2 + 3$, $1 + 4$, $5 + 0$.
- Understand the complementary or reversible character of addition and subtraction? ($7 + 3 = 10$, $10 - 7 = 3$, $10 - 3 = 7$).
- Watch an operation demonstrated using concrete material and then record this in written form?

- Translate a written equation into a practical demonstration (e.g. using Unifix cubes to demonstrate $12 - 4 = 8$)?
- Listen to a simple real-life situation described in words and then work the problem in written form? (Seven people were waiting at the bus stop. When the bus came only three could get on. How many were left to wait for the next bus?) Use numbers below twenty. Can the child work problems at this level mentally?
- Recognize and write numerals to fifty?
- Tell the time to the nearest half-hour? Read a digital clock correctly?
- Recite the days of the week? Recite the months of the year?

Level 3

If the child is able to succeed with most of the items in the previous levels, or if he/she seems reasonably competent in many areas of basic maths, consider these questions. Can the child:

- Read and write numbers to 100? To 1,000? Can he or she read and write sums of money correctly?
- Halve or double numbers mentally?
- Add money mentally? Give change by the counting-on method?
- Recite the multiplication tables correctly and answer random facts from these tables?
- Perform the correct procedures for addition of hundreds, tens and units, and thousands, hundreds, tens and units. Without carrying? Without carrying in any column?
- Understand place value with tens and units? With hundreds, tens and units? With thousands, hundreds, tens and units? Without exchanging in any column? with exchanging? It is important to note the actual method used by the child to carry out subtraction. Is it 'decomposition' using only the top line of figures, or the 'equal addition' method using top and bottom lines?
- Perform the correct steps in the multiplication algorithm? To what level of difficulty?
- Perform the correct steps in the division algorithm? To what level of difficulty?
- Recognize fractions: $\frac{1}{2}$, $\frac{1}{4}$, $3\frac{1}{2}$, $7\frac{1}{4}$, $\frac{1}{10}$, $5\frac{3}{10}$, 0.8, 5.9 etc.?
- Read and interpret correctly simple word-problems?

Over to you

Prepare the materials and questions needed in order to carry out assessments at one of the three levels described above.

Devise a simple check-list to enable you to record an individual child's responses to your assessment items. For Level 3 you may be able to locate published arithmetic tests to include in your assessment; but failing this, teacher-designed questions and items are perfectly acceptable. Don't forget to grade your items in each area carefully and where possible to include several items at each level of difficulty.

SOME BASIC TEACHING POINTS

Clearly it is impossible within a single chapter to summarize teaching procedures across the complete field of mathematics. One must be selective and is helped in this by Bowd's (1990) opening statement that in teaching mathematics to slower learners the two biggest hurdles to overcome will be number fluency and problem-solving. These two areas will be developed in the following pages.

Basic number concepts and skills

Conservation   Basic to all number work is the concept of conservation of number; that is, a group or set composed of N separate items remains a set of that number regardless of how it is arranged or distributed. Up to the age of five or six years (and later with disabled learners) the number of items in a set may appear to alter if the members are rearranged spatially. Experience has to be given to children to help them understand conservation of number and not to be misled by what their eyes seem to tell them. Much of the pre-school and early school experience of sorting, counting, giving out materials, one-to-one matching of objects, etc., should be helping the basic concept of conservation to develop. For some children the process needs to be made more explicit.

The following activities and apparatus may help a child to develop the concept of conservation of number:

- teacher-made cards with pictures, dot patterns, and shapes in different groupings can be sorted into sets of equal size (numbers in sets should be below ten and no numerals will be introduced);
- matching or joining up various patterns with equal numbers of shapes presented on worksheets;
- counting activities to ten (or less) to establish one-to-one correspondence between the number rhyme 'one, two, three...' and the actual objects in given sets, and to establish 'equivalence' or 'difference' between sets;
- matching of objects (toys, unit blocks, etc.) with pictures or dot patterns containing different size groups.

The vocabulary of early number relationships needs to be introduced carefully and systematically alongside such experiences. For the least able students this vocabulary needs to be repeated and over-learned until completely mastered (for example, same, different, more than, less than, few, many, all, none, altogether, as many as). One must not allow a child's mathematical progress to be held back by lack of ability to verbalize; but the almost total inability to verbalize found in some children can be a major obstacle which must be overcome. If the child's understanding of the vocabulary associated with number and mathematics is very restricted, greater attention must be given to teaching and over-learning the appropriate terms in a meaningful context. It is not just the vocabulary itself which is important, but the syntactical patterns which accompany the verbalizations. For example, 'Are there more dogs than cats in the picture?', 'How many more cars than buses can you see?'

Counting   Counting is perhaps the most fundamental of all early number skills. As indicated in the previous section, it can assist with the development of conservation of number. If this skill of counting is deficient it can only be taught and improved by direct instruction, working with the child alone or as a member of a small group. Perhaps the problem may be that the child fails to make a correct one-to-one correspondence between the word spoken in the 'number rhyme' and the objects touched in order. If the physical act of counting a set of objects appears to be difficult for the child, manual guidance of his or her hands may be needed. For young or handicapped children the use of 'finger plays' and 'number rhymes and songs' may assist with the mastery of counting. Rote counting to ten and then to twenty should be given high priority in any special mathematics programme.

Counting of actual objects will eventually be extended to encompass 'counting-on' strategies for addition, and to 'counting up' strategies for subtraction, in the absence of real objects. These strategies may have to be taught directly to certain students (Fuson and Fuson 1992).

Recognition of numerals   The cardinal value of number symbols should, of course, be related to a variety of sets of different objects. Teachers can make numeral-to-group matching games (the numeral 11 on a card to be matched with eleven birds, eleven kites, eleven cars, eleven dots, eleven tally marks, etc.). Also useful are teacher-made lotto cards containing a selection of the number symbols being taught or over-learned (one to ten, or one to twenty, or twenty-five to fifty, etc.). When the teacher holds up a flash-card and says the number, the child covers the numeral on the lotto card. At the end of the game the child must say each number aloud as it is uncovered on the card. Later these same lotto cards can be used for basic addition and subtraction facts, the numerals on the cards now representing correct answers to some simple question from the teacher (5 add 4 makes...? The number 1 less than 8 is...?).

Activities with number cards can also be devised to help children sort and arrange the numerals in correct sequence from one to ten, one to twenty, etc. The early items in the Unifix mathematics apparatus can be useful at this stage (e.g. the inset pattern boards, number indicators, number line to twenty).

The writing of numerals should be taught in parallel to the above activities. Correct numeral formation should be established as thoroughly as correct letter formation in handwriting: this will reduce the incidence of reversals of figures in written recording.

Recording   There is a danger that some children will be expected to deal with symbolic number recording too early. Pictorial recording, tally marks, and dot patterns are very acceptable forms of representation for the young child. Gradually, the writing of number symbols will accompany such picture-type recording and then finally replace it, by which time the cardinal values of the numerals are really understood (Stoessiger and Wilkinson 1991).

Number facts   Ashcraft (1985) suggests that functional knowledge in arithmetic involves two major components: mastery of number facts which can easily be retrieved from memory (to $9 + 9$ and 9×9), and a body of knowledge about computational procedures. Both components are needed in typical arithmetic problem-solving situations. Number facts are involved in all steps of the sub-routines carried out later in more complex computations.

It is essential that children be helped to develop habit recall of the basic number bonds rather than having, for example, to calculate with fingers each time they need 7 + 3 = 10. Being able to recall number facts easily is important for two main reasons; it makes calculation easier, and it allows time for the deepening of understanding (Ginsburg and Baroody 1983). Knowing number facts is partly a matter of rote learning (remembered through constant exposure) and partly a matter of grasping a rule (e.g. that zero added to any number doesn't change it: 3 + 0 = 3, 13 + 0 = 13, etc. or if that 7 + 3 = 10 then 7 + 4 must be 'one more than ten', etc.).

Many children with learning disabilities have problems in learning and recalling number facts and tables, and require extra attention devoted to this key area (Jones, Thornton and Toohey 1985). The following suggestions may help.

Daily speed and accuracy sheets   One must not underestimate the value of a daily worksheet to practise recall of number facts and tables for those children still needing such experience. Children should aim to increase their own scores each day in, say, a three-minute session, thus competing against themselves, not the class average. They are likely to get responses correct because they are working at their own rate (and can use counters, tally marks, etc. if necessary). This procedure is preferable to the daily session using 'ten mental problems', which can become nothing more than a morning ritual and only teaches some children how poor they are at rapid mental arithmetic.

Daily speed and accuracy sheets must not be allowed to become an end in themselves. It is vital that a child has the opportunity to apply number facts and arithmetic skills to problem-solving.

Number games   Almost any simple game involving a scoring system can be used to practise recall of number facts or simple addition or subtraction. For example, a skittle game can be played using empty bleach or cordial containers with a value (score) painted on each. The child has to add the value for any knocked down with each roll of the ball. Card games can be designed which involve adding and subtracting scores at each turn.

Salmon (1990) has recommended that teachers devise or select games carefully in order to complement the objectives of the lesson, rather than provide amusement. Children must be taught the appropriate way to play a game, and they should be made aware of what the game is teaching them.

Computer programs have proved to be particularly useful in providing the necessary amount of drill and practice without boredom. Hasselbring, Goin and Brandsford (1988) combined drill sessions on a computer with training in recall of basic number facts from memory for students with learning difficulties. Their results suggest that such a procedure is effective in developing automaticity in recall of number facts.

Computation and algorithms   Once children have evolved their own meaningful forms of recording in the early stages, one must move on carefully to the introduction of conventional forms of both vertical and horizontal computation. A child should be able to watch as a bundle of, say, ten rods and two extra ones is added to a set already containing a bundle of ten rods and three extra ones and then write the operation as

$$12 + 13 = 25 \text{ or } \begin{array}{r} 12 \\ +13 \\ \hline 25 \end{array}$$

The reverse of this procedure is to show the child a 'number sentence' (20 − 13 = 7) and ask him or her to demonstrate what this means using some form of concrete material. Dienes' MAB blocks are particularly useful for this purpose. Stern's equipment and Unifix blocks, being larger in size, are more appropriate for children with poor manipulative skills.

This stage of development is likely to require careful structuring over a long period of time if the slower learner is not to become confused. The grading of the examples and the amount of practice provided at each stage are crucial for long-term mastery. Once the children reach this stage of applying the basic algorithms for addition (with and without carrying), subtraction (with and without borrowing), multiplication and division, the demands on their thinking and reasoning increase rapidly (Beattie 1986).

Skemp (1976) suggested that ideally students should achieve two levels of understanding in their application of arithmetical processes to problem-solving. The most basic level is termed 'instrumental understanding' (knowing what to do and when to do it in order to select an appropriate process to solve a problem and complete the calculation correctly). At this level the learner knows *what* to do but does not necessarily have an in-depth understanding of why or how the procedure works. An example would be the application of the rule to invert and multiply when dividing by a fraction. The higher level of understanding is termed 'relational under-standing'. At this level the learner understands fully how and why a particular process works, as well as when to use it. Ideally one would hope to assist all children to achieve both levels of understanding; but realistically the relational level may be beyond the grasp of lower-ability children. However, it is possible to teach many of these children who have mastered the basic number system to select and carry out the correct arithmetical procedure to solve a problem. For everyday purposes that ability is all that is required.

Indirectly, the issues above raise the question of the place of the pocket calculator as a means of bypassing the computational difficulties of some students. There is a valid argument that time spent on mechanical arithmetic is largely wasted on a child who cannot seem to retain the steps involved in carrying out a particular procedure when working through a calculation using pencil and paper. The use of the calculator as a permanent alternative is totally defensible in such cases. The use of the calculator removes a major obstacle for children with poor computational skills and they can all compute with speed and accuracy. The instructional time saved can then be devoted to helping the children learn to select the correct type of operation needed to solve particular problems. *More* time on problem-solving, not less!

However, it is likely that in the foreseeable future many teachers will still wish to teach computational procedures in traditional written forms before a child is permitted to use a calculator. It is to these teachers that the following paragraphs in this section are directed.

It is, of course, valuable to teach students verbal cues when carrying out the steps in a particular calculation. For example, using the decomposition method for this subtraction problem the children would be taught to verbalize the steps in some way similar to the wording below.

$$5 \; _7 8 \; ^1 1$$
$$\underline{1 \;\; 3 \;\; 9}$$
$$4 \;\; 4 \;\; 2$$

The child says: 'Start with the units. I can't take 9 from 1 so I must borrow a ten and write it next to the 1. Cross out the 8 tens and write 7. Now I can take 9 from 11 and write 2 in the answer box. 7 take 3 leaves 4 in the tens column. 5 take 1 leaves 4. Write 4 in the answer space. My answer is four hundred and forty-two.'

Rote learning of these verbal routines has fallen into disrepute in recent years (Davis 1984; Wilson and Sindelar 1991). It is felt that these methods inhibit the more able children's thinking and may prevent them from devising insightful and more rapid methods of completing a calculation. Slavishly following an algorithm may represent purely mechanical performance even below the instrumental level. Nevertheless, for children with poor aptitude for arithmetic it is essential that, if the teacher does decide to cover these paper and pencil skills, they be taught thoroughly to the point of mastery. Without the verbal and mechanical procedures for working through a calculation the slower children are likely to be totally confused and utterly frustrated. These procedures can be elevated above the rote learning level if they are accompanied by some degree of self-monitoring in the student (Frank and Brown 1992). Self-monitoring helps the student to remember how to complete the steps in a sequential task and how to self-correct where necessary. For example, in subtracting hundreds, tens and units use the cue 'Remember the 3Bs': *Begin* in the units column. *Bigger* : which number is bigger? *Borrow* : if bottom number is bigger I borrow. Is my answer correct?

A support teacher or parent who attempts to help a child in this area of school work *must* liaise closely with the class teacher in order to find out the precise verbal cues which are used in subtraction, multiplication, etc., so that the same words and directions are used in the remedial programme, to avoid confusion.

It is important that students also be taught other strategies for solving addition and subtraction problems, preferably those which will help to develop insight into the structure and composition of the numbers involved. For example, if the child is faced with $47 + 17 =$ he or she is encouraged to think of this (to regroup) as a set of $(40 + 7)$ added to a set of $(10 + 7)$. The tens are quickly combined to make fifty, and the two sevens make fourteen. Finally fourteen combined with fifty is obviously sixty-four. Fewer errors seem to occur with this method than with the 'carry ten under the line' type of vertical addition. This is almost certainly because the approach is meaningful and does help to develop insight into the structure of number. It can also be easily demonstrated using MAB blocks or similar concrete materials (Suydam 1986).

With subtraction the procedure may be illustrated thus:

$(53 - 27 =$)   53 can be regrouped as $40 + 13$
27 can be regrouped as $20 + 7$
Deal with the tens first: $40 - 20 = 20$
Now the second step: $13 - 7 = 6$
We are left with 26.

Once the method is established with relational understanding it appears to result in fewer errors than either 'decomposition' or 'equal addition' methods. Equal addition, once considered to be the best method for tackling more difficult subtraction problems, has fallen out of favour.

In the surveys which have been carried out to determine adult needs in arithmetic, multiplication and division do not appear to be of great value in everyday life. Certainly it is useful to be able to multiply, say, twenty-three lengths of wallpaper by 3 m to find out how much to order to paper a room; but the adult who has difficulty with multiplication will usually solve the problem correctly as an addition process (setting down twenty-three three times and adding). It seems that if teachers are to identify the priorities for curriculum content in mathematics, addition and subtraction should be given high ranking, multiplication moderate ranking, and division low ranking. For children of limited ability a pocket calculator may well be the most obvious answer for multiplication and division.

Over to you

The place of the pocket calculator in the mathematics course remains a vexed issue for many teachers. Set down your own views on the matter and address yourself particularly to its possible value for lower ability children.

What are your views on the teaching of computational skills in fairly traditional ways involving set algorithms and verbal cueing?

One final word on the paper and pencil performance of children with perceptual difficulties or co-ordination problems. It is often necessary to rule up the pages of their exercise books in ways which will make it easier for them to set down the digits in correct spatial positions. Heavy vertical lines will assist with the correct placement of hundreds, tens and units and thus maintain place values. Squared paper will usually assist with the general arrangement of figures on the page. Teachers must also anticipate the difficulties which some children will have in reversing not only single digits but tens and units (e.g. 61 written as 16). Much specific teaching, with cues and prompts such as small arrows or dots on the page, will be needed to overcome this tendency.

MENTAL ARITHMETIC: DOES IT STILL HAVE A PLACE?

Mental arithmetic – the 'daily ten' – has an almost sacred position in the primary mathematics lesson. If the activity is used to review and practise important skills or facts, and if there is corrective feedback provided for the children who make errors, then the time is well spent. However, in many classrooms the session really is nothing more than a ritual if the questions are posed, the answers given and a mark given out of ten, with no follow-up whatsoever for children with poor scores. The teacher must identify which questions caused difficulty and spend a few moments reteaching the necessary procedure to solve the problems.

One simple teaching strategy which is extremely helpful for children who are poor at processing purely auditory information is to write the numerals on the blackboard as the problem is posed orally. For example, the teacher says, 'Red team scored nine goals. Blue team scored seven goals. Green team scored twelve goals. How many goals were scored altogether?' The numerals 9, 7 and 12 are quickly written randomly on the blackboard. Having this key information available in a visual form will enable many more children to add numbers mentally.

It is worth commenting that hearing-impaired children may have particular difficulties with mental arithmetic when the questions are dictated by the teacher. A number such as 'sixty' may *look* exactly like 'sixteen' on the teacher's lips if the child relies heavily on speech reading. Again the use of the blackboard will help to prevent this confusion.

DEVELOPING PROBLEM-SOLVING STRATEGIES

In an article 'You can teach problem solving' LeBlanc stated optimistically, 'Teaching problem solving is a problem; but like most other problems it can be solved' (1977: 16). He then went on to present a framework to help children develop problem-solving skills. His ideas, together with those of Riley and Pachtman (1978), Darch, Carnine and Gersten (1984), Howell and Barnhart (1992) and Wilson and Sindelar (1991) are summarized in the following paragraphs. The instructional goal should be to help children learn strategies and procedures for problem-solving. They need to learn how to approach a problem without a feeling of panic or hopelessness. They need to be able to sift the relevant from the irrelevant information and to impose some degree of structure on the problem (Carpenter 1985).

Four steps to problem-solving

Example: A store sold 485 bottles of cold drink on one day in the summer. The drink bottles are packaged in cartons which hold six bottles each. How many cartons of drink were sold that day?

Step 1: Understanding the problem   The teacher focuses the children's attention on the relevant information in the problem through the use of questions.

'How many bottles were sold?'

'What does packaged mean?' 'What is a carton?' (Visual aid or blackboard sketch may be helpful even at this stage.)

'How were the bottles packed?'

'If one carton holds six bottles, how many bottles in two cartons?'
'What does the problem ask us to find out?' (Advice such as 'think!' or
'read it again!' may be of no help to the child.)

Step 2: Planning to solve the problem   The teacher encourages the
child or children to consider possible ways of solving the problem. If
necessary, the teacher may need to offer some suggestions.

'Well could we do it like this? Could we get 485 bottles and put them
into groups of six? Do we need to do that? How else could we do it? Could
we make up some form of chart or table? Will a sketch help us to visualize
what to do?'

Both Munro (1981) and Nelson (1983) stress the immense value of
having children draw sketches which help them to picture the actual
problem.

Step 3: Attempting a solution   The children might now attempt,
perhaps through trial and error to some extent, to come up with a plausible
answer.

Step 4: Reviewing the problem and its solution   In this final stage
the children are encouraged to consider the problem again and to check
to see if their solution is what was asked for.

'John, you've got 2,910 cartons. Does that make sense?'
'Linda, you have written "80 and a bit cartons"; tell us how you got
that.'

LeBlanc (1977) suggests that the final review stage in teaching problem-
solving is very important indeed. It benefits the child who is having to
think carefully *how* he or she solved the problem, and it is helping the other
children who hear (in language they can readily understand) how someone
else tackled the problem.

This 'verbal mediation' is also an essential part of the teacher's role when
demonstrating how to break a problem down into its component steps.
The teacher should describe the process aloud and then have the students
practise saying the various steps and make procedural decisions during the
guided practice (Howell and Morehead 1987). Problem-solving in mathematics is another area of curriculum which benefits from self-instruction
training (see Chapter 3).

Salend's (1990) approach to solving word problems involves seven steps:

- Read the problem. Look for clue words which suggest the procedure
  to use (e.g. altogether, lost, remain, spent, more than, etc.).

- Reread the problem. Identify key information. Ignore extraneous detail. What units will the solution be in? (pounds, centimetres, eggs?)
- Visualize the problem. Draw a picture or imagine the picture.
- Write the problem. Set down the computational steps on paper.
- Estimate the answer. What will a reasonable answer be like?
- Solve the problem. Carry out the necessary calculations.
- Check the answer. Compare answer to estimate. Check calculation. Check units against original question.

Polloway *et al.* (1989) suggest using a strategy, the initial letters of each cue word spelling 'SOLVES IT':

S – Say the problem yourself
O – Omit unnecessary detail
L – Listen for key vocabulary
V – Vocabulary which suggests procedure to use
E – Equation. Write the problem as a maths equation
S – Solve the equation
I – Indicate the answer
T – Test the answer against the original question.

Riley and Pachtman (1978) consider that the most important thing to teach is how to sift out the key information from the facts which are presented. Children must be helped to perceive the relationships between the statements in the problem and to detect the relevant facts. This is basically a reading comprehension problem; Darch, Carnine and Gersten (1984) developed a four-step programme for aiding this process. The children are taught to:

- write down the numbers from the problem;
- identify the process needed to work with the numbers;
- write the equation or algorithm;
- write the solution.

The teacher models these steps very carefully and directly instructs the children in their use. Darch, Carnine and Gersten found significant improvement in fourth grade children's problem-solving skills following this type of training. Similar improvement has been found with adolescents (Montague and Candace 1986).

Since there is evidence that children can be helped to become more proficient at solving problems, teachers of children with learning difficulties should devote more time to this area of work. As mentioned in an earlier section, perhaps the use of pocket calculators will enable teachers to find the time to do, this rather than restrict the children to a diet of mechanical arithmetic (Burns 1986).

Over to you

Briefly outline some strategies you would use to help some slower-learning children solve this problem.

'At the beginning of the new term Class 7, with twenty-five children in it, has been given a collection of 98 books to increase the size of their classroom library. Before the holiday they had 102 books in the library. The teacher says, "I want labels pasted in all the books, new and old. You can share the work out equally so that you all have a turn at pasting." If the work is divided up fairly, in how many books will each child have to paste labels?'

Do students with learning disabilities need different methods?

Just as there are no unique methods of teaching reading and spelling to learning-disabled students, so too there are no unique methods for teaching mathematical skills and concepts.

The following basic principles emerge from the literature on learning disability. The same principles apply for *any* student who experiences learning difficulties in mathematics.

- They need to be taught the language of the subject, particularly the vocabulary associated with classifying and ordering objects, performing operations with numbers, and solving word-problems.
- They benefit from material which provides visual representation of number or spatial relationships.
- Attention must be given to developing automaticity with basic number facts and operations.
- Sufficient time-on-task must be established to enable the student to gain adequate successful practice.
- More than ordinary amounts of attention must be given to correctly positioning numerals during written computation.
- Strategy training will help the students to learn how to approach the recording of mathematical operations and how to solve word-

problems. Research evidence indicates that LD students *can* be taught to use effective task-approach strategies.

- Regular, daily sessions will be required if the learning rate is to be accelerated and maintained.

CURRICULUM CONTENT

With slow-learning and disabled children, it is sometimes necessary to modify somewhat the actual content which one attempts to cover. Some traditional topics in mainstream mathematics courses are inappropriate for these children. Cockcroft (1982) supports the notion of a reduced-content maths course with a functional emphasis for children of limited ability. In trying to decide upon content for a 'core curriculum', one is helped by the results of surveys of community expectations of basic numeracy (Bourke 1981). Parents and employers agree that the key areas for functional numeracy are: counting, tables, use of the four basic processes, money management, time and measurement. Some grasp of common and decimal fractions and the ability to understand simple graphs are also useful in everyday life.

The following content was considered by a group of primary and secondary teachers to comprise a core of essential material basic to the needs of low-achieving school-leavers. Items marked with an asterisk could be omitted with children of very low ability.

Suggested core content

Basic number

- Digit (numeral) recognition. Ability to count actual objects correctly. Understanding of cardinal and serial aspects of number. Appreciation of place value. Emphasis on establishing basic number facts as 'habit responses'.
- Standard processes (algorithms) of arithmetic. Emphasis on addition and subtraction. Emphasis on 'estimating' reasonable results for calculations. Greatest emphasis on problem-solving using basic processes.
- Multiplication and division to be taught later using realistic numbers. Grouping. (No objection to table charts or desk calculators.) Counting in intervals (2s, 5s, 10s, 100s).

Money

- Coin and note recognition.
- Ability to handle money (count up totals using the coins; give change by 'counting-on' method).
- Ability to perform basic processes with £ and p, $ and cents (especially addition and subtraction).
- Experiences with simple budgeting and banking.

Problem-solving

- Emphasis to be placed on applying all the above skills and processes to solving problems.
- Emphasis also on practical mathematics.
- Use of measurement scale in simple mapwork and interpretation.★
- Ability to interpret simple graphs and charts.★

Fractions, decimals, percentages

- Understanding and recognition of simple common fractions (½, ¾, ¼, ⅒). No rote learning of operations with fractions. Equivalence of simple fractions.
- Understanding and recognition of tenths and hundredths and decimal notation, particularly in connection with measurement (linear, temperature, etc.) and money.★
- Awareness of meaning of 100 per cent, 50 per cent, 25 per cent, 10 per cent, and particular reference to sales and '10 per cent off', etc.★

Measurement

- Ability to measure and construct using mm, cm and metres. Awareness of distance (km). Speed (km/hr) (and associated road signs).★
- Ability to weigh in g and kg. Awareness of common weights of goods (e.g. packet of sugar, potatoes etc.). Basic understanding of tonne.★
- Ability to tell the time. Probably best to teach digital clock notation rather than 'quarter past', 'quarter to', etc.). Teach that clock face is really a curved number line 1 to 60. Awareness of the passage of time (e.g. thirty seconds; one minute; five minutes; one hour; twenty-four hours). Estimate 'how long will it take' to do a certain task, or to travel a certain journey, or to get to the bus stop, etc.).
- Know days of the week, months of the year, and seasons.

- Liquid measures (litre). Relate to petrol, cans of paint, carton of milk or juice, etc.★
- Temperature. Read thermometer.★

A suggested core for moderately to severely disabled children[†]

Number concepts

The child is able to perform the following skills without prompting or guidance:

- rote counts to ten;
- counts objects to ten;
- gives correct number of objects (up to ten) on request;
- matches numerals one to ten;
- counts and points to numerals one to ten in sequence;
- finds correct numeral on request;
- names numerals to ten (any order) when shown card;
- matches numerals to groups (up to ten);
- rote counts to twenty;
- copies numerals one to ten;
- writes numerals from dictation;
- adds with objects to ten (combines groups);
- counts objects to twenty;
- adds with numbers to ten;
- subtracts with objects to ten;
- subtracts with numbers to ten;
- combines objects to twenty;
- rote counts to one hundred.

Monetary concepts

- Matches coins and notes;
- identifies coins and notes on request;
- knows value of coins and notes.

Concepts of telling time

- Says days of week by rote;
- says months of year by rote;

† See also Gumblatt and McClennen 1991

- correlates general times of day;
- tells time (digital clock).

Personal information concepts

- Gives parents' full names;
- gives birthdate;
- names self as male or female;
- gives address;
- gives own telephone number;
- dials phone number.

SUMMARY

In this chapter brief attention was given to factors which may cause children to experience difficulty learning basic mathematics, particularly those related to quality of instruction.

Three levels of diagnostic assessment were presented. A teacher using the items listed at each level should obtain a fairly accurate picture of what a child can and cannot do in number work and simple problem-solving.

Priority attention was given to practical ways of helping a child develop number fluency since this is basic to all problem-solving work. It was suggested that for some students a pocket calculator be provided as a permanent alternative to paper and pencil computation.

Suggestions were provided for the teaching of problem-solving skills through modelling appropriate step-by-step procedures.

Finally, a suggested 'core curriculum in mathematics' was presented, first for slower and mildly disabled students and then for the moderately to severely disabled students.

Discussion points

- 'Mathematics teaching in today's classrooms is dominated too much by textbooks.' Discuss this comment.
- Describe the key features you would expect to find in a maths textbook designed for lower-ability students.
- 'All students should be exposed to the mainstream mathematics curriculum. To water-down the content for slower students is not in their best interests.' Argue the points for and against this viewpoint.

- Mathematics learning is an area where it is only too easy for a student to enter a 'failure cycle'. How might teachers prevent this situation?

Further reading

Baroody, A. and Hume, J. (1991) 'Meaningful mathematics instruction', *Remedial and Special Education* 12, 3: 54–68.

Bley N.S. and Thornton, C.A. (1989) *Teaching Mathematics to the Learning Disabled* (2nd edn), Austin: Pro-Ed.

Burton, G.M. (1985) *Towards a Good Beginning: Teaching Early Childhood Mathematics*, Menlo Park: Addison-Wesley.

Durkin, K. and Shire, B. *Language in Mathematics Education*, Milton Keynes: Open University Press.

Hembree, R. (1986) 'Effects of hand-held calculators in pre-college mathematics', *Journal of Research in Mathematics Education* 17, 2: 83–99.

Hughes, M. (1986) *Children and Number: Difficulties in Learning Mathematics*, Oxford: Blackwell.

Lloyd, J.W. and Keller, C.E. (1989) 'Effective mathematics instruction', *Focus on Exceptional Children* 21, 7: 1–10.

Miles, T.R. and Miles, E. (1992) *Dyslexia and Mathematics*, London: Routledge.

National Research Council (1990) *Reshaping School Mathematics*, Washington, DC: National Academy Press.

Polloway, E., Patton, J., Payne, J. and Payne, R. (1992) *Strategies for Teaching Learners with Special Needs* (5th edn), Columbus: Merrill.

Skemp, R. (1989) *Mathematics in the Primary School*, London: Routledge.

Thornton, C., Tucker, B., Dossey, J. and Bazik, E. (1983) *Teaching Mathematics to Children with Special Needs*, Reading: Addison-Wesley.

Chapter 11

Adapting the curriculum

Make only adaptations that foster learning rather than excuse one from learning....Make adaptations that promote inclusion of the disabled student in an activity.

(Asch 1989: 203)

So far in this book, attention has been devoted to what are commonly called 'the basic academic skills' – reading, writing, spelling and arithmetic. Strategies have been presented for adapting methods and curriculum content in these areas to meet the special needs of some students. Clearly the basic academic skills are not the only curriculum domains which may need adaptation. In this chapter some general principles for modifying any curriculum domain will be examined briefly, together with a summary of the way in which teachers can also modify their actual instructional approach to accommodate students' special needs.

A CURRICULUM FOR ALL?

Contemporary views on social justice and equality of opportunity for all have led some writers to suggest that *all* students have the right to be exposed to a mainstream curriculum in a reasonably unadulterated form (Goodlad and Oakes 1988; Ainscow and Muncey 1990). They highlight a need to reconsider the notion that individual differences among students must necessarily call for radically different curricula, since such curricula may provide a student with reduced opportunities to learn and reduced chances in life. Such programmes, they argue, may be perceived as being inferior offerings. Certainly the practice of 'watering down' the curriculum for students with disabilities and learning difficulties by reducing and simplifying the content (for example, as was suggested in the case of mathematics in the previous chapter), has come in for criticism over the years (Haigh 1977; Dyer 1991). The move toward national and state prescribed curricula and competency testing in several countries (e.g. Great Britain, the United States, Australia) reflects this concern for the right of every individual to receive a broad, enriching school programme. But creating such curricula for a wide ability range can be problematic.

In Great Britain, following the Education Reform Act (1988), all schools, including special schools and centres, were required to implement the National Curriculum, and to provide access to it for all students. While this may be seen by many teachers and parents as a very positive opportunity for students with special educational needs to be brought within the mainstream curriculum, the move has also been seen by some to be a 'highly ideological crusade' which fails to take account of the realities of learning difficulties in this population of students (Emblem and Conti-Ramsden 1990). As special schools and regular schools take audit of their existing programmes and make improvements where necessary, there is some concern voiced that students with significant disabilities may be placed in programmes which are not relevant to their needs or geared to their functional level. Certainly students with disabilities can be described as 'working towards the achievement of Level 1 targets' (the first rung on the ladder); but if they stand no chance of achieving those targets the work may be totally inappropriate. Fordham (1989) argues that there is adequate flexibility within the National Curriculum guidelines to allow for appropriate modifications for individual students, and it seems likely that further flexibility will be permitted. At present a somewhat cumbersome system of 'disapplication and modification' has evolved which allows for some exceptional arrangements to be made. Meanwhile practitioners are attempting to find ways of modifying access to the curriculum for a wide range of students (Lewis 1991; Ashdown, Carpenter and Bovair 1991; Peter 1991).

While the sentiment behind the demand that all students be allowed access to the mainstream curriculum is laudable, it overlooks the fact that equality of opportunity does not, and must not, mean equality of treatment. In order to give some students an equal opportunity to learn and to access the curriculum, the way in which they are treated may have to be somewhat different for at least part of the time. It should be evident from the pragmatic approach presented thus far in this book that much can be done to include students with learning problems and disabilities within the regular classroom programme and to personalize their education to some extent. However, practices which are *generally* inclusive can go only so far in providing equality of opportunity; at times it will be necessary to modify curriculum content and teaching methods for certain students. Such adaptations may then enable the student to participate fully in the main-stream curriculum, or may result in the preparation of an individual programme for that student (Brennan 1985). Teachers therefore need to know how curriculum content can be adapted for students' needs and abilities, and how individualized alternative programmes can be designed. The basic principles which should guide modification to curriculum content are summarized below. They extend beyond the curriculum domains of literacy and numeracy where adaptations have already been discussed.

Basic principles of curriculum adaptation

Based upon suggestions in Westwood (1979), Cook Tessier and Armbrus-ter (1987), Wang (1989), Lewis and Doorlag (1991), Cohen and Lynch (1991), Polloway *et al.* (1991):

- Select curriculum tasks which are likely to lead rapidly to successful accomplishments for the students. Quick, tangible results will build a student's confidence. Set achievable goals.
- Success is likely to be achieved if the demands of the task are within the student's current cognitive ability level. The task should be meaningful to the student, and linked to prior knowledge.
- Tasks which are similar to those already mastered by the student, but which take him or her one step further, are likely to maximize chances of success.
- The task may need to be broken down into small steps, each leading to successful completion.
- It may be useful to restate the general class objective to represent a modified goal which the student can achieve successfully.
- The selected task should not demand prerequisite knowledge or skills not possessed by the student (e.g. reading comprehension; fine motor co-ordination; arithmetical competence).
- Involvement and motivation are likely to be established and main-tained if the task is of relevance and interest to the student. For students with moderate to severe disabilities, the tasks should have some immediate functional value for daily living.
- Attention can be most readily established and held if the task has some degree of novelty value.
- Select, create, or modify resource materials which will match the student's current aptitudes (e.g. reading level) and which will provide

motivating practice. It is frequently necessary to adapt published classroom materials.

- Provide additional examples, exercises and activities over and above those needed by most students in the class. These are required at both guided practice and independent practice stages of learning. Where appropriate, such additional exercises can be used for homework or private study.
- Provide visual representations and concrete learning aids to give hands-on experience and to facilitate understanding.
- Wherever possible, integrate two or more areas of the curriculum to provide opportunities for basic skills to be reinforced and extended. An integrated curriculum is one which draws together content from various academic areas and enables students to generalize and apply the skills they have been learning. Even when the curriculum is prescribed (e.g. the National Curriculum) integration of subject matter is valuable for students with learning problems.

Most of these suggestions are self-explanatory. Issues of goal-setting, objective writing, and task analysis merit further discussion, as they impinge not only upon adaptation to the regular class curriculum but also upon the design of individualized education plans.

GOAL SETTING

To teach Stephanie to name three colours.
To teach the students to understand how to use the library catalogue system.
John will improve his computational skills in dealing with money transactions.
Sally will increase her reading comprehension skills.

Goals are the general statements which must be made to indicate the knowledge, skills, attitudes or values a teacher hopes to develop in the student. They are usually presented in the form of teaching aims which outline what the teacher intends to cover, and they provide a general direction for making programme decisions (e.g. type of resources needed; time allocation; activities; methods). They do not usually provide specific reference to observable outcomes in terms of knowledge, skills or behaviour the students will demonstrate on completion of the task or series of tasks. Goals are the starting points for planning a suitable teaching programme, but they lack the specificity necessary to enable a teacher to know if the desired learning has occurred. The next step is to translate a goal into specific student performance objectives which do describe precisely what the student will be able to demonstrate as a result of an episode of successful learning.

OBJECTIVES

When given a selection of coloured cards Stephanie will correctly pick up and name all three red, yellow and blue cards without prompting.

When given a book title and its author the student will correctly enter this information in the library computer catalogue and write down the shelf number of the book.

John will write down in horizontal form and correctly solve at least eighteen out of twenty money problems involving change from £10.00 (e.g., £10.00 − £7.80 =   ).

Sally will explain and demonstrate successfully the three steps involved in locating the main idea in a passage of text provided by the teacher.

A student performance objective states as clearly as possible what the student will be able to demonstrate. The performance, when tested, will indicate at once whether or not learning has taken place. A clearly stated objective leads to the appropriate form of evaluation of learning for that task. A single educational goal may have several sub-objectives which identify and describe the various components of the performance being assessed.

Although objectives can be written in an abbreviated form, they have maximum specificity if they embody three components: the observable behaviour to be demonstrated by the student; the conditions under which the behaviour is to be performed, and the level of proficiency expected (criterion for successful performance). The four sample performance objectives above illustrate these features.

Teachers often write objectives in terms which are too vague for easy evaluation. The verbs they select to describe the performance are non-observable behaviours (to know, to understand, to recognize, to appreciate, etc.). In such cases it is fair to ask 'How do you *know* the student "knows"?' 'How can you tell the student 'understands'?' Wherever possible, objectives should utilize verbs which do describe something the student can demonstrate overtly (e. g., to write, to underline, to state aloud, to recite, to point to, to touch, to perform, to construct, etc.).

One of the main advantages of using precise performance objectives is that a teacher's purpose can be communicated clearly to others – an important consideration when individual education plans are to be implemented or interpreted by other staff and by parents. They also help to provide a clear focus for programme decisions and facilitate effective evaluation of learning. In an ideal situation the student or students should help with the formulation of their own learning objectives.

There is sometimes a criticism voiced that comprehensive sets of performance objectives, typical of programmes in the 1960s and 1970s, can be daunting and off-putting for teachers. They may feel that an objectives-based programme is essentially rigid and incapable of adjustment to individual needs of students. This of course need not be the case. Stating a performance objective does not in any way dictate the methods to be used – which can be as many and varied as the teacher's imagination allows. The objective simply acts as a signpost, reminding the teacher and others where they are heading by whatever route is chosen. The excesses of the 1960s and 1970s, when performance objectives became almost an obsession, have given way to a more judicious use within individual education plans.

The topics of goal-setting and objective writing are covered in detail in the following texts: Mager (1975), Ainscow and Tweddle (1979), Solity and Bull (1987) and Bigge (1988). A valuable critique of the advantages and disadvantages of an objectives approach is provided by Miller and Seller (1990).

TASK ANALYSIS

Task analysis involves the process of breaking down a learning task into its component steps (teachable units), and ordering these steps into the most effective sequence to facilitate achievement of the instructional goal and performance objectives.

There are several steps involved in carrying out a task analysis. They may be summarized thus:

- The teacher personally performs the task several times to observe the actual steps involved.
- The teacher identifies any prerequisite knowledge or skills necessary for performing the task.
- The task should be analysed at a metacognitive level as well as a practical performance level. (What do I need to think about at this stage? How will I know if I'm doing this well? Is this step going to be easy or difficult?)

- The task should be broken down into teachable units which are small enough to be mastered by the student. For some students it may be possible to group two or more of these steps together.
- If necessary, prepare a flow-chart showing the sequence of steps and the prerequisite skills.

Task analysis: two examples

Example A

Domain: Self-help (dressing)
A skill is identified which the student needs to master: for example, dressing: putting on socks.

The goal is stated: 'The child will be able to put on own socks without adult assistance when these are handed to him or her.'

The actual task of putting on socks is then analysed. What are the identifiable steps or stages involved?

These steps are listed in logical sequence:

1   Child adopts suitable position with knee raised (on floor; on chair; edge of bed; etc.).
2   Child picks up sock.
3   Identifies open end of sock.
4   Slides toes into open end while enlarging the opening with both hands.
5   Pulls sock towards heel of foot.
6   Pulls sock up to correct height.

(This example may be too simple. It assumes many prerequisite skills before step 1.)

The check-list of steps thus constructed is used to determine precisely how much of the task the child can do already (for example, he or she may achieve up to stage 5 but not beyond). A specific short-term performance objective is then stated for that child (usually based on the next step in the sequence).

The dressing example used above can also serve to illustrate the principle of 'back chaining'. In back chaining, the child actually masters a skill step by step, working in reverse order. For example, perhaps he/she cannot put on a sock. At first the adult puts the sock on the child's foot and does everything apart from pulling it up (step 6). The child does only the last action. When this is mastered, the child has to complete stages 5 and 6, then 4, 5, 6, etc., until finally, after a period of time, the child does all the steps set out in the example and successfully puts on the socks.

Example B

Domain: Mathematics: (TU subtraction 40)
$$-17$$
Steps involved in carrying out the procedure:

1 Identify the problem as subtraction.
2 Identify starting point.
3 Recognize that 7 cannot be subtracted directly from 0.
4 Regroup from tens column.
5 Cross out 4 and write 3 tens.
6 Place 1 ten before the zero (10).
7 Subtract 7 from 10.
8 Write 3.
9 Subtract 1 from 3 in tens column.
10 Write 2.
11 Read answer correctly as 23.
12 Check: $17 + 23 = 40$.

Task analytic approaches have been used intuitively by teachers for many years. It is only with the rise of interest in more precise methods of instructional planning that the approach has received more overt attention. It is now recognized that the tasks and skills to be presented to students with learning difficulties need to be precisely analysed and taught in small, incremental steps. When teachers do modify tasks in this way, children with learning difficulties experience greater success (Cohen and Lynch 1991). The fact that effective teachers analyse learning tasks carefully may account for their success in minimizing failure rates (Ainscow and Tweddle 1979).

There is, of course, a limit to how far one can go with this step-by-step reduction of the curriculum without creating separate learning tasks which, in themselves, are meaningless (Iano 1990). For this reason, task analysis is not regarded highly by some teachers. It looks too mechanistic to be appropriate for human learning and development. Some would argue quite rightly that we don't usually learn to do something by gradually learning all the separate 'bits' which can be identified in the total performance. We do tend to learn many things in rather holistic, all-embracing ways, not in the step-by-step sequential pattern suggested in task analysis schedules. Learning is random as well as sequential. Many of the most worthwhile outcomes of the educational process are just not capable of detailed analysis or expression in specific performance terms. Teachers shouldn't feel badly about this, provided that they think out their teaching sequences and objectives where appropriate. As a general rule, the greater the degree of disability experienced by the student, the more valuable it is to task analyse and adapt the curriculum.

Over to you

- Generate two long-term goals for the environmental education curriculum area.
- Generate two long-term goals for a *social skills* curriculum.
- Rewrite the following goals as student performance objectives:
  To teach the students how to construct an equilateral triangle.
  Brian will learn to tell the time.
  The students will understand the dangers of chemical pollution.
  Sarah will learn to catch a ball.
- In this chapter it was said that students should help to formulate their own learning objectives, when possible. Why would this be useful?
- Carry out a task analysis to identify the component steps involved in locating a specific word in a dictionary and writing down the definition.
- Identify the prerequisite skills required for using a dictionary efficiently.
- What prerequisite skills would be involved in each of the two 'task analysis' examples given above?

SELECTING CURRICULUM CONTENT

To help teachers select appropriate content for inclusion in the class curriculum or in individualized programmes, Brennan (1985) proposed a '4R test'. To apply the test, consider the proposed content under the following headings:

- Is it real? Does it figure in the child's life experiences?
- Is it relevant? Will it be of value to the child to know this or be able to do this?
- Is it realistic? Is the goal achievable for this student?
- Is it rational? Can the purpose of learning be made clear to the student?

These questions are not unique to planning curricula for students with special needs. Miller and Seller (1990) provide a very similar list for selecting curriculum content for *any* students.

In order to appraise curriculum content in this way it is first necessary to appraise students in terms of their relevant characteristics. Ainscow and Muncey (1990) suggest that the following factors should be examined:

- Previous experience – what sorts of experience has the student had inside and out of school?
- Current knowledge and skills – what does the student understand, and what is he or she able to do?
- Interests – what are the student's particular interests and enthusiasms?
- Attitudes – does the student have any positive or negative feelings which may influence learning?

Some characteristics of the students will significantly influence the priorities given to certain aspects of the curriculum. For example, students with hearing impairment will always need to have maximum attention devoted to vocabulary development and oral–aural communication skills. Students with intellectual disability will always need attention given to self-help and daily living skills, social skills and communication. Students with physical disabilities which severely restrict mobility and access to real-life learning experiences and social contact will need curriculum content which is designed to compensate for this deprivation of experience. Students with emotional disorders need a curriculum containing many success situations which consistently build confidence and self-esteem, develop self-management skills, and foster social and interpersonal communication. Lewis and Doorlag (1991) suggest that high priority must be given to teaching emotionally or behaviourally disordered students independent study skills.

Brennan (1985) suggests that some learning is so important that it should be regarded as core content which must be mastered by all children. Beyond this core there is a periphery of knowledge, skills, attitudes and values which it is desirable, but possibly not essential, for students to acquire. Special schools frequently organize their programmes under a 'core + enrichment' model, and design alternative curricula to ensure that core content is thoroughly covered. In recent years general education has also grappled with the notion of a core curriculum (Print 1992), and students with special needs are likely now to have to attempt to achieve within that mainstream core.

It cannot be denied that placement of students with disabilities in regular classrooms has made the task of identifying core content and adapting curricula much more difficult than it was when students were placed in special groups (Polloway *et al.* 1991). Perhaps one of the few advantages of a segregated programme was the opportunity it presented for designing a relevant *alternative* curriculum for students with special needs. The challenge of the 1990s is to modify mainstream curricula where necessary, and provide some individual educational programming for certain high-risk students.

INDIVIDUALIZED EDUCATION PLANS

The 1970s saw the advent of individualized education plans (IEPs) in the United States of America, as a direct result of Public Law 94–142: The Education of All Handicapped Children Act. Without necessarily using the term 'Individual Education Plan', and without the legal requirement to do so, several other countries have adopted a similar model (e.g. Australia, New Zealand); and in Great Britain the process of producing a statement indicating a student's special educational needs serves much the same purpose under the 1981 Education Act.

The IEP, as required by law in America, is drawn up through a process of consultation and collaboration between class teacher, special education teacher, parents and school principal, with input from relevant specialists (psychologist, speech pathologist, physiotherapist, etc.). Taking into account the child's current strengths and weaknesses, long-term goals and short-term objectives are carefully prepared. Time lines are established for the achievement of objectives and for regular review of progress. Personnel responsible for implementation and monitoring of the programme are identified.

The underlying concepts of IEP development are philosophically and educationally sound. In theory at least the IEP holds education service providers accountable, and offers the best possible chance for a student to receive an appropriate educational programme. It also allows parents to have some input into the process of curriculum adaptation.

The broad framework of the IEP should serve as a basis for subsequent development of individualized instructional plans at classroom level relating to specific areas of the curriculum. For example, what modifications, if any, are necessary to the learning objectives for social studies, for physical education, for science, or for geography? Equally important, the IEP should help to identify areas of the curriculum where no modification is required and where the student can be counted in with the general class. Notwithstanding the legal requirement, and the potential value of generating IEPs, in reality the process does not always achieve the ideal (Ashman and Elkins

1990). It is important for teachers and others involved in negotiating individual programmes for students with special needs to reflect upon some of the problems encountered in America. These problems are not insurmountable and should receive due attention in the coming years.

IEP-Panacea or paper tiger? (Westwood 1991)

A review of the literature dealing with the design, implementation and evaluation of individualized education plans has identified the following difficulties or weaknesses:

- Members of multidisciplinary teams frequently lack the experience or training to prepare collaborative plans using input from specialist areas and relating this to the curriculum.
- Too often, IEPs are based on the provision of one-to-one tuition or assistance, even when personnel are not available to provide this. IEPs must recognize the realities of class size.
- An IEP seems to be equated too readily with the notion of a totally different work programme for the student throughout the school day. IEPs should focus on inclusive practices, since it is in the student's interest to be part of the class programme whenever practicable.
- Recommendations in some IEPs are impressive, but unrealistic in terms of resources, time and outcomes.
- Resources and support are often promised at the planning stage but fail to materialize later.
- Plans are drawn up to satisfy the legal requirements, but then fail to be implemented.
- Negotiation and consultation are time-consuming, expensive and labour-intensive processes.
- Parents may lack confidence, knowledge and skills to participate fully, preferring to leave the decisions to others.

ADAPTING INSTRUCTION

Modifying the curriculum content, either by adapting the mainstream classroom programme or by providing individualized education plans, is only part of the solution in meeting students' special needs. It is also necessary to consider ways in which the actual process of instruction can be adapted where necessary for these students. Below there is a summary of the ways in which teachers can adjust their instructional procedures.

Adapting instruction

In Chapter 1 several suggestions were made to indicate how teachers can 'personalize' their approach within a whole-class or group lesson. Such adaptations to instruction should result in improved success rates for lower-ability students. The suggestions from Chapter 1 are summarized here, together with other adaptations described by Lewis and Doorlag (1991) and Cohen and Lynch (1991).

Demonstrations   Provide additional demonstrations for certain students, using a step-by-step approach.

Instructions   Clarify and shorten instructions. Provide clues or hints to facilitate student responses.

Practice   Give additional time to guided practice (e.g. by setting more practice items requiring more responses in the time available, by scheduling extra time for guided practice within the lesson, by using time outside the lesson for further practice and homework. Increasing successful response rates accelerates learning.

Assistance   Give more direct assistance and frequent feedback to some students during guided practice.

Questioning   Use different levels of complexity when asking questions to different students. At least 80 per cent of questions asked should be answered easily by all students. Ask many questions. Ask questions that build confidence (Clopton 1992).

Wait time   Allow a few seconds longer for the oral response from certain students.

Response mode   Do not rely solely on written responses. Consider other modes (e.g. drawing, selecting from multiple choice answers, tape recording, etc.).

Personal interests and abilities   Draw on personal interests and talents of students when possible.

Praising   Use more frequent and more descriptive praise for some students.

Rewards Increase incentives for some students by using reward systems and graphic charting of progress.

Work output Expect different quantity and quality of work from students.

Revision Provide more frequent reviews and revision for certain students.

Short-term goals For some students, set easily attainable goals within the lesson, and discuss these with the students.

Seating Ensure that students with attention difficulties, or students with sensory impairments, are seated where they can see or hear the teacher and the other students clearly. Seat students together who are least likely to antagonize or distract one another.

Student–teacher interaction Deliberately set out to interact more frequently and positively with lower ability students. Research findings suggest that teachers tend on average to spend much less time with these students in whole-class lessons.

MODIFYING INSTRUCTIONAL MATERIALS

Often a simple modification to teaching materials (worksheets, texts, diagrams, audio-tapes, etc.) allows a student with mild disabilities to access the mainstream curriculum without further adaptations. When selecting or modifying materials, consider alternative methods of presentation if reading and writing are major problem areas (e.g. use audio tape, video tape, computer programme, pictorial recording. Use graphic organizers and word webs to prepare the way for reading and writing. Preview texts before reading, etc.).

When preparing teaching materials apply the following principles from Currie (1990) and Meese (1992):

- highlight critical features;
- reduce extraneous detail;
- simplify language (use short sentences: substitute simple words for difficult terms);
- pre-teach critical vocabulary;
- provide clear illustrations or diagrams;

- use cues or prompts where responses are required;
- make response items self-correcting where possible;
- improve legibility of print and layout.

SUMMARY

This chapter provided suggestions for selecting curriculum content for students with special needs, and for adapting regular class programmes where appropriate. Attention was given to goal-setting, objective writing, task analysis and modification of instructional materials. The advantages of individual programming were briefly discussed, and some of the problems associated with the preparation of IEPs were presented.

Discussion points

- Take a particular curriculum domain (e.g. science) and translate the principles of adaptation given on pp. 176–7 for a specific topic to be taught in that domain.
- What problems are likely to be encountered by teachers when required to implement a national or state compulsory curriculum with all students?
- When students are withdrawn from class to receive individual or small group tuition, what impact is this likely to have upon their contact with the regular class curriculum? What can be done to minimize these problems?

Further reading

Ainscow, M. and Muncey, J. (1990) *Meeting Individual Needs*, London: Fulton.

Ashdown, R., Carpenter, B., and Bovair, K. (1991) *The Curriculum Challenge: Access to the National Curriculum for Pupils with Learning Difficulties*, London: Falmer.

Baine, D. (1982) *Instructional Design for Special Needs*, Milton Keynes: Open University Press.

Branwhite, T. (1986) *Designing Special Programmes*, London: Methuen.

Brennan, W.K. (1985) *Curriculum for Special Needs*, Milton Keynes: Open University Press.

Cook, R.E., Tessier, A. and Armbruster, V.B. (1987) *Adapting Early Childhood Curricula for Children with Special Needs*, Columbus: Merrill.

Goldstein, H. (ed.) (1981) *Curriculum Development for Exceptional Children*, San Francisco: Jossey-Bass.

Hart, M. (1992) 'Diversity at secondary level', British Journal of Special Education 19(1): 32–4.

Lewis, A. (1991) *Primary Special Needs and the National Curriculum*, London: Routledge.

Lewis, A. (1992) 'From planning to practice', *British Journal of Special Education* 19, 1: 24–7.

Morgenstern, F. (1981) *Teaching Plans for Handicapped Children*, London: Methuen.

Simmons, D.C., Fuchs, D. and Fuchs, L. (1991) 'Instructional and curricular requisites of mainstreamed students with LD', *Journal of Learning Disabilities* 24, 6: 354–9.

Chapter 12

School-based and regional support systems

Throughout the 1980s in-class support teaching increased. This was matched by a corresponding decline in withdrawal groups and special classes. Withdrawal was discouraged as it was seen as another form of segregation.

(Lewis and Howell-Jones 1991)

This final chapter looks briefly at the issues involved in providing support for children with special needs and for the regular class teachers who work with them. When the integration of disabled children was first undertaken in earnest in America, Australia and Britain it was always agreed that an effective support system would be crucial for the success of the venture. Unfortunately, in all three countries the amount of support available to a school or to a particular teacher is not always adequate. Many teachers with disabled children in their classes are left to work out their own salvation. Large schools, particularly those in metropolitan areas, may be able to justify extra staff and will have easy access to any centralized support service. Small schools, particularly in isolated rural areas, experience the greatest difficulty in receiving regular and effective help. Even when a support service is available there may be problems involved in its staffing or its operation.

In recent years the actual role of support teachers and special needs co-ordinators has changed considerably (Dyson 1991), and schools have been left more and more to their own devices in setting up support systems to meet students' special needs.

It will be useful at this point to consider what a school can do to help itself cope with children demanding more than the ordinary amount of assistance.

HELPING STRATEGIES WITHIN THE CLASSROOM

One of the major problems faced by the teacher who has a child with a learning difficulty or disability placed in the regular class is how to organize in such a way that, if necessary, he or she can spend a little time with that child each day. This individual attention must not be achieved at the expense of other children in the group. The following options are worth consideration:

- peer tutoring;
- cross-age tutoring;
- teacher aides and para-professionals;
- parents;
- volunteer helpers;
- secondary school, college and university students;
- team teaching;
- principal or deputy principal;
- support teachers;
- computer-assisted instruction.

Peer and cross-age group tutoring

Bloom (1978), in a book dealing with peer-group and cross-age tutoring, describes the creation of a system whereby students can help each other to learn. This should not always be seen as 'the more able helping the less able' but rather as students working in the role of tutor and tutee and applying the principle, 'One who teaches also learns'. The value of peer tutoring is well documented (Cole and Chan 1990).

All the advocates of peer-group or cross-age tutoring stress the importance of having preparation sessions for the tutors so that they may adopt appropriate skills and techniques. Bloom has written:

In my own work in training tutors for peer tutoring at the elementary school level, I have found that the tutors need:
(a) Clear directions as to what they are to do and how they are to do it.
(b) A specific learning task and specific instructional materials for that task.
(c) A model of appropriate tutoring behaviours for the task.
(d) An opportunity to role play or practise with feedback and correction and possibly, a second opportunity to review the model and practise further.

(e) Some opportunity to make a choice of materials or games and even the possibility of creating or reinterpreting learning materials.

To meet these conditions, where the student tutor has already learned the content to be taught, only a short training period is necessary.

(1978: 11)

Peer-group tutoring at various ability levels has the advantage of reducing the time a teacher needs to spend interacting with a whole class. It thus increases the amount of time he or she has to work directly with students who have learning problems. Alternatively, a child with a problem, for example in mathematics, reading or writing, may well be helped very efficiently by a friend in the class or by a child from a higher grade. Many schools make use of older children to help younger children, to the benefit of both. It appears that the 'tutors' use simple, direct language and demonstrate more rapidly and effectively what is required than do many teachers. Payne (1991) reports great success in using peer-tutoring at secondary level not only in language arts but also in science and mathematics. Her system is so well accepted by the students that those with learning difficulties now take the initiative and ask for a tutor to assist them.

Teacher aides and para-professionals

An aide can either work individually with the child on material and activities planned by the teacher, or the aide could supervise in a general way the rest of class on work set by the teacher while the teacher works with the child. The aide should not be expected to determine what the child needs – that is clearly the teacher's responsibility.

Aides can fulfil the role of 'trusted adults' who have time to listen to individual children's interests and worries. They are therefore instrumental in improving the child's communication skills, while acting as counsellor and friend.

Parents

Many schools now involve parents in the educational programme. The parents usually require some degree of training and preparation by the teacher in order to be used to maximum advantage (e.g. how to talk with children and be encouraging; how to listen to children read; how to operate paired reading or conference writing sessions; how to use particular word-building, spelling or number games, etc.). The suggested training to be given to peer tutors described above might apply equally to parent helpers. This structured use of parental involvement appears to yield the best results in terms of gains in student achievement (Topping 1991).

Parents are not necessarily natural teachers, particularly of their own children. Without some initial guidance on strategies for working with children, parents tend to require them to perform *perfectly* in tasks such as reading, writing and spelling, and are too critical and negative, rather than encouraging in their feedback. In reading they tend to have students focus attention too much on isolated words or letters, rather than helping them develop strategies for using context and reading for meaning (Builder 1991). Similarly, parents tend to want students to read for unreasonably long periods of time, particularly when tutoring the child at home. With guidance they can become much more effective in their supporting role, and can grow in both confidence and competence.

Parental involvement need not be confined to the reading programme. Hawkins (1991) reports very positive effects when using parents as tutors in mathematics.

The involvement of parents in schools can have some real benefits for the parents as well as the students with whom they work (Payne 1991). They develop an understanding of the aims of the school and of the methods being used. They learn new approaches they can use at home (e.g. in managing behaviour and in encouraging reading). They can share interests and concerns with other parents; and if their own child has a learning difficulty they can often be relieved to discover that many other students have problems too. They grow in confidence as people and establish a much more positive relationship with the teachers. As Wildlake has said, 'When teachers and parents acknowledge their complementary expertise and arrange to share it, the result can be an educational institution richer in experience, innovative in its day-to-day practices, and more responsive to change in a democratic society' (1987: 27).

Volunteer helpers

Volunteers are often used to excellent advantage in both special schools and regular classrooms. With unemployment running at a high level, many volunteers could be found for such a role. Some retired people who wish to remain active have been used very successfully as tutors in secondary school programmes and as mentors in gifted children's projects. The preparation they need is similar to that described for peer tutors and parents.

Secondary school and college students

Many high school students are gaining experience from working with children in kindergartens and junior primary schools. This is usually as part of a work-experience or community-involvement programme for senior students. If their presence is timetabled on a regular basis, the teacher can make use of their services for group work or individual help.

Team teaching

If two or more teachers are prepared to work together for at least part of each day, the organizational options are at once increased. Quite large groups may be taken for certain activities (e.g. films, TV, story, etc.) by one teacher, so releasing the other to work with quite small groups of individuals. Team teaching also allows teachers to discuss and share their problems, and to learn from one another.

Principal or deputy

The head teacher or deputy may take a regular time slot with the class thus releasing the teacher for individual work with certain children.

Support teachers

Usually if a child with special needs is to be integrated into the class, the services of a special education support teacher will be provided for at least a few hours a week. Some aspects of this support service have already been mentioned above; others are dealt with in more detail later in the chapter.

Computer-assisted instruction

The use of computers has already been discussed in chapters on literacy and numeracy. In effect, a computer can act as an additional 'person' in the classroom, providing instruction and giving feedback. Students may work collaboratively in pairs at the computer, or parents or volunteers may elect to work with certain students. With some students receiving computer-assisted instruction there is at once the possibility to reduce the class size and allow for more individual contact from the teacher.

THE RESOURCE ROOM MODEL

In some schools, children who have been mainstreamed may still need to receive additional help from personnel outside the classroom setting. The resource room model as a school-based support system appears to meet the needs of some schools. Sceptics will argue that that is nothing more than the old 'remedial withdrawal room' given a more palatable name. Advocates will point out that the resource room operates in a much more flexible manner than the traditional remedial room and provides a base from which the support or resource teacher can operate. Children may go to the room for special help, but it is equally likely that the teacher may go to the child's classroom to provide the needed help. The resource room is also seen as the collecting house for materials and ideas for the *most able* as well as the least able students.

Resource room programming may involve the resource teacher in setting up such strategies as peer-group or cross-age group tutoring in specific classes. Resource teachers can produce greater impact when they manage a support system involving other personnel than when they merely instruct small groups or individuals themselves.

In some of the American literature dealing with resource rooms, it is quite clear that in certain schools they do function much as a traditional remedial centre, catering mainly for children with reading problems. For that reason they must be open to the same doubts in terms of long-term benefits which have plagued remedial programmes, i.e. that the children make gains while in the programme but fail to maintain these, or even regress, as soon as the extra help is withdrawn. Doubts have been voiced about the overall success of resource-room programming. The problems appears to be that much of individualized special help given in the resource room does not transfer to the regular classroom, since the learning environment there remains unchanged. Demands in the regular classroom may still be too great for the particular child's existing skills, so that for every half-hour spent in the resource room in a success situation, five hours may be spent failing in the regular class. This is why there has been a shift towards providing support for the children within the regular class situation (Lavers, Pickup and Thomson 1986).

Sindelar and Deno (1978) reviewed seventeen studies concerned with the efficacy of resource programming. They conclude that in the academic domain, learning disabled and mildly disturbed children seem to benefit more than intellectually disabled children from resource room programmes.

ESTABLISHING MUTUAL HELP NETWORKS

The time has gone when schools could expect to receive such a comprehensive support service from visiting special education teachers that all they needed to do was identify the children and pass over the problem for outsiders to solve. Most schools cannot easily call upon regular outside help and must now look far more thoroughly at their own resources, using existing expertise within the school to establish a support system for staff and students. This usually calls for a high degree of teamwork and willing collaboration among the teachers, but has the advantage of forcing the school to acknowledge and address its own problems.

One scheme which appears to operate well is the establishment of a 'teacher assistance team' (TAT) within the school (Hayek 1987; Chalfant and Pysh 1989). The 'team' is made up from willing staff who have some basic knowledge of special education strategies, or who understand some of the flexible ways of managing classroom procedures for a wide ability range. A teacher who has a student with learning or behaviour difficulties is encouraged to join the team and to share the problem with colleagues. By calling upon their existing pool of knowledge and experience, many classroom problems can be solved or minimized by team action and mutual help between teachers. Referral of a problem to a TAT usually brings far more rapid action and assistance than referral to outside agencies could achieve. The system is also said to help individual teachers to become more confident in sharing problems with colleagues, and eventually more self-sufficient in dealing with students' difficulties.

Networks for mutual help can extend beyond the school itself. It is extremely helpful for staff with similar concerns across a number of different schools to be able to contact one another to discuss problems and possible solutions. Sometimes such networks become established informally; but it should be part of the role of visiting advisers to help establish contact between teachers with similar professional needs.

WHOLE-SCHOOL APPROACHES

Increased interest is being shown in Australia, the United States and Great Britain in what is called 'the whole-school approach' to special needs (Ainscow and Florek 1989). This usually involves the writing and adoption of a whole-school policy on children with special needs, and also seeks to find practical ways of involving all staff in catering for the needs of these students. To a large extent it is a 'survival response' to the change of emphasis from segregated to integrated placement for disabled students in times of shrinking resources.

The establishment and maintenance of a whole-school approach is difficult. Not only is the approach exceedingly difficult to implement, but in practice 'the whole school approach may consist of no more than cosmetic changes which actually serve to sustain the status quo' (Dyson 1990: 116). Unless the approach results in some major rethinking of the curriculum to make it more inclusive of a diverse range of learners, and changes to school organization, it is unlikely to be much more than a grafting-on of traditional 'remedial' teaching to general classroom work.

The ways in which a school can marshal its resources, both material and personnel, should be formalized to some extent through the establishment of a school policy created by, and genuinely 'owned' by, the whole school staff (Ashman and Elkins 1990). The key components of a school policy on special education needs are summarized below.

Bines (1989) has concluded that developing a whole-school policy document is a useful and important method for clarifying beliefs, accepting responsibility at school level and making the best use of available expertise and resources.

Elements of a school policy

Situational analysis   Describe the school population, with particular reference to special educational needs and available personnel and resources.

Belief statements   Summarize the consensus of opinion within the school staff concerning the identification of students with special needs, and the most effective ways of meeting these needs in terms of instruction, management and placement. Link beliefs with existing policies on social justice and equal opportunities, etc.

Aims   Describe what the staff identify as the key aims to be achieved in providing some form of assistance to special-needs students.

Internal arrangements   Specify the range of options to be made available at classroom level and at school level (e.g. in-class support; withdrawal; resource room; teacher assistance teams; team teaching; learning assistance programmes; etc.).

Links with outside agencies and services   Identify all outside sources of assistance and the procedures to be used in liaising with them. Co-ordination of services.

Staff roles and responsibilities   Indicate clearly who is directly responsible for identification, referral, decision-making and resource allocation. Specify how mutual help networks can operate and ensure mechanisms exist to enable them to be established. Identify key staff to arrange in-service training and development programmes.

Assessment and reporting procedures   How will student progress be determined? How will it be recorded and reported? How will support systems be evaluated over time? Establish time lines.

Liaising with and working with parents   Specify how parental communications can be optimized, and how parents may become involved in educational programmes related to special-needs students.

MULTIDISCIPLINARY APPROACHES

It has been realized for many years that the provision of special services for children with disabilities must be multidisciplinary and must involve co-operation between and among several professional groups. For example, when a child with a disability or impairment is placed in a regular class, his or her needs should be determined and agreed upon by at least the following individuals: regular class teacher, special education teacher (for example, support teacher; visiting teacher for hearing impaired services), guidance officer (educational psychologist), school principal and the child's parents. In some cases an even more varied group will need to consult together to plan the best approach to use to optimize the child's chances of success. As a result of consensus on the child's needs, short-term objectives and longer-term goals are formulated; and the regular class programme is adapted or an individualized education plan is designed (Lewis and Doorlag 1991). This type of group consultation and planning is not alway easy to achieve, of course, and one has to realize that the more individuals are involved, the slower will be the process of decision-making, and the greater the likelihood that the eventual outcome will be a compromise (Moore *et al.* 1989).

One of the new demands placed on teachers by the team approach is the emerging role of 'educational synthesizer'. In other words, the teacher is the key professional who can combine the observations and recommendations of other team members and incorporate them into daily procedures for the student. Phillips and McCullough (1990) indicate clearly that teachers should reject suggested programmes or interventions if they feel that they are unrealistic in their demands. The teacher is obviously the person who needs to monitor the practicalities of suggestions made *before* they become 'written policy' in terms of a child's programme plan.

What do regular class teachers need to know?

What is it that regular class teachers need to know in order to judge the suitability of the recommendations from multidisciplinary teams; and what do they need to be able to do in terms of implementation?

The teacher with a disabled child in his or her class needs to know:

- how to establish specific objectives for the child in both the academic and the social areas; and how to use these objectives as the basis for regular assessment of progress;
- how to teach diagnostically and adapt teaching procedures to match the characteristics and needs of the child;
- how to provide learning situations which will enable the child to be 'counted in' as much as possible with the other children and make a contribution to the lessons (instructional integration);
- how to create situations where social skills and group-working skills are developed through interaction between the child and the peer group (social integration);
- how to plan and implement individual assignments or tasks if these are necessary for the child in order to provide training to overcome specific areas of weakness (individual programming);
- how to train a child in self-management skills and how to encourage independence and initiative;
- how to liaise effectively with parents in order to establish a situation of mutual trust and mutual help;
- how to liaise with specialists where necessary (e.g. speech therapist; psychologist);
- how to make optimum use of available support (both material and personnel);
- how to apply the strategies and tactics which are associated with high-quality education for all children.

Hegarty has commented: 'Particular care must be taken with monitoring pupils' progress and ensuring that their overall programme is balanced'(1982: 102). 'Balance' in this context involves all of the following:

- sufficient group activities to foster social development and acceptance;
- sufficient guidance to provide help for the child without maintaining his or her dependence;
- sufficient opportunity for the child to show initiative, develop self-management skills and discover areas of strength and interest.

THE ROLE OF THE SUPPORT TEACHER AND SPECIAL NEEDS ADVISER

The support teacher is in the school to provide a service to children with special needs by assisting the classroom teacher develop or adapt appropriate learning programmes to cater for exceptional children. He or she may spend time teaching children individually or in small groups within the classroom or in withdrawal situations. The support teacher works in co-operation with the class teacher and his or her work should supplement the regular class teacher's programme, not replace it (Lewis and Howell-Jones 1991).

The following duties are usually seen as part of the support teacher's role.

- Educational assessment and diagnosis using formal and informal methods in conjunction with information provided by specialists or agencies.
- Collating and disseminating such information.
- Regular discussion with class teachers about suitable educational programmes and activities for children with special needs.
- The provision or loan of resource materials to assist with the teaching of specific skills or concepts where necessary.
- Regular evaluation of the progress made by children receiving direct support; and the keeping of appropriate records.
- Teaching of individuals or small groups within the classroom or elsewhere.
- Team teaching with the regular class teacher.
- Taking the class while the class teacher works with a small group.
- Providing some school-based in-service staff development seminars.

If support teachers are working across a region they should be deployed in such a way that they do not have too many schools or too many children to service. Efficiency will be lessened if the service is spread too thinly. It is best that a thorough job be done intensively in a small number of schools or with a small number of students for a viable period. As class teachers become more adaptive in their approach to children with special needs it should be possible to withdraw much of the direct help which was required initially.

The role of the special needs adviser or co-ordinator is increasingly becoming one of consultant on general matters of curriculum and teaching (Dyson 1990), and change-agent to influence teachers' attitudes toward students with special needs (Kelly 1991). They also have a major role in helping to generate whole-school policies in relation to students with special needs (Malone 1991), and to provide in-service professional development for their colleagues (Dyson 1991).

WHAT DO SUPPORT TEACHERS AND ADVISERS NEED TO KNOW?

Regardless of whether a special education teacher provides help to a regular class teacher via a resource room programme, team teaching, through advice or through any combination of these, certain issues are important. Little (1978) highlighted the vital importance of support and resource teachers having what he calls 'change-agent skills'. They need to be able to relate appropriately to the teachers with whom they work and consult, and with school principals who may be the key individuals in agreeing or not agreeing to vary organizational patterns, provide particular materials or set up and support specific programmes. The 'change-agent/support teacher' role is a very difficult one. To be able to relate to and influence the behaviour of colleagues requires enormous tact and subtlety. One of the most obvious temptations for the support teacher is 'coming the expert'. The 'I-know-all-there-is-to-know-about-the-things-you-don't-understand-or-can't-cope-with' attitude will not establish the necessary helping relationship through mutual trust. From the first moment of contact with a teacher who has requested advice or help, the support teacher should establish the idea that he or she is there to work out possible solutions or strategies jointly, that there are no ready-made answers or panaceas, but that *together* they will try various solutions (Lewis and Howell-Jones 1991).

It is vital that the support teacher recognizes from the start that a teacher who seeks help has certain attitudes and expectations concerning the child referred for special help. These attitudes and expectations may be very positive and very realistic, or they may be totally unrealistic. That teacher will also have certain expectations of the support teacher which may be unrealistic. Whatever the attitude and expectations, they will not be changed overnight. Establishing a working relationship with the teacher should be seen as a process of mutual adaptation.

A SUPPORT TEACHER/ADVISER'S CHECK-LIST OF POSITIVE INTERACTIONS

Do be a good listener   Indicate clearly that you are genuinely interested in all that the teacher wants to tell you (even if you don't, at the time, agree with some of what is said). Your role as a listener will be conveyed more by non-verbal cues than by anything you say. Such things as eye contact, facial expression, physical stance and proximity to the speaker are all important. To get others to talk, you need to talk less yourself and to ask open-ended questions which invite longer answers.

Do seek information which is to the point   For example, ask to see examples of a child's work or school report. Discuss these. Ask for more detail about some of what is said (e.g. if the teacher has described some incidents of bad behaviour, ask if he or she knows what triggers them off; do they happen at the same time of day; or in the same type of lesson; or the same type of classroom grouping? etc.).

Do find something in the classroom or lesson to praise   Be precise in your reasons for praising it.

Do stress the need to 'collaborate' with the teacher   Agree from the start that you will work together to find solutions to the problems. Do not give the impression that you can work miracles.

Do try to 'read between the lines'   Ask yourself: 'Is this teacher really asking for help and advice, or hoping that I will confirm that there is nothing anyone can do?'; 'Where is this teacher's locus of control? Does the teacher really think that there is anything he or she can do to change the situation; or does she really believe that the child's difficulties are determined by factors beyond his or her control?'

Do bring the conversation around to focus on some attainable, short-term goal which you can both work towards during the coming week   It is helpful to set down some short-term objectives. Get the teacher to do something between your first and second visits. Perhaps get them to note more systematically when certain behaviours occur; or note more precisely what causes a child to produce such a small amount of written work in a given period; or determine precisely what phonic knowledge the child does have. You may be able to leave check-lists for the teacher to use, but make these fairly simple and quick to apply. If some ideas occur to you during your visit, make some suggestions but do not guarantee success and do not overload the teacher.

Do observe the child in various situations and try to spend some time working with him or her, even on the first visit.

Do allow the teacher to see what you are doing with the child when you work with him or her   This should not be in the form of a 'demonstration'; merely approach the task in a very open manner which enables the teacher to notice any particular strategies you use.

Do bring suitable resource materials and leave these with the teacher   However, avoid giving the impression that kits and games or worksheets are going to provide the answer to all the problems. Select your materials carefully: if they are too simple or too difficult and the child does not like them, the result will undermine your credibility.

Do work in close co-operation with other specialist personnel (e.g. educational psychologist, play therapist).

Do suggest the need for reassessment if you think that the child is not coping adequately, even with the extra support   The class teacher may feel reluctant to do this, as he or she may feel that it will reflect some degree of incompetence.

Do offer your services to any network of staff the school has established.

Do facilitate contact between teachers in different schools.

A SUPPORT TEACHER/ADVISER'S CHECK-LIST OF STRATEGIES TO AVOID

Don't take over the entire responsibility for a disabled student's programme.

Don't promise regular visiting services unless you are certain that you can provide these.

Don't bite off more than you can chew in terms of programme planning and the provision of resources.

Don't give the impression that certain methods or materials are infallible   If they fail, your credibility will be questioned and the teacher's confidence will be undermined.

Don't give the impression that you are pushed for time and must dash off to the next school.

Don't gloss over the amount of time and effort that may be needed if a certain approach is to be introduced   If the time involved is not feasible, look for other alternatives.

Don't openly criticize a teacher's way of working, organizing the classroom or dealing with difficulties   If change is necessary, it will need to be brought about by more subtle means.

Don't appear to be a mere courier of material and resources   Your colleagues may consider that you are too highly paid to act as a delivery agent.

Over to you

- Your school may have a significant number of children with special educational needs. How might you determine the size of the problem in your school?
- Given an ideal situation, how would you organize the timetable and deploy teaching staff and other available personnel to create a viable support system?
- Identify and list the main obstacles which would need to be overcome in order to implement such a programme in your school.
- If your school already has a support system established for children with special needs, evaluate its present positive and negative features. How might it be improved?

SUMMARY

This chapter has presented some basic models for school-level support services, and has indicated how schools may become more self-sufficient in meeting students' special educational needs. The contribution of outside agencies, advisers and special education support teachers has been considered. The specific roles and responsibilities of class teachers, support teachers and advisers have been presented in detail.

Discussion points

- Most research literature on problems involved in educational change (e.g. Fullan 1991) indicates that teachers are reluctant to change unless the benefits of doing so obviously outweigh the personal costs. Mainstreaming of students with disabilities frequently requires teachers to change in ways which they may perceive to be threatening and unreasonable. How might the problems involved in implementing an integration policy be minimized?
- Given an ideal situation, what outside services and personnel do you feel are necessary for really effective educational support for students with disabilities in the mainstream?
- Support teachers and advisers need to be knowledgeable across a broad range of issues in special and in regular education. Specify the key areas of knowledge which these teachers need to possess.

Further reading

Baker, D. and Bovair, K. (eds) (1989) *Making the Special Schools Ordinary*, London: Falmer.

Butt, N. (1991) 'A role for the SEN Coordinator in the 1990s', *Support for Learning* 6, 1: 9–14

Dean, J. (1989) *Special Needs in the Secondary School: The Whole School Approach*, London: Routledge.

Dissent, T. (1987) *Making the Ordinary School Special*, London: Falmer.

Morsink, C.V., Thomas, C.C. and Correa, V.I. (1991) *Interactive Teaming: Consultation and Collaboration in Special Programs*, New York: Macmillan.

Topping, K.J. and Wolfendale, S.W. (eds) (1985) *Parental Involvement in Reading*, London: Croom Helm.

West, J.F. and Idol, L. (1990) 'Collaborative consultation in the education of mildly handicapped and at-risk students', *Remedial and Special Education* 11, 1: 22–31.

Wiederholt, J.L., Hammill, D. and Brown, V. (1983) *The Resource Teacher* (2nd edn), Austin: Pro-Ed.

References

Adelman, H.S. and Taylor, L. (1987) *An Introduction to Learning Disability*, London: Scott Foresman.

Ainscow, M. and Florek, A. (1989) *Special Educational Needs: Towards a Whole School Approach*, London: Fulton.

Ainscow, M. and Muncey, J. (1990) *Meeting Individual Needs*, London: Fulton.

Ainscow, M. and Tweddle, D.A. (1979) *Preventing Classroom Failure: an Objective Approach*, Chichester: Wiley.

Allington, R.L. and McGill-Franzen, A. (1989) 'Different programs, indifferent instruction', in D.K. Lipsky and A. Gartner (eds), *Beyond Special Education*, Baltimore: Brookes.

Anderson, J. (1990) 'Computers as learning tools in remedial teaching', *Australian Journal of Remedial Education* 22, 2: 8–12.

Anderson, K.F. (1985) 'The development of spelling ability and linguistic strategies', *The Reading Teacher* 39, 2: 140–7.

Asch, A. (1989) 'Has the law made a difference?', in D. Lipsky and A. Gartner (eds) *Beyond Separate Education*, Baltimore: Brookes.

Ashcraft, M.H. (1985) 'Is it far fetched that some of us remember our number facts?', *Journal for Research in Mathematics Education* 16, 2: 99–105.

Ashdown, R., Carpenter, B. and Bovair, K. (1991) *The Curriculum Challenge*, London: Falmer.

Asher, S.R. and Dodge, K.A. (1986) 'Identifying children who are rejected by their peers', *Developmental Psychology* 22, 4: 414–49.

Ashman, A. and Conway, R. (1989) *Cognitive Strategies for Special Education*, London: Routledge.

Ashman, A. and Elkins, J. (eds) (1990) *Educating Children with Special Needs*, New York: Prentice Hall.

Au, W.K. and Bruce, M. (1990) 'Using computers in special education', *Australian Journal of Remedial Education* 22, 1: 13–18.

Auten, A. (1983) 'Help for reluctant writers', *Language Arts* 60, 7: 921–6.

Baarda, W. (1982) 'The place of phonics', *Australian Journal of Reading* 5, 3: 166–7.

Baker, E.L., Herman, J.L. and Yeh, J.P. (1981) 'Fun and games; their contribution to basic skills instruction', *American Educational Research Journal* 18, 1: 83–92.

Ball, E.W. and Blachman, B.A. (1991) 'Does phonemic awareness training in kindergarten make a difference in early word recogntion and developmental spelling?', *Reading Research Quarterly* 26, 1: 49–66.

Baroff, G.S. (1991) *Developmental Disabilities*, Austin: Pro-Ed.

Barone, D. (1992) 'Whatever happened to spelling?', *Reading Psychology* 13, 1: 1–17.

Beattie, I.D. (1986) 'Modelling operations and algorithms', *Arithmetic Teacher* 33, 6: 23–8.

Bendell, D., Tollefson, N. and Fine, M. (1980) 'Interaction of locus of control and the performance of learning disabled adolescents', *Journal of Learning Disablilities* 13, 2: 83–6.

Bentley, D. (1990) *Teaching Spelling: Some Questions Answered*, Earley: University of Reading.

Berrill, R. (1982) 'The slow learner and the gifted child', in M. Cornelius *Teaching Mathematics*, London: Croom Helm.

Bigge, J. (1988) *Curriculum-based Instruction for Special Education Students*, Mountain View: Mayfield.

Bines, H. (1989) 'Whole school policies at primary level', *British Journal of Special Education* 16, 2: 80–2.

Bloom, S. (1978) *Peer and Cross-age Tutoring in the School*, Hawthorn, Victoria: Australian Council for Educational Research.

Borkowski, J.G. (1992) 'Metacognitive theory: a framework for teaching literacy, writing and math skills', *Journal of Learning Disabilities* 25, 4: 253–7.

Bos, C. (1988) 'Process-oriented writing: instructional implications for mildly handicapped students', *Exceptional Children* 54: 521–7.

Bourke, S. (1981) 'Community expectations of numeracy in schools', *SET Research Information for Teachers, No. 1*, Hawthorn, Victoria: Australian Council for Educational Research.

Bowd, A. (1990) *Exceptional Children in Class* (2nd edn), Melbourne: Hargreen.

Boyle, G. (1990) 'Time out: a remedial strategy', in S. Butler (ed.) *The Exceptional Child*, Sydney: Harcourt Brace Jovanovich.

Brandt, R.S. (1985) 'Success through adaptive education', *Educational Leadership* 43, 1: 3.

Brennan, W.K. (1985) *Curriculum for Special Needs*, Milton Keynes: Open University Press.

Brophy, J.E. (1979) 'Teacher behaviour and student learning', *Educational Leadership* 37, 1: 33–8.

Bryant, P. and Bradley, L. (1985) *Children's Reading Problems*, Oxford: Blackwell.

Builder, P. (1991) *Exploring Reading: Empowering Readers with Special Needs*, Hawthorn, Victoria: Australian Council for Educational Research.

Burmeister, L.E. (1978) *Reading Strategies for Middle and Secondary School Teachers*, Reading, Mass: Addison-Wesley.

Burns, M. (1986) 'Teaching "what to do" in arithmetic vs. teaching 'what to do and why'', *Educational Leadership* 43, 7: 34–8.

Burton, G.M. (1985) *Towards a Good Beginning: Teaching Early Childhood Mathematics*, Menlo Park: Addison-Wesley.

Butler, S. (1990) *The Exceptional Child*, Sydney: Harcourt Brace Jovanovich.

Butt, N. (1991) 'A role of the special needs coordinator in 1990s', *Support for Learning* 6, 1: 9–14.

Byrnes, D.A. (1984) 'Social isolates and the teacher', *Educational Forum* 48, 3: 373–81.

Calf, B. (1990) 'Educational implications', in S. Butler (ed.) *The Exceptional Child*, Sydney: Harcourt Brace Jovanovich.

Canino, F.J. (1981) 'Learned-helplessness theory', *Journal of Special Education* 15, 4: 471–84.

Carpenter, T.P. (1985) 'Research on the role of structure in thinking', *Arithmetic Teacher* 32, 6: 58–60.

Casazza, M.E. (1992) 'Teaching summary writing to enhance comprehension', *Reading Today* 9, 4: 26.

Cashdan, A. and Wright, J. (1990) 'Intervention strategies for backward readers', in P. Pumfrey and C. Elliott (eds) *Children's Difficulties in Reading, Spelling and Writing*, London: Falmer.

Cawley, J.E., Baker-Kroczynski, S. and Urban, A. (1992) 'Seeking excellence in mathematics education for students with mild disabilities', *Teaching Exceptional Children* 24, 2: 40–3.

Center, Y. and Bochner, S. (1990) 'Integration at the the pre-school level', in S. Butler (ed.) *The Exceptional Child*, Sydney: Harcourt Brace Jovanovich.

Chalfant, J.C. and Pysh, M.V. (1989) 'Teacher assistance teams: case studies', *Remedial and Special Education* 10, 6: 49–58.

Chall, J. (1989) 'Learning to read: the great debate ten years later', *Phi Delta Kappan* 70, 7: 521–38.

Chan, L. (1991) 'Metacognition and remedial education', *Australian Journal of Remedial Education* 23, 1: 4–10.

Chapman, J.W. and Tunmer, W.E. (1991) 'Recovering reading recovery', *Australian and New Zealand Journal of Developmental Disabilities* 17, 1: 59–71.

Church, J. and Langley, J. (1990) 'Behaviour disordered children', *SET Research Information for Teachers*, Hawthorn: Australian Council for Educational Research.

Clarke, D.J. (1992) 'Activating assessment alternatives in mathematics', *Arithmetic Teacher* 39, 6: 24–39.

Clay, M.M. (1985) *The Early Detection of Reading Difficulties* (3rd edn), Auckland: Heinemann.

Clay, M.M. (1990) 'The Reading Recovery Programme, 1984–1988', *New Zealand Journal of Educational Studies* 25, 1: 61–70.

Clopton, E.L. (1992) 'Ask questions that build confidence', *Mathematics Teacher* 85, 1: 30.

Clutterbuck, P.M. (1990) *The Art of Teaching Spelling*, Melbourne: Longman-Cheshire.

Cockcroft, W.H. (1982) *Mathematics Counts*, Report of Committee of Enquiry into the teaching of mathematics in schools, London: HMSO.

Cohen, N.J. and Minde, K. (1983) 'The hyperactive syndrome in kindergarten children', *Journal of Child Psychology and Psychiatry* 24, 3: 443–55.

Cohen, S.B., and Lynch, D.K. (1991) 'An instructional modification process', *Teaching Exceptional Children* 23, 4: 12–18.

Cole, P. and Chan, L. (1990) *Methods and Strategies for Special Education*, New York: Prentice Hall.

Coleman, M.C. and Gilliam, J.E. (1983) 'Disturbing behaviours in the classroom; a survey of teachers' attitudes', *Journal of Special Education* 17, 2: 121–9.

Conway, R., (1990) 'Behaviour disorders', in A. Ashman and J. Elkins (eds) *Educating Children with Special Needs*, New York: Prentice Hall.

Conway, R. and Gow, L. (1990) 'Moderate to mild disability: teaching and learning strategies', in S. Butler (ed.) *The Exceptional Child*, Sydney: Harcourt Brace Jovanovich.

Cook, R., Tessier, A. and Armbruster, V.B. (1987) *Adapting Early Childhood Curricula for Children with Special Needs* (2nd edn), Columbus: Merrill.

Cornoldi, C. (1990) 'Metacognitive control processes', *Learning Disability Quarterly* 13, 4: 245–55.

Cripps, C. (1978) *Catchwords. Ideas for Teaching Spelling*, Sydney: Harcourt Brace Jovanovich.

Cripps, C. (1983) 'A report of an experiment to see whether young children can be taught to write from memory', *Remedial Education* 18, 1: 19–24.

Cripps, C. (1990) 'Teaching joined writing to children on school entry as an agent for catching spelling', *Australian Journal of Remedial Education* 22, 3: 13–15.

Crux, S.C. (1991) 'HELP: A whole language literacy strategy that works', *Education Canada* 31, 2: 16–21.

Csapo, M. (1983) 'Effectiveness of coaching socially withdrawn and isolated children in specific social skills', *Educational Psychology* 3, 1: 31–42.

Currie, H. (1990) 'Making texts more readable', *British Journal of Special Education* 17, 4: 137–9.

Darch, C., Carnine, D. and Gersten, R. (1984) 'Explicit instruction in mathematics problem solving', *Journal of Educational Research* 77, 6: 351–9.

Davis, R.B. (1984) *Learning Mathematics*, London: Croom Helm.

DeFord, D.E. (1991) 'Fluency in initial reading instruction: reading recovery', *Theory into Practice* 30, 3: 201–10.

Dempster, F.N. (1991) 'Synthesis of research on reviews and tests', *Educational Leadership* 48, 7: 71–6.

Dickson, L., Brown, M. and Gibson, O. (1984) *Children Learning Mathematics: A Guide to Recent Research*, Eastbourne: Holt Rinehart & Winston.

Dixon, R. (1976) *Morphographic Spelling*, Chicago: Science Research Associates.

Dixon, R.C. (1991) 'An application of sameness analysis to spelling', *Journal of Learning Disabilities* 24, 5: 285–91.

Dole, J., Duffy, G., Roehler, L.R. and Pearson, P.D. (1991) 'Moving from the old to the new: research in reading comprehension', *Review of Educational Research* 61, 2: 239–64.

Donaldson, J. (1992) 'Whole Language: a working definition for administrators', *Reading Today* 9, 2: 18.

Doorlag, D.H. (1989) 'Students with learning handicaps', in R. Gaylord-Ross (ed.) *Integration Strategies for Students with Handicaps*, Baltimore: Brookes.

Dyer, C.(1991) 'An end to the slow lane: a critique of the term "slow learner"', *Support for Learning* 6, 2: 66–70.

Dykes, B. and Thomas, C. (1989) *Spelling Made Easy*, Sydney: Hale and Iremonger.

Dyson, A. (1990) 'Effecting learning consultancy: a future role for the special needs coordinator', *Support for Learning* 5, 3: 116–27.

Dyson, A. (1991) 'Rethinking roles, rethinking concepts: special needs teachers in mainstream schools', *Support for Learning* 6, 2: 51–60.

Eeds-Kniep, M. (1979) 'The frenetic fanatic phonic backlash', *Language Arts* 56, 8: 909–17.

Ekwall, E. (1985) *Locating and Correcting Reading Difficulties* (4th edn), Columbus: Merrill.

Ekwall, E.E. and Shanker, J.L. (1985) *Teaching Reading in the Elementary School*, Columbus: Merrill.

Eldredge, J.L. (1990) 'Increasing the performance of poor readers in the third grade with a group-assisted strategy', *Journal of Educational Research* 84, 2: 69–76.

Eldredge, J., Quinn, B. and Butterfield, D. (1990) 'Causal relationships between phonics, reading comprehension and vocabulary in the second grade', *Journal of Educational Research* 83, 4: 201–14.

Elkins, J. (1991) 'Current perspectives on learning difficulties', *Australian Journal of Remedial Education* 23, 4: 20–5.

Emblem, B. and Conti-Ramsden, G. (1990) 'Towards Level 1 – reality or illusion?', *British Journal of Special Education* 17, 3: 88–90.

Englehardt, J.M. (1982) 'Using computational errors in diagnostic teaching', *Arithmetic Teacher* 29, 8: 16–19.

Espiner, D., Wilton, K. and Glynn, T. (1985) 'Social interaction and acceptance of mildly retarded children in a mainstream setting', *Australian Journal of Special Education* 9, 2: 8–15.

Fennell, F. (1991) 'Diagnostic teaching: writing and mathematics', *Focus on Learning Problems in Mathematics* 13, 3: 39–50.

Finch, M. and Hops, H. (1983) 'Remediation of social withdrawal in young children', in C.W. LeCroy *Social Skills Training for Children and Youth*, New York: Haworth.

Fletcher, P. and Presland, J. (1990) 'Contracting to overcome adjustment problems', *Support for Learning* 5, 3: 153–8.

Flynn, J.M., Deering, W., Goldstein, M. and Mohammad, H.R. (1992) 'Electrophysiological correlates of dyslexic subtypes', *Journal of Learning Disabilities* 25, 2: 133–41.

Fordham, D. (1989) 'Flexibility in the National Curriculum', *British Journal of Special Education* 16, 2: 50–2.

Franco, D., Christoff, K., Crimmins, D. and Kelly, J. (1983) 'Social skills training for an extremely shy adolescent', *Behaviour Therapy* 14: 568–75.

Frank, A.R. and Brown, D. (1992) 'Self-monitoring strategies in arithmetic', *Teaching Exceptional Children* 24, 2: 52–3.

Franklyn, B. (ed.) (1987) *Learning Disability: Dissenting Essays*, London: Falmer.

Fullan, M. (1991) *The New Meaning of Educational Change*, London: Cassell.

Fuson, K.C. and Fuson, A.M. (1992) 'Instruction supporting children's counting on and counting up', *Journal for Research in Mathematics Education* 23, 1: 72–8.

Gable, R., Enright, B., and Hendrickson, J.M. (1991) 'Curriculum-based assessment and instruction in arithmetic', *Teaching Exceptional Children* 24, 1: 6–9.

Gagne, R.M. (1983) 'Some issues in the psychology of mathematics instruction', *Journal of Research in Mathematics Education* 14, 1: 7–18.

Gersten, R. and Carnine, D. (1986) 'Direct instruction in reading comprehension', *Educational Leadership* 48, 7: 70–8.

Gillet, S. and Bernard, M.E. (1989) *Reading Rescue* (2nd edn), Hawthorn, Victoria: Australian Council for Educational Research.

Ginsburg, H. and Baroody, A. (1983) *TEMA: Test of Early Mathematics Ability*, Austin: Pro-Ed.

Gloeckler, T. and Simpson, C. (1988) *Exceptional Students in Regular Classrooms*, Mountain View: Mayfield.

Gollasch, F.V. (1982) *Language and Literacy: Selected Writings of Kenneth Goodman*, London: Routledge.

Goodlad, J.I. and Oakes, J. (1988) 'We must offer equal access to knowledge', *Educational Leadership* 45, 5: 16–22.

Goodman, K.S. (1967) 'Reading: a psycholinguistic guessing game', *Journal of the Reading Specialist* 6: 126–35.

Goodman, K.S. (1986) *What's Whole in Whole Language,?* Portsmouth: Heinemann.

Goodman, K.S. (1989) 'Whole language is whole: a response to Heymsfeld', *Educational Leadership* 46, 6: 69–70.

Goswami, U. and Bryant, P. (1990) *Phonological Skills and Learning to Read*, Hove: Erlbaum.

Gow, L. and Ward, J. (1991) 'Progress towards integration: Impressions from a national review', *Australian Disability Review* 4–91: 8–19.

Graham, S. and Harris, K.R. (1989) 'Improving learning disabled students' skills at composing essays: self-instructional strategy training', *Exceptional Children* 56, 3: 201–14.

Graham, S., Harris, K.R. and Sawyer, R. (1987) 'Composition instruction with learning disabled students: self-instructional strategy training', *Focus on Exceptional Children* 20, 4: 1–11.

Graham, S. and MacArthur, C. (1988) 'Improving learning disabled students' skills at revising essays on a word processor', *Journal of Special Education* 22: 133–52.

Graves, D.H. (1981) 'Writing research for the eighties', *Language Arts* 58, 2: 197–206.

Graves, D.H. (1983) *Writing: Teachers and Children at Work*, Exeter: Heinemann.

Gresham, F.M. (1982) 'Social skills instruction for exceptional children', *Theory into Practice* 21, 2: 129–33.

Gresham, F.M. (1984) 'Social skills and self-efficacy for exceptional children', *Exceptional Children* 51, 3: 253–61.

Groff, P. (1990) 'An analysis of the debate: teaching reading without conveying phonic information', *Interchange* 21, 4: 1–14.

Gronlund, N.E. (1985) *Measurement and Evaluation in Teaching* (5th edn), New York: Macmillan.

Gross, H. and Gipps, C. (1987) *Supporting Warnock's Eighteen Percent*, London: Falmer.

Grossman, H.J. (1983) *Classification in Mental Retardation*, Washington DC: American Association on Mental Deficiency.

Gulliford, R. (1969) *Backwardness and Educational Failure*, Slough: NFER.

Gumblatt, L. and McClennen, S. (1991) 'Math is more than counting', in S. McClennen *Cognitive Skills for Community Living*, Austin: Pro-Ed.

Gurry, D. (1990) 'The physician and the politics of learning difficulties', in S. Butler (ed.) *The Exceptional Child*, Sydney: Harcourt Brace Jovanovich.

Haigh, G. (1977) *Teaching Slow Learners*, London: Temple Smith.

Hallahan, D.P. and Kauffman, J.M. (1986) *Exceptional Children* (3rd edn), Englewood Cliffs: Prentice Hall.

Hallahan, D.P. and Kauffman, J.M. (1991) *Exceptional Children* (5th edn), Englewood Cliffs: Prentice Hall.

Harris, K.R. and Pressley, M. (1991) 'The nature of cognitive instruction', *Exceptional Children* 57, 5: 392–403.

Harste, J.C., Short, K.G. and Burke, C. (1988) *Creating Classroom Authors*, Portsmouth: Heinemann.

Hasselbring, T.S. and Goin, L.I. (1989) 'Enhancing learning through microcomputer technology', in E.A. Polloway *et al. Strategies for Teaching Learners with Special Needs* (5th edn), Columbus: Merrill.

Hasselbring, T.S., Goin, L., and Bransford, J. (1988) 'Developing math automaticity in learning handicapped children: the role of computerized drill and practice', *Focus on Exceptional Children* 20, 6: 1–7.

Hawkins, W. (1991) 'Parents as tutors of mathematics', *Australian Journal of Remedial Education* 23, 4: 16–19.

Hayek, R.A. (1987) 'Teacher assistance teams', *Focus on Exceptional Children* 20, 1: 1–8.

Heddens, J.W. (1986) 'Bridging the gap between concrete and abstract', *Arithmetic Teacher* 33, 6: 14–17.

Hegarty, S. (1982) 'Integration and the comprehensive school', *Educational Review* 34, 2: 99–105.

Hewson, J. (1990) 'Paired spelling', *Support for Learning* 5, 3: 136–40.

Heymsfeld, C.R. (1989) 'Filling the hole in whole language', *Educational Leadership* 46, 6: 65–9.

Hickerson, B. (1992) 'Reading and thinking with content area texts', *Reading Today* 9, 3: 32.

Hickson, F. (1990) 'The socialization process', in S. Butler (ed.) *The Exceptional Child*, Sydney: Harcourt Brace Jovanovich.

Holdaway, D. (1982) 'Shared book experience: teaching reading using favourite books', *Theory into Practice* 21, 4: 293–300.

Holmes, E.E. (1990) 'Motivation: an essential component of mathematics instruction', in T.T. Cooney and C.R. Hirsch (eds) *Teaching and Learning Mathematics in the 1990s*, Reston: National Council of Teachers of Mathematics.

Horne, M.D. (1982) 'Facilitating positive peer interactions among handicapped and non-handicapped students', *Exceptional Child* 29, 2: 79–86.

Howell, K.W. and Morehead, M.K. (1987) *Curriculum-based Evaluation for Special and Remedial Education*, Columbus: Merrill.

Howell, S.C. and Barnhart, R.S. (1992) 'Teaching word problem solving at primary level', *Teaching Exceptional Children* 24, 2: 44–6.

Hughes, C.A., Korinek, L. and Gorman, J. (1991) 'Self-managment for students with mental retardation in public school settings: a research review', *Education and Training in Mental Retardation* 26, 3: 271–91.

Humes, A. (1983) 'Putting writing research into practice', *Elementary School Journal* 84, 1: 3–17.

Hynd, G., Marshall, R. and Gonzalez, J. (1991) 'Learning disabilities and presumed central nervous system dysfunction', *Learning Disability Quarterly* 14, 4: 283–96.

Iano, R.P. (1990) 'Special education teachers: technicians or educators?', *Journal of Learning Disabilities* 23, 8: 462–5.

Isaacson, S.L. (1987) 'Effective instruction in written language', *Focus on Exceptional Children* 19, 6: 1–12.

Jackson, M.S. (1987) 'The treatment of severe reading disability: dyslexia', *Australian Journal of Remedial Education* 19, 2: 10–16.

Jackson, M.S. (1991) *Discipline: An Approach for Teachers and Parents*, Melbourne: Longman-Cheshire.

Jenkins, J.R., Pious, C.B. and Jewell, M. (1990) 'Special education and the Regular Education Initiative: basic assumptions', *Exceptional Children* 56, 6: 479–91.

Johns, J. (1986) *Handbook for Remediation of Reading Difficulties*, Englewood Cliffs: Prentice Hall.

Johnson, D.W., Johnson, R.T. and Holubec, E. (1990) *Circles of Learning* (3rd edn), Edina, Minn. : Interaction Books.

Johnson, R. and Johnson, D.W. (1980) 'The social integration of handicapped students into the mainstream', in M.C. Reynolds *Social Environment of the Schools*, Reston: Council for Exceptional Children.

Johnson, R.T. and Johnson, D.W. (1991) 'Cooperative learning: the best of the one-room schoolhouse', *The Teacher Educator* 27, 1: 6–13.

Johnson, T. and Johnson, R. (1977) 'The use of comics in remedial teaching', in P. Widlake (ed.) *Remedial Education: Programmes and Progress*, London: Longman.

Johnson, T.D. and Louis, D.R. (1987) *Bringing it all Together*, Melbourne: Nelson.

Jones, G., Thornton, C. and Toohey, M. (1985) 'A multi-option programme for learning basic addition facts', *Journal of Learning Disabilities* 18, 6: 319–25.

Kamii, C. and Lewis, B.A. (1991) 'Achievement tests in primary mathematics: perpetuating lower-order thinking', *Arithmetic Teacher* 38, 9: 4–9.

Kavale, K., Forness, S., and Lorsbach, T. (1991) 'Definition for definitions of learning disability', *Learning Disability Quarterly* 14, 4: 257–66.

Keith, R.W. and Engineer, P. (1991) 'Effects of methylphenidate on the auditory processing abilities of children with Attention Deficit-Hyperactivity Disorder', *Journal of Learning Disabilities* 24, 10: 630–40.

Kelly, M. (1991) 'The role of learning support: a trefoil catalyst', *Support for Learning* 6, 4: 170–3.

Kemp, M. (1980) *Reading-language Processes: Assessment and Teaching*, Adelaide: Australian Reading Association.

Kemp, M. (1987) *Watching Children Read and Write*, Melbourne: Nelson.

Kerin, M. (1990) 'The writing process with a computer', *Australian Journal of Remedial Education* 22, 1: 25–6.

Kraayenoord, C.V. and Elkins, J. (1990) 'Learning difficulties' in A. Ashman and J. Elkins (eds) *Educating Children with Special Needs*, New York: Prentice Hall.

Lavers, P., Pickup, M. and Thomson, M. (1986) 'Factors to consider in implementing an in-class support system', *Support for Learning* 1, 3: 32–5.

Lawrence, E.A. and Winschel, J.F. (1975) 'Locus of control: implications for special education', *Exceptional Children* 41, 7: 483–9.

LeBlanc, J.F. (1977) 'You can teach problem solving', *Arithmetic Teacher* 25, 2: 16–20.

LeGere, A. (1991) 'Collaboration and writing in the mathematics classroom', *Mathematics Teacher* 84, 3: 166–71.

Leinhardt, G. (1986) 'Expertise in mathematics teaching', *Educational Leadership* 43, 7: 28–33.

Levy, F. (1990) 'The role of the child psychiatrist', in S. Butler (ed.) *The Exceptional Child*, Sydney: Harcourt Brace Jovanovich.

Lewis, A. (1991) *Primary Special Needs and the National Curriculum*, London, Routledge.

Lewis, G. and Howell-Jones, M. (1991) 'Perspectives on support teaching', *Education 3–13* 19, 3: 44–9.

Lewis, R.B. and Doorlag, D.H. (1987) *Teaching Special Students in the Mainstream* (2nd edn), Columbus: Merrill.

Lewis, R.B. and Doorlag, D.H. (1991) *Teaching Special Students in the Mainstream* (3rd edn), New York: Merrill.

Lindsley, O.R. (1992) 'Precision teaching: discoveries and effects', *Journal of Applied Behaviour Analysis* 25, 1: 51–7.

Little, T.L. (1978) 'The teacher-consultant model', *Journal of Special Education* 12, 3: 345–55.

Loughrey, D. (1991) 'Hands on computer experience and the child with special educational needs', *Support for Learning* 6, 3: 124–6.

Lovitt, T.C. (1991) *Preventing School Dropouts*, Austin: Pro-Ed.

Lynch, E.M. and Jones, S.D. (1989) 'Process and product: a review of the research on LD children's writing skills', *Learning Disability Quarterly* 12: 74–86.

Lyndon, H. (1989) 'I did it my way. An introduction to "OldWay: New Way"' *Australasian Journal of Special Education* 13, 1: 32–7.

Madden, N.A. and Slavin, R.E. (1983) 'Effects of co-operative learning on the social acceptance of mainstreamed academically handicapped students', *Journal of Special Education* 17, 2: 171–82.

Mager, R.F. (1975) *Preparing Instructional Objectives* (2nd edn), Belmont: Fearon.

Malone, G. (1991) 'Special needs forever', *Support for Learning* 6, 1: 15.

Malone, L.D., and Mastropieri, M.A. (1992) 'Reading comprehension instruction: summarization and self-monitoring', *Exceptional Children* 58, 3: 270–9.

Mather, N. (1992) 'Whole Language reading instruction for students with learning disabilities: caught in the crossfire', *Learning Disabilities Research and Practice* 7: 87–95.

McCormick, W. (1979) 'Teachers can learn to teach more effectively', *Educational Leadership* 37, 1: 59–60.

McKinney, J.D. (1988) 'Research on conceptually and empirically derived sub-types of specific learning disability', in M.C. Wang, M. Reynolds, and H.J. Walberg (eds) *Handbook of Special Education Vol 2*, Oxford: Pergamon.

McManus, M. (1989) *Troublesome Behaviour in the Classroom*, London: Routledge.

McNaughton, S. (1981) 'Low progress readers and teacher instructional behaviour', *Exceptional Child* 28, 3: 167–76.

Meese, R.L. (1992) 'Adapting textbooks for children with learning disabilities', *Teaching Exceptional Children* 24, 3: 49–51.

Merrett, F. and Wheldall, K. (1984) 'Classroom behaviour problems which junior school teachers find most troublesome' *Educational Studies* 10, 2: 87–92.

Meyen, E.L., Vergason, G.A. and Whelan, R.J. (1972) *Strategies for Teaching Exceptional Children*, Denver: Love.

Miles, E. and Miles, T.R. (1990) 'Specific difficulties in reading and spelling', in R.M. Gupta and P. Coxhead (eds) *Intervention with Children*, London: Routledge.

Miller, J.P. and Seller, W. (1990) *Curriculum Perspectives and Practice*, Toronto: Copp Clark.

Montague, M. and Candace, S. (1986) 'The effect of cognitive strategy training on verbal math problem solving performance', *Journal of Learning Disabilities* 19, 1: 26–33.

Moore, K., Fifield, D., Spira, D. and Scarloto, M. (1989) 'Child study team decision making in special education: improving the process', *Remedial and Special Education* 10, 4: 50–8.

Morgan, S.R. and Reinhart, J.A. (1991) *Interventions for Students with Emotional Disorders*, Austin: Pro-Ed.

Moyle, D. (1982) 'Recent developments in reading and their effects upon remedial education', *Remedial Education* 17, 4: 151–5.

Munro, J. (1977) 'Language abilities and mathematics performance', *Australian Journal of Remedial Education* 9, 3: 24–31.

Munro, J. (1981) 'Diagnosis in mathematics', *Australian Journal of Remedial Education* 13, 4: 11–20.

Murray-Seegert, C. (1992) 'Integration in Germany', *Remedial and Special Education* 13, 1: 34–43.

Naidoo, S. (1981) 'Teaching methods and their rationale', in G. Pavlidis and T. Miles, *Dyslexia Research and its Application to Education*, Chichester: Wiley.

Neale, M.D. (1988) *Neale Analysis of Reading Ability* (2nd edn), Hawthorn, Victoria: Australian Council for Educational Research.

Neale, M.D. (1989) *Neale Analysis of Reading Ability* (Revised British edition), Windsor: NFER-Nelson.

Nelson, D.W. (1983) 'Math is not a problem when you know how to visualize it', *Instructor* 93, 4: 54–5.

Newman, J.M. (1984) 'Language learning and computers', *Language Arts* 61, 5: 480–3.

Newman, J.M. and Church, S.M. (1990) 'Myths of whole language', *Reading Teacher* 44, 1: 20–6.

Olson, M.W. (1990) 'Phonemic awareness and reading achievement', *Reading Psychology* 11: 347–53.

Omanson, R.C. (1985) 'Knowing words and understanding texts', in T.W. Carr, *The Development of Reading Skills*, San Francisco: Jossey-Bass.

Paris, S.G. and Oka, E.R. (1986) 'Self-regulated learning among exceptional children', *Exceptional Children* 53, 2: 103–8.

Paris, S.G. and Winograd, P. (1990) 'Promoting metacognition and motivation in exceptional children', *Remedial and Special Education* 11, 6: 7–15.

Payne, E. (1991) 'Parents at work in special education in a middle school', *Australian Journal of Remedial Education* 23, 3: 27–9.

Perrott, E. (1982) *Effective Teaching*, London: Longman.

Peter, M. (1991) 'Progress report on curriculum change', *British Journal of Special Education* 18, 4: 162.

Peters, M.L. (1967) *Spelling: Caught or Taught?* London: Routledge.

Peters, M.L. (1985) *Spelling Caught or Taught: A New Look* (2nd edn), London: Routledge.

Phillips, V. and McCullough, L. (1990) 'Consultation-based programming: instituting a collaborative ethic in schools', *Exceptional Children* 45, 4: 291–304.

Pinsent, P. (1984) 'Some current perspectives on the writing of young children', *Early Child Development and Care* 14: 125–39.

Polloway, E.A., Patton, J., Payne, J. and Payne, R. (1989) *Strategies for Teaching Learners with Special Needs* (4th edn), New York: Merrill.

Polloway, E.A., Patton, J.R., Smith, J.D. and Roderique, T.W. (1991) 'Issues in program design for elementary students with mild retardation: emphasis on curriculum design', *Education and Training in Mental Retardation* 26, 2: 142–50.

Preen, B. and Barker, D. (1987) *Literacy Development*, Sydney: Harcourt Brace Jovanovich.

Print, M. (1992) *Curriculum Development and Design*, Sydney: Allen & Unwin.

Radlauer, E. and Radlauer, R. (1974) *Bowmar Reading Incentive Programe*, Glendale: Bowmar.

Reason, R. and Boote, R. (1986) *Learning Difficulties in Reading and Writing*, Windsor: NFER-Nelson.

Reetz, L.J. and Hoover, J.H. (1992) 'The acceptability and utility of five reading approaches as judged by middle school LD students', *Learning Disabilities Research and Practice* 7: 11–15.

Reid, D.K. and Stone, C.A. (1991) 'Why is cognitive instruction effective?', *Remedial and Special Education* 12, 3: 8–19.

Reisman, F.K. (1972) *A Guide to the Diagnostic Teaching of Arithmetic*, Columbus: Merrill.

Reynolds, M. and Dallas, S. (1991) *Reading Success*, Sydney: Prince of Wales Hospital.

Richards, P. (1982) 'Difficulties in learning mathematics', in M. Cornelius *Teaching Mathematics*, London: Croom Helm.

Richardson, S.O. (1992) 'Historical perspectives on dyslexia', *Journal of Learning Disabilities* 25, 1: 40–7.

Rickleman, R. and Henk, W.A. (1991) 'Parents and computers: partners in helping children learn to read', *Reading Teacher* 44, 7: 508–9.

Riley, J.D. and Pachtman, A. (1978) 'Reading mathematical word problems', *Journal of Reading* 21, 6: 531–4.

Rogers, G. (1982) *Truckin' with Kenny*, Berri: South Australian Education Department.

Rogers, H. and Saklofske, D.H. (1985) 'Self-concept, locus of control and performance expectations of learning disabled children', *Journal of Learning Disabilities* 18, 5: 273–8.

Rogers, W. (1989a) *Decisive Discipline*, Geelong: Institute of Educational Administration.

Rogers, W. (1989b) *Making a Discipline Plan*, Melbourne: Nelson.

Roseman, L. (1985) 'Ten essential concepts for remediation in mathematics', *Mathematics Teacher* 78, 7: 502–7.

Rosenshine, B. (1986) 'Classroom instruction', in N.L. Gage (ed.) *The Psychology of Teaching Methods*, Chicago: NSSE.

Rowe, M.B. (1986) 'Wait time: slowing down may be a way of speeding up', *Journal of Teacher Education* 37, 1: 43–50.

Salend, S.J. (1984) 'Factors contributing to the development of successful mainstreaming programs', *Exceptional Children* 50, 5: 409–16.

Salend, S. (1990) *Effective Mainstreaming*, New York: Macmillan.

Salmon, B. (1990) 'The role of games in the primary curriculum', *Teaching Mathematics* 15, 2: 24.

Salvia, J. and Hughes, C. (1990) *Curriculum-Based Assessment*, New York: Macmillan.

Sawyer, D.J. and Fox, B.J. (1991) *Phonological Awareness in Reading*, New York: Springer-Verlag.

Schunk, D.H. (1989) 'Self-efficacy and cognitive achievement', *Journal of Learning Disabilities* 22, 1: 14–22.

Searle, D. (1984) 'Scaffolding: who's building whose building?', *Language Arts* 61, 5: 480–3.

Sears, H.C. and Johnson, D.M. (1986) 'The effects of visual imagery on spelling performance', *Journal of Educational Research* 79, 4: 230–3.

Sewell, G. (1982) *Reshaping Remedial Education*, London: Croom Helm.

Sheppard, J.L. (1990) 'The CATCH project: a social skills training unit', in S. Butler (ed.) *The Exceptional Child*, Sydney: Harcourt, Brace Jovanovich.

Sileo, T.W. (1985) 'Cognitive approaches', in B. Gearheart (ed.) *Learning Disabilities: Educational Strategies* (4th edn), St Louis: Mosby.

Simmons, D.C., Fuchs, D. and Fuchs, L.S. (1991) 'Instructional and curricular requisites of mainstreamed students with learning disabilities', *Journal of Learning disabilities* 24, 6: 354–60.

Sindelar, P. and Deno, S.L. (1978) 'The effectiveness of resource programming', *Journal of Special Education* 12, 1: 17–28.

Sippola, A.E. (1985) 'What to teach for reading readiness', *Reading Teacher* 39, 2: 162–7.

Skemp, R. (1976) 'Relational understanding and instrumental understanding', *Mathematics Teaching* 77: 20–6.

Slade, D.L. (1986) 'Developing foundations for organizational skills', *Academic Therapy* 21, 3: 261–6.

Slavin, R.E. (1991) 'Synthesis of research on cooperative learning', *Educational Leadership* 48, 5: 71–82.

Smith, F. (1978) *Understanding Reading*, New York: Holt, Rinehart & Winston.

Smith, F. (1985) *Understanding Reading: A Psycholinguistic Analysis*, New York: Erlbaum.

Smith, N.B. (1969) 'The many faces of reading comprehension', *Reading Teacher* 23, 3: 249–59.

Snider, V.E. (1992) 'Learning styles and learning to read: a critique', *Remedial and Special Education* 13, 1: 6–18.

Solity, J. and Bull, S. (1987) *Special Needs: Bridging the Curriculum Gap*, Milton Keynes: Open University Press.

Sowder, L., Moyer, M. and Moyer, J. (1986) 'Diagnosing a student's understanding of operations', *Arithmetic Teacher* 33, 9: 22–5.

Stainbeck, W., Stainbeck, S. and Wilkinson, A. (1992) 'Encouraging peer support and friendships', *Teaching Exceptional Children* 24, 2: 6–11.

Stobart, G. (1986) 'Is integrating the handicapped psychologically defensible?', *Bulletin of the British Psychological Society* 39: 1–3.

Stoessiger, R. and Wilkinson, M. (1991) 'Emergent mathematics', *Education 3–13* 19, 1: 3–11.

Stott, D.H. (1962) *Programmed Reading Kit*, Edinburgh: Holmes McDougall.

Stott, D.H. (1978) *Helping Children with Learning Difficulties*, London: Ward Lock.

Stott, D.H. (1981) 'Teaching reading; the psycholinguistic invasion', *Reading* 15, 3: 19–25.

Stott, D.H., Green, L. and Francis, J. (1983) 'Learning style and school attainment', *Human Learning* 2: 61–75.

Sutton, G. (1992) 'Cooperative learning works in mathematics', *Mathematics Teacher* 85, 1: 63–6.

Suydam, M.N. (1986) 'Manipulative materials and achievement', *Arithmetic Teacher* 33, 6: 10–32.

Taylor, A. (1991) 'Real myths and reading screams: some thoughts about using literature to teach children to read', *Education 3–13* 19, 3: 10–15.

Taylor, R.L. and Sternberg, L. (1989) *Exceptional Children: Integrating Research and Teaching*, New York: Springer-Verlag.

Thomas, D. (1986) 'Special educational needs: translating policies into practice', *Journal of Curriculum Studies* 18, 1: 100–1.

Thomas, D. (1991) 'A framework for teaching reading', *Support for Learning* 6, 3: 103–7.

Thompson, R., White, K. and Morgan, D. (1982) 'Teacher–student interaction patterns in classrooms with mainstreamed mildly handicapped students', *American Educational Research Journal* 19, 2: 220–36.

Thornton, C.A. and Wilmot, B. (1986) 'Special learners', *Arithmetic Teacher* 33, 6: 38–41.

Thurman, S.K. and Widerstrom, A.H. (1990) *Infants and Young Children with Special Needs* (2nd edn), Baltimore: Brookes.

Topping, K. (1991) 'Achieving more with less: raising reading standards via parental involvement and peer tutoring', *Support for Learning* 6, 3: 112–15.

Treiman, R. (1985) 'Phonemic analysis, spelling and reading', in T.H. Carr (ed.) *The Development of Reading Skills*, San Francisco: Jossey-Bass.

Tunmer, W.E. (1990) 'The psychology of learning to read: current trends in theory and research', *Education Research and Perspectives* 17, 1: 34–49.

Underhill, R.G., Uprichard, A.E. and Heddens, J.W. (1980) *Diagnosing Mathematical Difficulties*, Columbus: Merrill.

Vallecorsa, A.L., Ledford, R.R. and Parnell, G.G. (1991) 'Strategies for teaching composing skills', *Teaching Exceptional Children* 23, 2: 52–5.

Van Daal, V.H.P. and Van der Leij, A. (1992) 'Computer-based reading and spelling practice for children with learning disabilities', *Journal of Learning Disabilities* 25, 3: 186–95.

Walberg, H.J. (1988) 'Synthesis of research on time and learning', *Educational Leadership* 45, 6: 76–85.

Walden, T.A. and Ramey, C.T. (1983) 'Locus of control and academic achievement', *Journal of Educational Psychology* 75, 3: 347–58.

Walker, H.M. (1988) *The Walker Social Skills Curriculum*, Austin: Pro-Ed.

Wallace, G. and Kauffman, J.M. (1986) *Teaching Students with Learning and Behaviour Problems* (3rd edn), Columbus: Merrill.

Wang, M.C. (1981) 'Mainstreaming exceptional children: some instructional design and implementation considerations', *Elementary School Journal* 81, 4: 195–221.

Wang, M.C. (1989) 'Adaptive instruction', in D. Lipsky and A. Gartner (eds) *Beyond Special Education*, Baltimore: Brookes.

Wang, M.C. and Stiles, B. (1976) 'An investigation of children's concept of self-responsibility for their school learning', *American Educational Research Journal* 13, 3: 159–79.

Wang, M.C. and Walberg, H.J. (1985) *Adapting Instruction to Individual Differences*, Berkeley: McCutchan for NSSE.

Wang, M.C. and Zollers, N.J. (1990) 'Adaptive instruction: an alternative service delivery approach', *Remedial and Special Education* 11, 1: 7–21.

Weinstein, C.E., Ridley, D.S., Dahl, T. and Weber, E.S. (1989) 'Helping students develop strategies for effective learning', *Educational Leadership* 46, 4: 17–19.

Wendon, L. (1989) *Letterland System*, Barton: Letterland Ltd.

Wepner, S.B. (1991) 'Linking technology to genre-based reading', *Reading Teacher* 45, 1: 68–9.

Westwood, P.S. (1975) *The Remedial Teacher's Handbook*, Edinburgh: Oliver & Boyd.

Westwood, P.S. (1979) 'Planning units of work for less able students', in *Catering for Children with Special Needs in the Primary School*, Adelaide: Education Department of South Australia.

Westwood, P.S. (1982) 'Strategies for improving social interaction of handicapped children in regular classes', *Australian Journal of Remedial Education* 14, 4: 23–4.

Westwood, P.S. (1984) 'Asking the crucial question: "Is integration working for this child?"', *Australian Journal of Remedial Education* 16, 1: 10–12.

Westwood, P.S. (1985) 'When writing is a problem', *Australian Journal of Remedial Education* 17, 1: 23–4.

Westwood, P.S. (1986) 'Contemporary view on the teaching of reading', *Australian Journal of Remedial Education* 18, 2: 9–13.

Westwood, P.S. (1991) 'Negotiated curriculum plans – panacea or paper tiger?', *Australian Association for Special Education Bulletin*, July 1991.

Whitehead, D. (1990) *Language across the Curriculum: Teaching Strategies*, Carlton: Australian Reading Association.

Whitehead, D. (1991) 'Whole language: dialogue or debate?', *Reading Psychology* 12, 4: 3–10.

Widlake, P. (1983) *How to Reach the Hard to Teach*, Milton Keynes: Open University Press.

Widlake, P. (1987) 'When parents become partners', *British Journal of Special Education* 14, 1: 27–9.

Williams, R. (1986) 'Top ten principles for teaching reading', *English Language Teaching Journal* 40, 1: 42–5.

Wilson, C.L. and Sindelar, P.T. (1991) 'Direct instruction in Math Word problems: students with learning disabilities', *Exceptional Children* 57, 6: 512–19.

Wong, B.Y. (1986) 'A cognitive approach to teaching spelling', *Exceptional Children* 53, 2: 169–73.

Workman, E.A. (1982) *Teaching Behavioural Self-Control to Students*, Austin: Pro-Ed.

Wragg, J. (1989) *Talk Sense to Yourself*, Hawthorn, Victoria: Australian Council for Educational Research.

Wray, D. (1989) 'Reading: the new debate', *Reading* 23, 1: 2–8.

Wray, D. and Medwell, J. (1989) 'Using desk-top publishing to develop literacy', *Reading* 23, 2: 62–8.

Yates, G.C.R. (1988) 'Classroom research into effective teaching', *Australian Journal of Remedial Education* 20, 1: 4–9.

Zimmerman, B. and Schunk, D. (1989) *Self-regulated Learning and Academic Achievement*, New York: Springer-Verlag.

Index